Still Breaking Normal

A Fat, Black, Femme, Geek Navigating an Anti-Black World

By TaLynn Kel

Credits and Copyright

Cover photo
Nikki Rau-Baker of Geek Behind the Lens Photography

Photo edits
Acdramon's Artist Cove

Essays were written by TaLynn Kel during 2016, 2017, and 2018 and originally published on Breaking Normal (www.talynnkel.com), Black Girl Nerds (www.blackgirlnerds.com), and The Establishment (www.theestablishment.co).

Printed in the United States of America

First Printing, February 2018

Introduction

Hello and welcome to my life. My fat, Black, femme geek life. This is the second collection of essay from my blog, Breaking Normal. The first collection, *Breaking Normal: Essays from My Fat Black Geek Life*, captured my take on 2016, the year the white supremacists stop pretending to want anything less than full domination of everyone who isn't white, male, cisgendered, able-bodied, and heterosexual. It was a shocking year on many levels for many people and its effects are devastating communities throughout the country and all over the world. They will for years to come.

I've watched my circle grow smaller as I've better understood how these power dynamics affect me and others around me. I've better understood how I am complicit and how I am resisting. And while I've always been aware that misogynoir has impacted my relationships and ambitions, this year I became more attuned and capable of seeing more nuance in how it's affected me. As I pushed back on the racism and sexism that tries to define my space, my relationships began to struggle. It's been amazing to see the impact that controlling my space and insisting on receiving the same respect people want from me can have on my relationships. Amazing and challenging in ways I didn't imagine but manage to navigate.

My marriage is still a tap dance of diplomacy and love. My relationship with fandom is a tango, full of love, hate and everything in between. Misogynoir is the Kizomba, an intimate dance that taught me to embrace my self-hate – a dance I hope I can shape into the joy of self-love. Anti-Blackness is the waltz, imperialistic and exclusive, laced with rules of respectability. And accountability is not a dance. It is prostration, a position white people love to enforce on Black people, Indigenous people, and people of color yet never feel the need to impose upon themselves. These forced dances are how I navigate life as a Black woman in america and they are exhausting.

But my life is not sad. It's demanding in ways I wish I didn't have to manage but there are many things to celebrate. It was late in 2016 that I realized I couldn't keep focusing on the same depressing shit as it was eroding too much of my joy. I needed and wanted more for myself, so I chose to acquire new projects. I found people with whom to collaborate. I found ways to work with other creatives and expand my skill set, while still exploring ideas and experiences with my writing. Since then, I've created new YouTube content and joined a newly created podcast, while also pushing myself to do more creative writing. That creative writing is still a work in progress, but I'm getting there. And I love it.

I'm still learning and growing, something I hope to continue for the rest of my life. I love being able to see the growth in my writing...the confidence I've gained over time. I can feel myself stepping into who I've needed to be, and it feels glorious. Far from simple, but worth the effort.

This book, *Still Breaking Normal: Essays from My Fat, Black, Femme, Geek Life*, is not just about breaking social norms. It's about breaking the norms I've accepted for myself. I don't have to stay in the same place, doing the same things I've done in the past. I can take everything I thought I was, break it, and shape myself into someone new. It's a type of rebirth and reclamation of self that I celebrate each time. As I reshape me, I reshape the world around me, hopefully for the better.

So, if you read my first book, thank you for continuing this journey with me. Full transparency, I've included essays from the first book in here because they provide context for the 2017 essays. As I have more content to pull from, I've noticed some strong themes in my life and while they all coexist, some topics stand out more than others. Organizing them resulted in some unpublished essays that take a more overarching view of these themes. You don't need to read the overviews, but they do provide some insight and context because contrary to popular belief, context matters.

Again, thank you for sharing your time with me as I learn to live my truth and embrace my joy.

With love, anger, and joy,

TaLynn Kel

P.S.
I included a list of free online books on race, gender, and class at the start of the Reference section. If you haven't read them, it's a great place to start.

Table of Contents

My Marriage

AKA Why I Write About White People

Despite having spent the majority of my life surviving whiteness, I probably wouldn't be writing about white people if it weren't for my marriage. Weird, right? One would think that I'd have totally swallowed the color-blind kool-aid when I married a white man, but I hadn't. What I did believe was that white people wanted to and were capable of profound change.

I was wrong.

That is not to say some won't try, but after years of living with the harm that they delude themselves into thinking is for my own betterment, I've learned that in order to change, one must first admit there's a problem. White people seem to have a really difficult time with this. They can admit a general problem but are knee-jerk defensive when it comes to admitting their role in it. They struggle to come to terms with their apathy and casual racism and segment their lives, desires, hopes, and fears to maintain the illusion of their anti-racism. They lie to themselves at every opportunity to avoid any acknowledgement of privilege and access due to their whiteness. And they refuse to confront any conscious or subconscious beliefs they have about whiteness, Black people, Indigenous people, and People of Color (BIPoCs).

Because I only interacted with whiteness at work and out in public, I was unaware of how deeply entrenched the denial was. I am very clearly Black and because of that, I was not privy to the private conversations white people had about Black people. My relationship with my significant other (S.O.) changed that...at least among his friends and family. My relationship with him signaled in some way that I was "safer" than other Black people. It wasn't an immediate shift. It took over a year of tense exchanges and awkward social situations before they started relaxing around me. And when they did, the casual oppressive shit flowed freely, and I was unequipped to handle it.

Don't get me wrong. They let shit slip throughout our entire relationship, but as I was unsure of myself in these new circumstances, I didn't challenge them on it. Instead, I chose to remove myself from their presence and process what was happening. I struggled more with coded language back then because we're conditioned to give white people the benefit of the doubt. The benefit of the doubt is a lie when we're never meant to make people aware of their transgressions - all it does is maintain the status quo, and this in intentional.

Constantly being exposed to people who, not only refused to acknowledge a problem but also sought to silence any potential acknowledgement of one was eye-opening. Having any kind of conversation on oppression was shut down instantly. Protestors were always depicted as criminals or greedy people always trying to take things they hadn't "earned." They would talk about poverty as though it was an indicator of morality, not an intentionally curated and maintained lifestyle. And I was never supposed to challenge any of their prejudices. I mean, look at me - I was a college graduate and in grad school. Apparently, racism wasn't real if I could achieve what I had. All other Black people needed to do was work hard, avoid drugs, and obey the law.

The bullshit flowed so fast and free among these people that even while giving them the benefit of the doubt, I could only tolerate them for two hours at a time. It was an emotional torture I'd never experienced. In addition to spending my personal time with them, I was expected to spend holiday time. I was expected to open my home to them. Initially it was a challenge, and I like challenges, but I finally realized that it was damaging. Eventually, I stopped torturing myself and walked away with a deeper understanding of how shitty white people choose to be.

Once the lies were exposed, I couldn't go back. And with the constant exposure of racially motivated policing, murders, housing, gentrification…the micro- and macro-aggressions of co-workers, the ever-worsening political climate as the illusion of equality was hammered away, I couldn't go back to unseeing it. I didn't want to, despite the stress and emotional pain it caused. And while I couldn't go back, I knew I couldn't have these disingenuous discussions with white people who would pretend to engage in these topics when really working towards the goal of shutting me down or reminding me that I should be grateful to be in this country. Former classmates and "friends" would respond to my social media posts with accusations of racism and oversensitivity whenever I shared my experiences. White people would pop into my life to bird shit a "shut up" or a "get over it" whenever they felt comfortable until finally I said no more.

These feelings, these experiences need to be expressed, especially when I was seeing liars and racists given platforms any and everywhere. I needed to stop being invisible and share my reality, my truth with more than my immediate circle, who, by the way, were often protective of whiteness because, well, conditioning works.

The other thing I found was that when I had issues with racism in my relationship, I had little to no support. Everyone would say silly shit like, "he can't be racist if he married you." They were wrong.

Black people would say, "what did you expect? You knew he was white. You brought this on yourself," while self-identified, anti-racist white people would advise me to be patient and approve my tolerance, regardless of the pain it caused me. I couldn't find honest, empowering accounts of interracial relationships. Often, it was people pretending that love erased racism, while protecting whiteness at the expense of the Black partner. I knew more people were living my story, and since I couldn't find them, I decided to share mine, so others could find it.

Despite the pain and the difficulties, this experience has been revelatory and empowering for me. I wouldn't recommend it, because it feels overwhelming at times, but it has helped me embrace aspects of myself that I'd ignored. Knowing what I know now, I'm not sure I would make the same choices, but I love who I am so maybe I would. And I share these experiences when I write, for me and for other Black women who can't find support when shit goes sideways with their white partner. And I write about white people because, apparently, they need to hear some truths they've spent too long suppressing. So much so that they can't even recognize it.

The essays in this section talk about different aspects of my marriage. It's a progression from learning how to address the racism in our relationship, to dealing with in-laws, to learning time and time again that my S.O. has a lot more work to do. I write from my experience and I write from my heart, so if you feel pain reading my words, understand that it took a lot for me to put it to the page and share it with you.

My Husband's Unconscious Racism Nearly Destroyed Our Marriage

I wrote this because...well, because I had to. It was cathartic in many ways and it helped me deal with an aspect of my relationship that I didn't want to face...something nobody else seemed to be talking about. And with the way the discussions around racism were changing, how it was so much harder to hide that to not see it meant you were actively looking away, it felt right to talk about how it impacts my relationship. It still feels right to talk about it and we still struggle with it.

People read this many different ways. Some read it as though I am ignorant and self-harming. Others read it as a story of love triumphing hate. It's really just a story about two people who are committed to growing together, but who also recognize that it may not be meant to be. But if it fails, it won't be because we didn't try our hardest to make it work.

Also, in retrospect, I should have called his racism "unchallenged" instead of "unconscious." It was conscious; it's just that no one around him thought it was wrong.

✻✻✻✻✻

When I was in my teens, I figured I'd be married at least three times. The first would be the young, practice marriage. My second marriage would be the passionate one through which I would become a better version of myself, and my third would be the one that stuck. As you can see, I never really had a lot of respect for the institution.

By the time I was 30, after years of never sleeping with anyone for more than two months, much less actually dating them, I'd revised

"

my prediction from three to zero. I'm not religious; I didn't want kids; and I sure as hell didn't want someone in my home that felt like they had any control over my decisions. Why get married at all? That shit looked ridiculous to me.

Then I met *Kevin. We met in the geekiest way possible: He saw a picture of me in a cosplay outfit, wanted to know more, found my blog, and then found my profile on a dating site and asked to meet at DragonCon. Everything about that impressed me. I loved the idea of someone being willing to do a little legwork to find me, especially since exercising my curiosity and putting in some effort to satisfy it is how I engage with the world. His approach spoke to me. Also, he asked me out—no hedging, no game playing. He stated up front that he wanted to get to know me better and asked me on a date. In a society where people are "hanging out" and "chilling" and "hooking up"—meaning anything from a light kissing session to a night of full-blown sex—being direct was important.

There was only one concern: He was white. I'd been in the dating scene for a while and while I didn't think race *should* matter, I definitely knew it *did*. I'd met my share of white men looking for a "Nubian goddess" (their words, not mine). Or the ones who believed that Black women would offer some kind of freaky, wild sexual experience. I'd met white men who wanted to demean and defile me, white men who wanted to dominate or be dominated by me, and white men who just wanted to check a Black woman off their sexual bucket list. Not to mention the ones who thought that being with me somehow made them "edgy" or proved they weren't racist. I mean, not every white guy has a "David Duke cock[1]" right?

---

[1] Clark-Flory, Tracy. "John Mayer's Johnson hates black women." Salon, 10 Feb. 2010. Web. 21 Feb. 2016.

Needless to say, dating white men was tiring. I had to constantly be on guard, preparing myself for their racist comments. And I knew they were coming. I knew there would be a point where I'd have to talk about why I could say n***** and they couldn't. I knew there'd be a conversation about Black on Black crime. I KNEW there'd be some fucked up assumption about Black people that I'd have to dismantle and then beat my white date over the head with—thereby ending whatever the fuck we were doing together. And I really wasn't there for that shit.

But you know how they say timing is everything? Kevin entered my life at a particularly vulnerable point. My father had passed three months before we met. He'd been sick for over a decade with cancer and I spent that entire time blocking out everyone. When he passed, all that energy I'd used protecting myself started to dissipate and my walls softened. I started letting people in. I was willing and capable of giving people opportunities to be a part of my life, and I was also willing to do the work to keep them there.

That's why I let Kevin in, but it's not why I kept him around. I'd always been told to be more feminine, more womanly, and to cater to some stranger's every need, but Kevin didn't expect that. He didn't try to mold me into the perfect woman. He didn't look for me to take care of him. He didn't minimize my accomplishments; we weren't competing, and my success did not undermine his masculinity. And he was nice to me and genuinely interested in me—something I'm sad to say wasn't common in my relationships. He listened, and he cared. He also had an important characteristic that I share: the willingness to examine his beliefs and change them when he learns that they're wrong. He doesn't state his beliefs as vocally as I do, but he shares my love of learning and adapting to shifts in our perception and awareness.

Being with Kevin felt like a refuge from sexism. At the time, that seemed more immediate—and easier to address—than the racism that surrounded me. But it didn't negate the fact that Kevin is white—and not just white, *extremely* white. He has ash blond hair and pale, easily sunburned skin. His close friends are all white men and their spouses. His family is mostly white. His co-workers are mostly white men. The more serious our relationship got, the more I was spending half my time—at least—surrounded by white people. While I'd gone to predominantly white schools and worked in mostly white companies, I'd never had so many white people suddenly in my intimate spaces. It's one thing to hit it and split it with a guy and another to interact in my personal time with entire groups of white people, sometimes in my home.

And it affected me a LOT. I was constantly pulled out of spaces where I felt comfortable and pushed into spaces that felt isolating. We live in Atlanta, where multi-racial, multi-ethnic options are everywhere, yet when we socialized with his friends, I was required to visit all-white neighborhoods, businesses, and events. Many of his friends lived in "white flight" zones, suburban areas where white people moved to avoid the "downfall" of urban areas. I was constantly required to go to the one Atlanta county still referred to as a "sundown town"—as in a town Black people shouldn't be in after dark. And while he and his friends were pretty clueless about these things, I was very aware.

It was in one of these predominantly white spaces, a restaurant with a mostly-white clientele, that I first ran headlong into Kevin's unrealized racism. I'd just learned that he and all his friends carried 4-inch pocket knives (or "box openers," as they liked to call them), and I was kinda freaked out by it. My weapons tend to be off-label weapons, like my keys, a pen, or my purse. I only had one friend who carried a gun, and nobody carried knives. Now, I was sitting surrounded by armed white men.

When I pointed out that they were all carrying weapons, they laughed—didn't I know the knives were just for opening boxes? I could have been arrested or killed for carrying something like that, regardless of what I planned to do with it—unlike them. They wouldn't face any consequences for bringing weapons into a restaurant; after all, they were white, and the restaurant was mostly white. Kevin shrugged at my observations and said, "At least we don't have to worry about being shot."

This was how I realized that I was dating a racist man.

Kevin didn't understand what he'd done wrong, but he knew he'd fucked up; he wanted to know how and why. I told him that his assumption—that we were safe from shootings because we were in an all-white restaurant, that a predominantly Black restaurant would be likely to have a shooting—was shitty, ignorant, and racist. When he pushed back, I pointed out that he and his friends were the ones carrying weapons. What the fuck did they need them for at dinner? Were they expecting a package? But, of course, it's always okay for white people to be armed. If they have a knife, it's probably just for opening boxes. If they have a gun, it's probably for protection—despite all the shootings to the contrary. Kevin stammered and backpedaled, but the damage was done. I'm not sure how far we were into our relationship, but that was the first moment I wondered if this was a huge mistake.

To this day, I look back and question how and why I stayed. I can see now that, this early in my relationship with Kevin and my own personal development, I was still in a lot of denial about what racism is and how it manifests. Ironically, choosing to stay with

Kevin after I realized he wasn't immune to racism, and later choosing to marry him, helped me sort that out. Being exposed to so many white people, including some who were now my family, helped me recognize racist buzzwords like "conservative," "social conservative," "Republican," "traditionalist," and "older generation." These code words make racism more palatable and less offensive to those that engage in it. It also makes it easier to lie to ourselves about it.

Being with Kevin also helped me realize how much anti-Blackness I'd internalized. Growing up Black in America, you learn to ignore a lot of racist shit, especially if you are moving in white spaces. I was taught that white spaces were aspirational, that access to these spaces meant success. That's a white supremacist ideology, but we live in a white supremacist society, so it's also true: all-white spaces are where a lot of power brokering happens. This often means that the more power you achieve, the more you face casual social racism. You sit in meetings where people openly say that Black people are lesser—but not you, they add. You're different! That is, you're different until you do something of which they don't approve. Then you're "just like the rest of them" or "you don't know your place." And to teach you your place, they revoke some of your privileges, like a naughty child, until you understand that you are there by their sufferance. To survive in that environment, you learn to stay quiet.

I learned this in school, at work, in certain social groups...in order to keep your spot, or move "up the chain," you learn to let casual racism slide. Your ability to stay silent in the face of racist bullshit becomes the norm. So, you do it, because you think that's your only feasible option and the price you pay to succeed in white America. The side effect is that this type of talk, this dislike and hatred of

Black people, becomes not just the white noise but also the internal harmony of your life. It goes from being something you actively ignore to something you actively hum, and eventually sing. You stop noticing it, and then you stop fighting it, because it no longer sounds wrong to you. It sounds normal.

Dating Kevin jarred the melody. Hearing him parrot anti-Black shit I said helped me hear the discordance in my life. I was suddenly super-aware of my audience, and it forced me to listen to what I was saying—and then to change what I was saying, not from a "fit in at any cost" ideology but from an internal assessment. I started listening to and correcting myself more. Then I started sharing my realizations and pushing back on the bullshit. It's been a shake-up for all of my relationships; I've had more than one non-Black friend express apprehension at talking with me, because I don't divorce personal experiences from the larger, external factors that shaped them. And I don't tolerate racism in my relationships anymore...which was scary for me and Kevin.

We hit a point where he had to change, or we were going to separate. That point was the Trayvon Martin trial and verdict. From the moment Trayvon's murder became visible, I dismissed the idea that his murderer's actions were justifiable in any way. Imagine my surprise when Kevin said that the evidence supported the murderer's account. It was in that moment, when I saw that the man I'd married believed that a 17-year-old teenager visiting his dad presented a threat to a 30+-year-old man who randomly patrolled his neighborhood with a gun, that I started to fear our relationship was beyond hope.

I talked to my white therapist about it and she commended me for being willing to work through these tough issues. I didn't feel support. Instead, I felt betrayed by the two white people I'd allowed into my intimate confidence. When I was a child, my father had told me never to trust white people, and now I felt that his warning had been validated. If my white husband couldn't acknowledge the humanity of a Black teenage boy who'd been stalked and murdered, if he could believe it was just for this child to be profiled and found dangerous based on nothing but a visit to the store, I KNEW that this person wasn't someone with whom I could spend my life. And I started preparing my exit strategy—exactly one year after our wedding.

I'd realized that, although being with Kevin had helped me to recognize the racist attitudes I'd unconsciously swallowed, he hadn't been able to do the same. He wasn't willing to face his own racism, and this meant I didn't trust my husband with my Blackness. I am not naïve; I do not expect another person to ever understand and accept the whole of me. I think that is highly unrealistic and self-centered. But my Blackness defines how the world engages with me, and it is something that he had to understand and embrace for us to be together. And in order for him to do that, he had to own his racism. He had to acknowledge he was racist, harbored racist thoughts, and said and did racist things. He had to confront this part of himself that he'd denied all his life...that he had the privilege of ignoring until he decided he wanted to share his life with me.

The thing that amazes me about him is that he did it and continues to do it. As I write this, it's been almost three years since I realized that I couldn't live with my husband's racism, and we are still together. It wasn't easy for either of us, but when he realized that I could not trust him, that his inability to admit his racism made him a liar, he knew he had to change. My promise is to give him the space to educate himself and make mistakes, and the time to grow from it.

I also made a fundamental change in how I interacted with him and with the world: I stopped treating my Blackness as a burden. I stopped feeling bad about being Black. I stopped feeling like I had to prove I was different, "one of the good ones." I hadn't even realized I was doing it, and it's still something I struggle with. When I'm in a situation where I feel silenced, or singled out, I don't blame myself anymore. There is nothing wrong with me, my Blackness, and recognizing my skills and accomplishments. I am worthy. I share my experiences and amplify the narratives of others without shame. I invoke the privilege of my intelligence, education, and support network to learn more and write more about the impact of racism in various parts of my identity. I work to center myself in my narratives, instead of the men or the white people who surround me. I have reached a place where I feel safer without all the games I've been forced to play in this society. I'm still not 100% safe, but I'm not sure if that will ever be the case.

This also changed how I interacted with Kevin. Instead of focusing on how my Blackness affected us, we started focusing on how his whiteness affected us. He continues to confront his racism and doing the work to change his thinking and his reactions. He is rewriting himself and learning that his perspective is fucked up and he needs to continually straighten that shit out. It is his job to shoulder the burden of his ancestors and their history of genocide, rape, theft, and destruction of other cultures as they falsely promoted their illusion of dominance. It's his job to check the racism of his family and friends. This is his role he took by being with me. It's not an easy battle for us. He knows when I talk about oppression he doesn't have a seat at the table. He knows that my understanding of racism overrides his.

In exchange, I work to keep our communication about racism as safe as it can be for him—without doing harm to myself. Among other things, this means my anger is accepted without my having to explain or justify it. He knows he is not an authority and that his ally work is in white spaces, not Black ones. He is continually unlearning white supremacy and how to de-center himself in these conversations. It's no longer focused on his hurt feelings or fears that I hate all white people. Instead, it's about knowing that all white people in this country are racist until they take on the continuous task of unlearning what everyone and everything has taught them about race in America.

It's not an easy battle, but it's the one I've chosen. I'm just happy that I'm with someone willing to fight the battle with me.

Name has been changed.

This story first appeared at TheEstablishment.co, a multimedia site entirely run and funded by women on May 26, 2016.

To this day, I look back and question how and why I stayed. I can see now that, this early in my relationship with Kevin and my own personal development, I was still in a lot of denial about what racism is and how it manifests.

– TaLynn Kel, My Husband's Unconscious Racism Nearly Destroyed Our Marriage

The Danger of Unchallenged Racism in Interracial Relationships

It shouldn't surprise me that interracial relationships are here to stay, considering that I'm in one. Still, I worry about the people in them. When I started dating "Kevin," I was concerned about the demographics of the relationship. I worried about how it would play out with our families and friends, the rest of the world.

The one thing I didn't really understand was how it would play out between us.

So, I wrote about it. I wrote about how I'd desensitized myself to a lot of casual racism[2] in my life as a survival tactic. I wrote about how I'd internalized anti-Blackness. Then I wrote about retuning myself to hear the anti-Blackness in my relationship, and subsequently having to address it with my white spouse[3] before we ruined our marriage.

My husband was willing to change. He continues to change and address his racism. Because he's willing to do this work, we work.

I am one of the lucky ones.

I'm lucky because even though it's hard for him, he admits his racism and actively works to dismantle it. He'll have the hard conversations. He accepts that there were things he supported in the past that were disgusting. He unmasks his lies and owns his mistakes. We both do. That we don't have children helps. We don't

---

[2] Kel, TaLynn. "Othering the Self – Learning to Recognize My Anti-Blackness." Black Girl Nerds, 02 March 2016. Web. 20 July 2016.

[3] Kel, TaLynn. "My Husband's Unconscious Racism Nearly Destroyed Our Marriage." The Establishment, 05 May. 2016. Web. 20 August 2016.

have the additional stress of inadvertently encoding any children with racism or self-hate. It is a humbling way to live, but it's real, raw, and truthful. We don't mask our ugly. We sit it right beside the pretty and figure out how we're going to live with it.

When I read the blogs of other interracial couples, I rarely hear about the ugly. I don't hear about how those couples confront the elephant in the room and fight to keep it from trampling everything. Instead, I hear odes to colorblind love and admiration for the white people who dared the ostracization of their white families and friends—something you don't hear about the Black partner because it's presumed that dating a white person is a come-up, not a downgrade. I read about the white person's bravery and their struggle.

What I see, though, is their internalized racism.

Just yesterday I read a blog about an interracial family[4]. The woman has a white son from a previous relationship and is currently married to a Black man, with whom she has a two-year-old son. In this essay, she reflects on her relationship as she has had to admit to herself the racism her husband experiences and realize the future her toddler son faces. They have been together for years and now she is beginning to understand the inherent danger this country presents for people with brown skin. Now she sees that minor things like spending time alone with their white child or driving with a broken tail light are potentially lethal for her Black spouse. Finally, she is starting to see what's been in front of her all of her life. Finally.

---

4 Chelsie. "When Suddenly No Lives Matter." 2 boys 1 blog and me, 09 July 2016. Web. 20 August 2016.

Her response? To tell her two-year-old Black child this: "You better make smart decisions. Safe decisions. No robbing a gas station. No walking down the street swinging a sword around. No rioting. You are to be respectful. You are to be a member of society that contributes to the world. You are to be proud of who you are and your heritage. If you are anything less than these things, you might not come home to me one day."

There was so much in that one quote that I wished I still smoked. I love how she made it all about her potential loss. Not fear about the life he may have to live, but her fear that he may not come home...to her. She told her child, "Don't be a kid. Grow up. Don't make mistakes. Don't confront the system. Don't rebel. Be quiet. Be still. Be invisible. Do what people say, but be proud of who you are, as long as it doesn't look like any kind of protest or disobedience."

On top of that, she threw in a few gems about only doing legal things because robbing a gas station is every Black person's aspiration unless they fight *really* hard not to. I also liked the shout out to Darrien Hunt[5], the young Black man who was murdered for cosplaying with an ornamental sword. They sell those swords at the mall, you know. I have six of them.

What she forgot to mention, however, was how being respectful, productive, proud, and lawful can still get Black people "legally" murdered by police and scared white people. How it can get you lynched in police custody[6]. How Black people are refused medical

---

[5] Broadnax, Jamie. "Cosplay or No Cosplay: The Homicide of Darrien Hunt." Black Girl Nerds, 17 Sept. 2014. Web. 20 August 2016.

[6] Graham, David A. "Sandra Bland and the Long History of Racism in Waller County, Texas." The Atlantic, 21 June 2015. Web. 20 Aug. 2016.

care by the police[7] until they die in custody. How scared white people kill Black people[8] asking for help. How Black people are killed by police for sleeping in their cars[9]. Did she forget this? Or has she just not acknowledged it yet? I wonder…

I wonder if she tells her white son these things. Does she think he'll be killed for being disrespectful?

I wonder how her husband responds to her casual racist attitude towards their child. I wonder how he feels when she dismisses his fears as "crazy paranoia." I wonder if it bothers him that it took another Black man being murdered for her to begin to understand his legitimate concerns.

I wonder how he feels when he reads her statement that everyone has the same opportunities and choices, completely ignoring the hundreds of years that many choices were illegal for Black people. I wonder if he questions himself when he hears her dismiss the hundreds of laws that explicitly forbade Black people from accessing the same benefits as white people. I know I questioned myself when Kevin did it. I questioned him, myself, and our relationship. I asked myself how much work was I willing to do to stay and how much I was willing to compromise for him. It was more than I would do now; my patience was in a different place

---

[7] Neyfakh, Leon. "50-Year-Old Black Woman Who Died in Jail Was Denied Water and Medication, Court Filings Allege." Slate, 25 Feb. 2016. Web. 20 Aug. 2016.

[8] Manuel-Logan, Ruth. "Police: Man Says He Killed Teen Seeking Help After Crash 'Accidentally.'" NewsOne, 2014. Web. 20 Aug. 2016.

[9] Agorist, Matt. "Parents on a Date Were Asleep in Car When Cops Arrived and Killed Them Both." The Free Thought Project, 25. Feb 2016. Web. 20 Aug. 2016.

then, but it's less than other people think it should be, as evidenced by every person asking if Kevin is okay with my essays.

For the record, Kevin is okay with my essays. He supports what I do and accepts that sometimes my writing will be about our relationship. He listens and learns and he calls out my hypocrisy—not to silence me, but to remind me of who I want to see in the mirror.

And I hold a mirror, so he can see himself and ask if he's being the person he wants to be.

Then we hold up a mirror so that we can see ourselves, together, because honesty and accountability are everything.

I wonder who holds up the mirrors for the couple from the blog post, if they even have mirrors at all.

*****

As hard as everything is right now, this social environment is an improvement. No longer are Black people silenced as easily as they were during my childhood. More Black people have voices than ever before. Injustice is called out, spread, the veil of American freedom lifted, our bullshit now visible to the rest of the world. It is both glorious and heartbreaking to see the volume of injustices across the country. It isn't surprising, though. Black people have been discussing this for decades.

For a long time, I gave white people the benefit of the doubt. I told myself that they didn't know what they were doing. They were ignorant. If only we explained it to them, helped them relate, then they'd understand. Over the past three years I've seen explanation after explanation and still people deny racism. They deny profiling. They deny persecution of Black people. They deny and when they can't deny, they lie. It was in the past six months that I finally accepted that all of this is 100% deliberate, including the "ignorance." It is willful. It is a choice.

My denial of this was the only thing that made me feel slightly safe in this world. It was what helped me stay optimistic about the future and aided me in giving white people the benefit of the doubt. I don't give them the benefit of the doubt anymore. Now I just understand that if they aren't challenging racism, they support it. I can no longer call my husband's racism unconscious. It was unchallenged. Now we both live with the challenge of what that means and how he needs to continue to change and grow.

Interracial couples are going to need to challenge the racism in their relationships. If you haven't yet, you will. Some of your relationships will end. Others will grow. Regardless, you need to unbury the lie. It is toxic to both you and your partner, but especially to your children. Don't raise them to hide and hate themselves.

I hope this woman's racism is challenged before she does more harm to her family. I get that this is her experience and she is doing her best.

But her best isn't good enough.

This story first appeared at TheEstablishment.co, a multimedia site entirely run and funded by women, on July 18, 2016.

I questioned him, myself, and our relationship. I asked myself how much work was I willing to do to stay and how much I was willing to compromise for him.

– TaLynn Kel, The Danger of Unchallenged Racism in Interracial Relationships

Why I Cut My Racist In-Laws Out of My Life

I won't lie and say that I never had issues with the demographics of my mixed-race marriage. I definitely did. I worried about what my mom would think, and what my dad would say were he alive. I worried about what his parents thought. I worried about how the world would treat us.

I still worry.

After all, 2016 has all the hallmarks of an impending racial schism, and interracial couples are straddling a fence that may not be tenable.

When I entered my own relationship, I told myself that my significant other (S.O.) was different. That he wasn't with me because of some fetish. That he loved me, all of me. That my brown skin didn't matter to him. Over time came the revelations of his racism. I shouldn't actually call them revelations, as they were more a matter of me acknowledging the truth. I repeatedly pulled the veil over my eyes and told myself that love was enough. Over and over again, I'd feel this buildup of dread as time would reveal some other facet of his racism. Then we'd talk. Then we'd fight. Then we'd talk some more. It is painful and confusing to have someone love you, cherish you, support you, and then wound you with their inability to accept the whole of you. But how our love and communication about racism evolved[10] is another story.

This is the story of the kind of love I have with my in-laws.

$$*****$$

---

[10] Kel, TaLynn. "My Husband's Unconscious Racism Nearly Destroyed Our Marriage." The Establishment, 26 May 2016. Web. 31 July 2016.

You know the expression about how you don't just marry the person, you marry their entire family? This is both true and false, as it depends on how close your partner is with them. I am close with some members of my immediate family, but not others, and I have no relationship with my brother at all. My S.O. has a superficial relationship with his immediate family. We say hi and occasionally spend holidays together, but for the most part, we live in different parts of the country and rarely interact. We are casual Facebook friends, but have limited face-to-face time. When my S.O. goes to visit them, I go with him for support, but truly, these people are still kind of strangers to me.

I know that he has some resentment toward his family, which is something I've tried to help him work through. I'd just lost my father when I met my S.O., and while I was close with my dad, I still felt guilt about the many ways I wasn't there for him. I don't want my S.O. to experience that, so I encourage his relationship with his family as much as I can without forcing him into it. All I can do is champion and love him as he figures it out.

Yet even though I want him and his family to be closer, there is a part of me that is comfortable with the emotional and physical distance.

When I married my S.O., I married into whiteness and the bullshit that comes with it[11]. He doesn't remember this, but when he told his parents my name, there was a moment of pause from his mother. He mentioned that she expressed some concern about my being Black, but as he isn't invested in her opinion, he didn't pursue

---

[11] Kel, TaLynn. "White People, You Have A Lying Problem." The Establishment. 07 July 2016. Web. 31 July. 2016.

it. I, of course, was ravenous for information and completely unaware of how non-confrontational his family is. This family is comprised of passive aggressive people who will never confront you with their feelings and will visibly back away from you if you try to confront them. If you've read any of my other essays, you know that I am the complete opposite of that; if you are bothering me, chances are I'm just going to tell you. Not his family, though. If you bother someone, rather than tell you, they will tell another family member, and then another family member until everyone knows there's a problem except you. They will make snide remarks, but the moment you try to talk about it, they will retreat behind the wall of, "Oh, I meant nothing by it. It's not a big deal. Sorry."

Habitual liars, the whole lot of them. And in fact, this was a habit I had to help my S.O. break. He would agree to things just to make me go away. One time he replied with something that was so obviously a lie that I had to ask, "Why'd you lie about that?" He replied, "I don't know. It just...I don't know." Now he's more honest about such things, and I love watching him assert himself and break away from that toxic dynamic he grew up in.

Old habits die hard, though, and when he and his family get together, I see him revert back to the passive-aggressive liar I once knew. He changed because it was damaging our relationship. Suppressing his needs to avoid conflict isn't healthy, and because this is how his family operates, our relationship with them is not healthy.

I didn't want it to be this way, a relationship full of meaningless lies and petty obfuscations. Yet, any opportunity we had to improve our relationship was met with banality and superficial happiness. We talk about the weather and good restaurants. When the conversation finally begins to attain some depth, it's about work and people who don't matter. The dance to avoid any topic that may contain meaning is intricate and empty. I do not like socializing with people who are afraid of themselves, afraid of making mistakes, afraid of being wrong. I do not like people lying to me and avoiding important topics because they make them uncomfortable. As much as they think they are hiding behind the curtain, it's transparent and nothing is unseen. It's just ignored.

A part of me feels guilty about not pushing to change our relationship, but the rest of me is glad that I can recognize emotional danger when I see it. They are dangerous in their deceptions. The honesty my S.O. and I share is too much for them. His mom was constantly taken aback at holidays when I would speak my mind. They worked so hard to maintain a veneer of civility and calm, but the veneer is thin. Easy to break. Just a little nudge and they are frantic in their attempts to mask the hole. I struggled to tiptoe through their world—it is ugly to me, and I want as little contact as possible. I often laugh to cover my distaste, but my laughter is often filled with bitterness and my disgust is apparent.

Because we had such little contact with them, there were few opportunities for their casual racism to show. But every opportunity they had, they took. Each and every visit there was one moment when my friends would be referred to as a gang, or there would be mention of some lack of Black something, be it angels, ornaments, cards...with no acknowledgement as to why that is. There would be a question asking how Black people did some common thing, as though there was some mystical secret passed down orally from mother to daughter, carefully hidden from prying white eyes. There would be some reference to pretty, interracial babies with lovely skin or an inquiry about the best plantations to visit while in Georgia. For the limited exposure I had to them, his family managed to slip in some amazingly racist comments. And out of a mistaken sense of duty, I ate the pain and let many of them pass.

The first time I truly learned what I was dealing with was when I confronted his sister for asking me about plantations to visit. She asked via Facebook, so she did not see me visibly recoil from the question. When I told my S.O. about his sister's question, his response was, "She thinks of plantations like vineyards. She doesn't know what she's asking."

I thought about that for several minutes. I know American history has been whitewashed into complete fiction in order to protect white people from the atrocities of their ancestors, but *that* level of ignorance was shocking to me. What I didn't understand at the time was that white people care so little about the wrongs they've done to Black people throughout history that they don't bother to get educated about the people they've wronged. I'd married into the intersection of intentional ignorance, casual disregard, and the mistaken perception of supremacy—what I like to call the white bubble of bullshit that continues to poison this country.

I took the time to craft a polite, but clear explanation about why this was not just an insensitive question, but fucking shitty as hell. Her response was to blow it off—she didn't mean to upset me; no harm, no foul. Her casual dismissal and closing of the conversation sent me into a whole other level of rage. Between her dismissal and my S.O.'s defense of her fuckery, I was done.

That day, I told him that he was responsible for his family's ignorance. No longer could he avoid addressing the shit they said. No longer could he defend them or their whiteness. We'd already addressed this with his friends, but now it applied to family, too. The one pass I gave him was his delayed recognition of racist shit, because for him it just sounds like everyday conversation. But once that shit was identified, it was his job to confront it.

For a while, this worked. Then his mother posted some video of a Black man co-signing on America's racism and police brutality by asking for patience in collecting the evidence in the murders of Alton Sterling and Philando Castile[12]. She captioned it with, "If only we could get everyone to understand this."

Have I mentioned that his parents remain silent about anything having to do with racism? They avoid the topic like the plague. Then, when she finally says *anything*, it's about waiting to find some reason to validate the murders of these two men who were visibly unarmed and shot by government-approved murderers. This post was so vile that I decided to remove her from my life.

Her replies to my telling her I no longer wanted her toxicity in my life?

"No matter what I say it's going to be wrong."

"I have friends that are black."

"Shootings, no matter who does them are not always justified."

"I love you both. I don't understand. I am NOT for any group (BLM) or whatever."

It's times like this that I am grateful and sad for the internet. Grateful because I now recognize her responses for what they are— intentional blindness. This is someone who chooses to ignore and acknowledge the wrongness of this country because it makes her

---

[12] Wright, Kai. " Why Alton Sterling and Philando Castile Are Dead." The Nation, 07 July 2016. Web. 31 July 2016.

feel bad. Instead she chooses to pretend that she's neutral, something I recognize better because, thanks to the internet, I see it more often. The downside is that thanks to the internet, I see white people ducking and weaving the truth on a national scale. It is a hard thing to witness. It feels impossible to fight.

She is not neutral. A part of me wonders if one of her Black friends got shot, would she wait for all the evidence? Actually, I don't wonder. They aren't really her friends and I don't believe she is capable of having a discussion about racism with a Black person. I don't think she's brave enough to try. And her husband stands by her. They are a team and she is their representative, a person who cannot be honest about the country we live in.

That day I accepted that my S.O. cannot protect me from his family's racism. That day I decided to be my own hero and remove them from my sphere of influence. I won't make him choose between us; I know he needs his parents. I just won't let them in my home or my life. Their values are incompatible with mine.

Some people will say that I should give them a chance. That I should keep working to meet them halfway. To them I say that while I chose to attach whiteness to my personal life through my significant other, I also choose to set limits on the amount of damage I will allow it to wreak upon my life. I will not tolerate being tolerated. I will not tolerate liars. I will not cuddle you in your white fragility and co-sign on your racist bullshit so that you can feel good about yourself. If you lack the humanity to see that my skin, my body, my mind is human just like you, then you are not deserving of me, my time, or my energy. I will not continue to prove my worth to people who are not worthy, even if I am legally bound to you. That brown skin is such a goddamn deal breaker for white people makes me vacillate between rage and despair for this country, for this world.

Releasing people from your life isn't easy, and I don't expect this to be easy. It's only been a couple of weeks, so we'll see how this eventually plays out. 2016 has been a shitty year for a lot of reasons. I stopped speaking to people I've known for years, and I'm watching many friends struggle with doing the same. This is the year of cutting ties and closing doors.

But let's hope that this is also lighting the path to a better future.

This story first appeared at TheEstablishment.co, a multimedia site entirely run and funded by women, on August 2, 2016.

That day I accepted that my S.O. cannot protect me from his family's racism. That day I decided to be my own hero and remove them from my sphere of influence. I won't make him choose between us; I know he needs his parents. I just won't let them in my home or my life. Their values are incompatible with mine.

– TaLynn Kel, Why I Cut My Racist In-Laws Out of My Life

When the Space You Promised Hurts Like Hell

Last night my significant other (S.O.) and I got into a discussion about the oppression-driven division in this country and it sucked. It sucked for so many reasons. It sucked because I promised him the space to be wrong as he learns more about racism and oppression. I promised him the space to fuck up and grow from his mistakes. I promised him that I would continue to help him address and dissect his cultivated white supremacist education...and it sucked. It sucked because he didn't see how he was wrong. It sucked because I thought we were past this bullshit where we gave any legitimacy to the "other side." The side that doesn't respect my humanity. The side that thinks I am subhuman. The side that is actively fighting to keep me in a space where white people can use, abuse, and discard me at their discretion. The side that is fighting to ensure their perceived superiority.

A side that he was raised to think is the way things are supposed to be.

But he's white and white people have controlled the narrative of who deserves equality and who doesn't for hundreds of years. Apparently, it takes more than seven years with me for him to understand that it's a lie. Not just a lie, but flat out wrong. And immoral. And dehumanizing. And a violation of my personhood; my humanity; my life.

He doesn't understand how dangerous all this is.

It all started with Trevor Noah and Charlamagne the Sucka's radio interview[13]. I've been irritated at Trevor for his New York Times op-

---

[13] The Breakfast Club Power 105.1 FM. "Trevor Noah Talks Tomi Lahren, Donald Trump, Racism in America & More." YouTube, 07 Dec. 2016. Web. 09 Dec. 2016.

ed since I read it on Monday and decided he wasn't about shit. In fact, I'd written an essay a couple of weeks ago[14] that went live the same day as his op-ed[15] about exactly what Trevor was doing – legitimizing and doing the work for white supremacy. This work was done by inviting Tomi Lahren, a known racist, on his platform and then going out of his way to be nice and accepting of her. He gave legitimacy to her brand and, with this interview, doubled down on his promotion of her as someone worth listening to - as though the shit she spews doesn't actively hurt people. It's almost like he's part of the racist Barbie promotional tour, complete with cupcakes. Thanks to this one act, that nasty little hatemonger gained access to an entirely new audience and he made that possible. His op-ed explains why he thought that bullshit was the right thing to do. For him to willingly share his following with an active and vocal, intentionally ill-informed white supremacist is baffling to me and I've be openly and actively vocal about what bullshit this was.

Then Charlamagne, a personality I've never paid any attention to, started being a Tomy-ite all while conveniently claiming on Twitter that Black women don't do exponentially better shit than that vapid, racist shit storm... It was just a week where Black women found themselves being attacked and de-legitimized by Black men claiming they were being fair. Isn't it interesting how fair is about letting someone who shouts ignorant, informed, racist shit access

---

[14] Kel, TaLynn. "Becoming an Agent of Whiteness." The Establishment, 05 Dec. 2016. Web. 09 Dec. 2016.

[15] Noah, Trevor. "Trevor Noah: Let's Not Be Divided. Divided People Are Easier to Rule." The New York Times, 05 Dec. 2016. Web. 09 Dec. 2016.

to your audience and elevating their media profile. Bene Viera said it best in her essay for The Frisky[16]:

"Thanks to black men, Tomi Lahren has been all the buzz in media for over a week. She didn't have to do anything but cozy up with black men and let her mediocrity and proximity to them do the work. The way she hustled these fools reminds me that 13% of black men voted for Trump. As much as things change they remain the same."

As much things change they remain the same.

My relationship with my significant other has changed a lot over the past seven years. From his complete avoidance of talking about racism to him becoming active and vocal in speaking against it. Then he posted that interview between two agents of whiteness as though it's totally fine to have two black men advocate for racists. His reason: nothing will get better if the two sides don't talk to each other and that's what they were talking about."

Long stare in frustrated and disappointed Black woman

Two sides, he said. What two sides? The side that says "hey, we're all human and deserve equal rights and protections under the law" vs the side that says, "White people have run this shit and if you don't like what we've allowed you to have you can leave...or we can kill you and understand that we'll do both."

Another long stare in frustrated disbelieving Black woman

The conversation started with why what these men, Trevor and Charlamagne, were doing was problematic. How they were

---

[16] Viera, Bené. "Here's the problem with black men like Trevor Noah and Charlamagne Tha God." The Frisky, 07 Dec. 2016. Web. 09 Dec. 2016.

promoting rhetoric that was damaging to Black people and operated under the assumption that this conversation, this resistance to the dehumanization of Black people hasn't been going on for hundreds of years. That their whole "nothing's going to change if both sides aren't talking" ignores the hundreds of years that Black people have fought to get this far. It ignores that many, many white people don't want to have these conversations at all. It ignores the propaganda machine that operates expressly to devalue the needs of Black people; the systems that exist to actively destroy any cohesion and make every day a fight for survival. It ignores the escapes[17], the hiding[18], the building[19], the destruction, the casual, unjustified murders of Black people[20]. It ignores the violent and murderous rampages enacted by white people[21] on Black people who were doing nothing more than living their lives. It ignores how every fucking way we push back against this is somehow a problem.

It ignores the fact that many white people participate in the destruction of Black people, both explicitly and implicitly, including him. And yes, he needs to continue working on himself and the white people in his life to destroy this shit. And it's not going to happen in his lifetime, but he still fucking needs to work on it.

---

[17] History.com Staff. "Harriet Tubman." History.com. Web. 09 Dec. 2016.

[18] Loewen, James W.; Kaplan, Fran; Smith, Robert. "Sundown Towns: Racial Segregation Past and Present." America's Black Holocaust Museum. Web. 09 Dec. 2016.

[19] Sanders, Brandee. "History's Lost Black Towns." The Root, 27 Jan. 2016. Web. 09 Dec. 2016.

[20] The Establishment. "Every Day a Funeral." The Establishment, 20 Sept. 2016. Web. 09 Dec. 2016.

[21] Moore, A. "8 Successful and Aspiring Black Communities Destroyed by White Neighbors." Atlanta Black Star, 04 Dec. 2013. Web. 09 Dec. 2016.

Always. Just like I do. Like many Black people do. Like we *must* do because this is about the right to our humanity[22] and our survival.

I shared my personal experiences of racial discrimination with him and he said that there are white people who experience the same discrimination, bias, and threats of violence. Really? REALLY? Who? His response was that he could find someone online. Somebody online.

So, nobody he knows? Nobody he can call on the phone? Cuz I can invite 30 people over today who can tell him about the racist shit they've had to deal with. The threats. The discrimination. The inequities in the law and social imbalance.

And this is always my question for white people: who the fuck can you call who experienced racism from Black people? Who do you know? Who was assumed to be a bad influence and removed from classes as punishment? Who had their privileges revoked because they were NEAR an altercation? Who had their teachers, professors, counselors assume they didn't understand the lesson, accuse them of plagiarism, tell them not to aim high because that success wasn't meant for someone like them? Who do you personally know who lived on toxic land surrounded by white adults who would threaten to kill them for entering their neighborhood?

I don't need to read a fucking essay to understand what racism is and how it works. I live it. And I know I'm a goddamn privileged exception with my ivy league education and high paying job. I KNOW this. And despite all this fucking white approval, I still deal with racist co-workers and racist systems that explicitly deny me

---

[22] Oluo, Ijeoma. "You Don't Have To Like Me—You Just Have To Believe I'm A Human Being." The Establishment, 29 Nov. 2016. Web. 09 Dec. 2016.

entry to certain circles. I still work for unqualified white men who somehow "earned" their place despite having zero experience in that field. I still know that an interaction with police or some angry white person with a gun can result in my death and my corpse will be blamed for its murder.

But you got a fucking YouTube video. Get the fuck outta here.

This is the shit people in interracial relationships skate past. These discussions where you have to look at the white person in your life and realize this motherfucker is a white supremacist in denial. My S.O. has on more than one occasion admitted that he thinks this way and he's trying not to. He's trying. But all the information he's getting from white sources are feeding that belief system and he's fucking up.

He's hit his white supremacy reset button and that is a motherfucking problem.

While he no longer says that racism isn't real and no longer claims that he doesn't benefit from racism, he still seems to think racism isn't as dangerous as it is. He seems to think the people on the "other side" have the right to fight to oppress Black people and other people of color without repercussions. He seems to think that their fight for dominance is not problematic. That it's ok for them to fight to keep Black people beneath them and under their control.

He doesn't accept that the white people fighting to maintain this oppression don't think I'm equal. He doesn't grasp that there is a large part of the country that thinks he married a beast and is dirtying himself by being with me.

He doesn't accept that these people do not want to be at a table talking to me. They don't think I have anything worthwhile to say.

And he believes that my I'm being mean when I acknowledge this. He's fucking trying to protect them and their hate that he doesn't quite interpret as hate. To him, it's just a difference of opinion.

How did we get back here? How does the man who is astounded at the recent mistrial in South Carolina despite video evidence, who donated and supported Standing Rock and was outraged by the media's silence about it, say these things to me? Believe these things?

Did he lie to me about knowing these things aren't real? Did he lie to me about understand how racism works one way? And why is he making my conversations about racism about his feelings? Why is he trying to tell me to soften my stance about the shitty things white people do?

The more things change, the more they stay the same.

Right now, in this moment, I feel like I've wasted years of my life. Do I hate myself? I must hate myself to put myself through this.

Can I trust him? I'm starting to wonder...again. I'm starting to wonder again.

Is this worth it? I honestly do not know and whether I love him is irrelevant. I'm aware enough to know that loving a person doesn't mean they are healthy for you.

Last night he told me that he's scared that I'm talking about him when I talk about white fuckery. Well, sometimes I am. He does fucked up shit that is endemic to white people because of the privilege and power they hold in this society. One of those things is telling himself that he can't be racist or do racist shit because he married a Black woman. Another is pretending that white supremacy isn't the heartbeat of this country. He does this shit and he needs to keep pushing to change it, both within himself and those around him.

White people, if you are truly in this shit, in this fight for equal rights, you got a lot of fucking work to do. You got a lot of self-reflection, analysis, and introspection ahead. It's going to hurt. It's going to reveal some very hurtful things about yourself, and you're going to backslide because it sucks feeling like a shitty human. But this is your chance to work on changing that about yourself.

If something I'm saying hurts you, fucking examine that shit. Ask yourself why. If something I say makes you feel defensive, stop and ask why that is. Take the time. Do the work. Understand your reactions to POCs when they talk about racism, white supremacy, and white privilege. Learn why you fight so hard to deny it.

If you are about anti-racism work, this is a huge part of it. Embrace the pain that is fighting for the rights of everyone. Do the self-care so that you can stay in the fight. This is your time to fight for the rights of everyone.

People of Color, this is the shitty ass work of being with a white partner. This is the knife's edge you will find yourself perched upon as we establish our equality.

They will try to make us doubt ourselves. Don't let them.

They will try to undermine us. Fight them.

They will try to dismiss us. Understand and believe that you are right and deserve to be here, fighting for your rights and that if they can't see that, they are the problem.

We will hold our ground and make them bend. Our humanity is not in question. Our self-worth is not conditional. Our rights are not up for fucking debate.

There are not two sides to establishing my goddamn humanity and I will under no circumstances pretend that there is. I will not have a fucking conversation to debate my rights. I will not remotely entertain the idea that you are worth listening to. I am human. White people, you either fucking work the rest out or go join your brethren who are working so diligently to deny that.

Either way, get the fuck away from me.

This story first appeared at TheEstablishment.co, a multimedia site entirely run and funded by women, on January 3, 2017.

He doesn't accept that the white people fighting to maintain this oppression don't think I'm equal. He doesn't grasp that there is a large part of the country that thinks he married a beast and is dirtying himself by being with me.

– TaLynn Kel, When the Space You Promised Hurts Like Hell

"It's Fine..." How *Get Out* Has Me Questioning My Instincts (Again) About My Interracial Marriage

This article assumes you've seen the movie.

I wasn't going to see this movie. The trailers creeped me out that I knew I wouldn't be able to manage the experience. Then I started reading essays about it. I read Son of Baldwin's "Get the Fuck Outta Here: A Dialogue on Jordan Peele's *GET OUT*"[23] which completely piqued my interest. Another favorite essay is "What Becky Gotta Do to Get Murked? White Womanhood in Jordan Peele's *Get Out*"[24] which gets into the role white womanhood played in the movie. Both were great and are the standouts of the 20+ items I read about this movie. I decided to go to see how I would respond to it. I honestly didn't expect a lot. I was wrong.

Get Out fucked me up.

My very first reaction to the movie was "meh." Seriously. I came out unimpressed and cold. What I didn't realize was that the movie bothered me so much that I detached from my emotions to get through it. I often talk about how difficult it is to deal with the micro and macro-aggressions of interacting with white people. It's emotionally taxing. It's painful. And it's a part of my marriage. It has improved exponentially, but it's something that I control in my personal life as much as possible. Watching a movie full of them, and full of the casual lies white people tell Black people to keep them comfortable as they mine them for the parts they want was

---

[23] Son of Baldwin. "Get the Fuck Outta Here: A Dialogue on Jordan Peele's GET OUT." Medium, 27 Feb. 2017. Web. 17 Jan. 2018.

[24] Brooks, Kinitra. "What Becky Gotta Do to Get Murked? White Womanhood in Jordan Peele's Get Out." Very Smart Brothers, 03 March 2017. Web. 17 Jan. 2018.

overwhelming. They all feed into each other so seamlessly, that yes, that entire movie was a fucking terrible experience that showed me the many ways I've made myself vulnerable to white people by telling myself it's fine.

And afterwards I went home to my white husband and told myself, again, that it's fine.

But it wasn't. I was and continue to be shaken by this experience. It took me back to the time I realized that this man who cries at the pain of animals has trouble empathizing with Black people. This man who cannot watch violent anime without getting sad struggled to see that Trayvon Martin[25] was stalked and murdered. He still struggles to humanize Black people. And while he continues to confront this and work to change it, it's shocking to realize that it continues to be an issue. And as I sleep next to him every night, I am betting my life on him being an exception.

And I tell myself it's fine.

The movie reminded me of last time I spent xmas with him and his family, with whom I no longer interact[26]. We drove to Flori-Bama and I was the only Black person I saw for three days. His friends were sharing a vacation house with another family, who never spoke to me. I fielded questions from white children who'd never seen a Black person prior to that week. His mother told me how hard it was to find Black xmas décor, a child asked me why I was called Black if I'm brown, and I sat trying to engage but disengage

---

[25] Kel, TaLynn. "My Husband's Unconscious Racism Nearly Destroyed Our Marriage." The Establishment, 05 May. 2016. Web. 20 August 2016.

[26] Kel, TaLynn. "Why I Cut My Racist In-Laws Out Of My Life." Breaking Normal, 2 Aug. 2016. Web. 17 Jan. 2018.

because it was uncomfortable as hell. I still don't know exactly where we visited and if I'd lost my phone, I'd have been fucked. My only safety net was that it was my car and I had the keys.

And I told myself it was fine.

Early in our relationship, I constantly put myself in these environments. His friends live outside Atlanta where I see less and less Black people. Where we currently live is so diverse — not just Black people but also Asian-Americans, Middle Easterners, Latinx…so many different shades and experiences everywhere. Yet, when we'd visit his friends, suddenly I'd find myself surrounded by only white people. Every time I went to their homes, I was afraid. They lived in Forsyth County, a place I'd been told was a sundown town[27] that had been featured on an episode of Oprah in 1987. I remember expressing apprehension to my S.O. and he scoffed. At the time, the only way he would have believed me would have been if something happened.

And I told myself that it was fine.

Yesterday, I sat with my S.O. and told him this relationship isn't healthy for him. Because I'm not fine. I don't feel safe. Despite the seven years we've been together, I still sit and wait and watch for the moment that he says the indefensible thing. I am waiting for him to say or do something so racist that I can't ignore it. That I can't explain it away. The thing that we can't talk about enough to clear the air. And what *Get Out* showed me was that I let the racism

---

[27] NPR. "The 'Racial Cleansing' That Drove 1,100 Black Residents Out of Forsyth County, Ga." Fresh Air, 15 Sept. 2016. Web. 17 Jan. 2018.

minefield get too close to my home. When a mine goes off, and it's going to go off, I'm going to take heavy damage.

And I'm scared. I'm scared that my S.O. is Rose — the liar, the trickster. The psychopath who happily leads Black people to their demise. I am afraid that I am still not human enough to him and we just haven't found the right catalyst for his racism to bloom. I stay in this relationship wondering if and when there will be a big reveal.

And, because I have empathy, I know this is not fair to him.

How can I ask someone to continue to prove he's different? To continue to show me over and over again that he is confronting and dealing with his racism? How can that dynamic be an integral part of a healthy relationship? How can I keep asking and expecting this?

But this is the price of being with me. This is what I need to stay in this relationship because I still don't feel safe. He is not Black and because of that, I do not trust him with all my Blackness. I'm starting to think that the most I can do is trust him not to physically attack me for it. And still I'm not sure.

We talk about it. He tells me that all he can do is continue being who he is, keep learning, and keep supporting me. I asked him if it hurts and he said it does. But, he says, that it's his problem and he's figuring it out too. And I'm worth the work. He loves me.

I love him, too. It's hard. Sometimes it feels too hard. I didn't think a movie could make me feel this way. I didn't think that we still had all this work to do. But it did and we do. We always do.

I don't know how people look at all these interracial relationships and think theirs is safe. I don't know how I live, breathe, and shout my wholeness into the face of someone conditioned to think I'm not as whole as him. But I do. And I fight the urge to apologize for being me because I have the right to be me. And he has the choice to stay and live with it or to leave. But my choice to stay is dangerous. I'd be a liar if I said it wasn't.

But I tell myself that it's fine.

Yesterday, I sat with my S.O. and told him this relationship isn't healthy for him. Because I'm not fine. I don't feel safe. Despite the seven years we've been together, I still sit and wait and watch for the moment that he says the indefensible thing. I am waiting for him to say or do something so racist that I can't ignore it.

– TaLynn Kel, "It's Fine…" How *Get Out* Has Me Questioning My Instincts (Again) About My Interracial Marriage

When Your White Significant Other Says Something Racist

I am a Black woman in an interracial relationship with a white man, and while sometimes things are great, sometimes things are terrible.

Last week, things were terrible.

It all started when we talked about the women-only concert[28] being planned in Sweden in response to four rapes and 23 sexual assaults[29] that were reported at this year's event, following several reports of assault[30] at last year's event as well. I'm in favor of excluding men from events. Since men cannot and will not police themselves — in fact, they often protect each other from the consequences of their actions[31] — I support enforcing policies that hold them accountable for the harm they cause.

My Significant Other (S.O.) received his information about the concert on reddit, which, he claims, is a balanced source of information. Based on what he'd read, he felt confident stating that refugees and immigrants were responsible for the sexual assaults at the Bravalla concert. He felt so safe saying this that when I snapped, he doubled down and insisted that I look at his "evidence" for it.

---

[28] White, Adam. "Swedish Music Festival to go 'Women-Only' Following String of Sexual Assaults." The Telegraph, 6 July 2017. Web. 17 Jan. 2018.

[29] Cauterucci, Christina. "After 27 Sexual Assault Reports, Swedish Music Festival Replaced with Man-Free Event in 2018." Slate, 5, July 2017. Web. 17 Jan. 2018.

[30] Pollard, Alexandra. "Blaming the Swedish Festival Rapes on Migrants Isn't Just Wrong – It's Dangerous." The Guardian, 6, July 2016. Web. 17 Jan. 2018.

[31] Kel, TaLynn. "American, Stop Protecting Your Monsters." The Establishment, 10 Oct. 2016. Web. 17 Jan. 2018.

Evidence that he says has since disappeared, as the officer who reported the information is now under investigation.

I didn't need his evidence to know that what he said was bullshit. Blaming people who are considered to be "other" for a community's ills is common practice. I would have needed him to show me police reports and arrests supporting his statements before I would give it any real consideration, because my experience is that people considered "other" are often blamed for problems in predominantly white spaces. Considering that Sweden is a predominantly white space and anti-Blackness and xenophobia are worldwide, I didn't expect the white people there to be any different from the white people in America.

But to hear my S.O. say it was the immigrants who did it, and with such conviction…We started arguing immediately.

We were at dinner, so we fought in public until I told him to leave because I couldn't stand to look at him any longer. We paid for our meal and he left as I sat there, trying to sort out what the fuck just happened. After 20 minutes, I finally got up and took a walk. Eventually, I found him, and we went home, but needless to say, we didn't speak or have anything to do with one another for the remainder of the day.

If anyone other than the person I married had made such an offensive statement, I would have cursed them out and stopped fucking with them permanently. But I signed on to work with my husband and to build a future together[32]. And the thing is, I love

---

[32] Kel, TaLynn. "I Promised My White Husband the Space to Fuck Up on Racism – And It Hurts Like Hell." The Establishment, 16 Jan. 2017. Web. 17 Jan. 2018.

him. I love him so much that I constantly choose to stay despite these betrayals.

But when these arguments happen, I have to wonder: Am I doing more harm to myself by staying?

*****

The following day, we talked via text. He offered apologies, recanted, and admitted he'd fucked up. When I asked him why he seemed so happy to say it was because of the immigrants, he claimed that it was because he felt like he could win this argument. He said that he had the chance to be right and he took it. Apparently, confronting his ignorance about racism and constantly being wrong was getting to him, and he wanted a win. But this isn't about winning an argument. The fight for our humanity is so much bigger than an intellectual pissing contest.

Following this discussion, we continued to avoid each other. Even though he realized how badly he fucked up — even after he saw that all the posts he was using as evidence were removed and his source discredited — it was evident that his apology only went so far. He didn't want to question the part of him that led him to parrot "it was the immigrants" with such confidence. I'd never seen him so gleefully say something racist and xenophobic to me. It was as though he'd had all his secret thoughts validated. And while I told myself I'd never seen him act like that before, I knew it wasn't true. It had just been a very long time since the last time. Years, even.

While these fights occur less often now — and even though the time between them spans more and more months — every time they do happen, I just feel tired. Tired of doing the heavy lifting on racism in our marriage. Tired of being patient. Tired of giving him space to learn. Because here's the thing — that's what it means to be with a white person.

If you are Black or a Non-Black Person of Color (NBPOC), you are the one who cannot opt out of racism. You are the one who will recognize the microaggressions and the looks and the snide comments. You are the one who will be doing constant threat assessments when you're out and about. You are the one who will have to correct your S.O.'s ignorance and help them fix their shit. Because if you are talking about these things, as you should be, it's your partner who must choose to opt in to a discussion about racism — and sometimes, more often than I'd like, that shit doesn't take.

We all know white people don't have to talk about racism. We all know that racism isn't a constant in their lives. At least, not the degradation of it. Not the dehumanizing aspects of it. Not the discrimination, lack of worthiness, silencing, or violence that affects Black people all of their lives. But when a white person chooses to be with a Black partner, they are choosing to make racism a constant part of their lives. And if that white partner wants to pretend racism isn't a part of the relationship, they are a liar and a shitty partner. They are toxic.

Eight years ago, I lived this and he changed...and while right now it doesn't feel like enough, I know he's different now. I also know that if I met him now, as he is, I don't think I'd date him because it's hard to trust white people and I'm fucking tired.

But this is my reality, part of which I chose without fully understanding what it would mean. That reality includes the fact that the racism I experience is still not quite real for the man I love. This despite the constant backdrop of anti-Black nonsense in our lives: Black women being trashed[33]. Black people being discriminated against[34] and murdered[35] worldwide. Interracial couples in the U.S. getting threatened[36] and stabbed[37]. Mistrials when white people murder Black people[38]…

Sometimes I wonder what it would take for all this to be real. My death? An obvious threat to my life? When will he understand that I am not exaggerating — that I've just carved out the safest environment I know how, and it protects us from a lot of this shit?

I'm tired of him not being able to understand. I'm tired of being tired.

*****

Several days after the fight, we still aren't right.

Even though it's been a long time since the argument, we are struggling to talk to each other. Just today I asked him why. Why be with me? We could break up and he could find a white woman who

---

[33] Pache, Juliana and Starling, Lakin. "A Candid Conversation About Rap Culture's Pervasive Disrespect Against Black Women." Fader, 09 May, 2017. Web. 17 Jan. 2018.

[34] Herriott, Arianna. "6 African Countries That Are Hostile Toward Black People." Atlanta Black Star, 03 June. 2017. Web. 17 Jan. 2018.

[35] Helm, Angela. "Recent College Grad Beaten to Death in Greece." The Root, 09 July 2017. Web. 17 Jan. 2018.

[36] Edwards, Breanna. "2 Brooklyn, NY, Men Charged with Shouting Racial Slurs at Interracial Couple, Beating Up and Threatening to 'Lynch' Black Boyfriend." The Root, 12 July 2017. Web. 17 Jan. 2018.

[37] Tesfaye, Sophia. "Washington Man Stabs Kissing Interracial Couple, Cites Donald Trump When Arrested." Salon, 19 Aug. 2016. Web. 17 Jan. 2018.

[38] Associate Press. "Third mistrial declared in case of white ex-cop accused of killing daughter's black boyfriend." Los Angeles Times, 08 July 2017. Web. 17 Jan. 2018.

would never subject him to this again. It's so fucking hard sometimes, and sometimes I hate that trashing white supremacy means hurting him. But that's the price. For white people, rejecting white supremacy means rejecting your specialness. It means pulling away that cushion that protected you from the truth of who you are: oppressors, descendants of rapists and murderers. The offspring of generations of people willing and able to capitalize off the use and murders of thousands of Black people. Your heroes are savages[39] and you live in the benefits of their savagery.

And the result is that our relationship hurts us.

He says it doesn't matter. He says that it's worth it. I'm worth it. But I still have to live with hurting someone I love and don't want to hurt. And he lives with knowing that he says shit that hurts me, and he has to learn how to stop.

Sometimes I wonder if it will ever stop, and I still question why I'm choosing this life. But while love isn't the answer — it is the reason. Love and the willingness to learn and grow. If he didn't try, didn't admit his mistakes, didn't ask me what he could do to grow, I'd leave. There isn't a doubt in my mind that I'd bounce, hurt, heal, and move on. But when he's acknowledging his mistake and working to gain better understanding, it's hard to walk away.

From this fight, we learned some things. We learned that he has been building resentment toward me because of his inability to fully understand and discuss racism. We learned that he needs to take more steps and delve deeper into understanding the intentional systems that maintain racial hierarchy. We learned that he has to

---

[39] Kel, TaLynn. "White People Are the Villains in This Narrative." Breaking Normal, 26 June 2017. Web. 17 Jan. 2017.

do more work, and that he has to reassure me that he's going to do the work. Right now, he has some reading I've given him. It's a test and he knows that it's a test. If he fails, then I truly have wasted years of my life with him.

Love isn't the answer — but it is the reason.

I know he's only engaging in anti-racism for me and I don't wonder if it matters anymore. I know it matters. I know that his care for me exceeds his need to protect himself. There will be hiccups and fuckups and "you need to shut ups." And when the rage passes and the hurt fades, we'll regroup and figure out what to do next. Because we aren't working on a small issue. This is something that exceeds the boundaries of our relationships. These attitudes shaped our foundations, and when we confront them, we're shaking our houses down.

He fucked up and he's trying to learn from it. For now, at least, that is enough.

This story first appeared at TheEstablishment.co, a multimedia site entirely run and funded by women, on July 25, 2017.

Just today I asked him why. Why be with me? We could break up and he could find a white woman who would never subject him to this again. It's so fucking hard sometimes, and sometimes I hate that trashing white supremacy means hurting him. But that's the price.

– TaLynn Kel, When Your White Significant Other Says Something Racist

When Protecting Yourself from Racism Is the "Selfish" Choice

My racist mother-in-law is dying.

Well, we think she may be dying. She is in the hospital and they are trying to figure out what's happening, but it's been three days and we have no answers. My significant other (S.O.) drove down to be with his family. I chose not to go because I choose not to have a relationship with them and it would be an additional expense during a time where we are barely keeping ourselves afloat financially. So, he went, and I stayed home.

He's angry at me now.

I knew he would be. Here he is, in crisis about his mother, and I am choosing not to physically be there for him. I'm not working a 9–5 so I wouldn't be missing work. I am available to go, but because I won't stay in the home of people who are casually, unapologetically "racist-lite," I'm not being supportive.

The last time someone in his immediate family was sick, I went to his family's place, worked out of a hotel, spent evenings with them at the hospital, and had his mom ask me silly shit like, "how do Black people remove facial hair?" and "Your children would be beautiful, cuz of the skin." Ridiculous, offensive questions that intentionally identified me as "other" in their presence and implied that an infusion of whiteness into my gene pool would benefit any potential offspring. His mom would tell me how she wanted a Black woman angel for her holiday mantle, but all the Black ones were unattractive, so she couldn't find one. His father constantly referred to my friends as a gang, despite repeated correction. It was always about me being different and how I was different and how my difference was some kind of problem in some way. And each time, my S.O. would look ashamed and embarrassed while never addressing their transgressions. And when I tried to address it with his family, I was met with false apologies and protestations of innocent ignorance because they just didn't know. The expectation was always that I needed to be patient. That I needed to excuse them. That these grown ass people, 30+ years my senior, were ignorant children stumbling through conversations about race, and I was meant to be the mature person educating them.

My S.O. knew this was fucked up, but it was his sister's wedding, or Xmas, or the health of his family member was the priority and I needed to remember that. And while he never explicitly said this, he hinted that his parents were not particularly bright or socially adept. He actively limits his contact with them because, sadly, while he loves them, he doesn't like them. I know he didn't understand how offensive their comments were; I know the particulars were lost on him and all he knew was that I was upset. And in the interest of getting in and out of whatever social obligation pulled me into their orbit, I needed to understand they were limited and let this ignorant shit go because the situation was always more important, and I shouldn't make it about me. Except this was about me--about how his family talks to me--and only I seemed to care about it.

It was after that visit, and some other choice comments his mother made about Black people murdered by police, that I decided not to fuck with his family anymore. Specifically, I decided that I wouldn't interact with them in any way. I didn't want any gifts from them, wouldn't let them in my home, and sure as hell wouldn't visit them for any reason. I said he could have a relationship with them but that I wouldn't and he could navigate that however he wanted. It's caused some hiccups, but I am willing to talk about them with him as needed. I just won't interact with them personally, or even through him.

Before cutting them off, I told him he needed to confront his parents about their bullshit, which he did. He received the same response I did--the lie of "I didn't think it was racist? I didn't know. I'm sorry" bullshit white women love to say. His father sided with my S.O. but never admitted to his role in it. In the end, my S.O. didn't see the point in trying to get them to change because they don't see anything wrong with their beliefs, and barely acknowledge them. This stance actually made me look at my S.O. differently because I felt like it was complete bullshit.

But then a few months later, they happily voted for the orange menace, and have since supported his agenda wholeheartedly. My S.O. attempted talking about politics with them only to find himself overwhelmed with their nonsense rhetoric. At one point, his mother said something along the lines of "I have to vote white. It's the only thing I know how to do." I remember my S.O. hanging up on her at that point because what is there to say to that? Over time, I watched him become more depressed and defeated as he saw the damage white people were willing to inflict upon everyone to uphold white supremacy.

In some ways I felt bad for my S.O., because the blinders had slid back even more, and he was faced with the reality of white people — people with whom he identified for the majority of his life. And because he was one of them, he hated what it said about him.

My S.O. has shown me that he's still figuring out how to manage oppression enacted by those he cares about. While he figures that out, I'll be somewhere else, managing my self-care. I will also offer my emotional support from a distance--by offering him any time he needs, managing the household responsibilities, dipping further into savings to supplement the income we're losing by him taking this time off, and letting him feel his pain without trying to cheer him up. I share stories about health crises that weren't as dire as they initially seemed, without minimizing the seriousness of his mother's current situation. I am here for him in a way that isn't damaging to me.

And if that isn't enough for him, he needs to figure that out. I am not sacrificing my well-being in this.

This choice is not easy. I am sitting here now, sorting through my thoughts as I try to figure out what's best. What's best for him. What's best for me. He called me when he got to the hospital to tell me that he was upset I wasn't there with him. I told him that I feel bad about it but that I was not going to put myself in a vulnerable situation with people who I do not have a relationship with.

This might break us. I realize that. I don't want it to, but it could.

*****

Our culture is inundated with images of Black women sacrificing themselves in every way imaginable for whatever greater good is in vogue. And when we collapse from the strain and die from the stress, people look around for the next martyr for the cause. But I'm not a martyr. I'm a Black woman trying to live her life under ridiculous circumstances, in a society that tells me I'm not enough. If sacrificing my physical and emotional safety is a requirement to support you, then fuck you. I deserve better than that.

And this isn't just about my S.O. As I began talking about the oppressive transgressions I've experienced at the hands of my S.O.'s family, people I called friends and family basically told me to be silent. They would ask me how my S.O. felt about the things I said. They told me I was being too militant and insensitive. That I was risking my relationship by confronting the misogynoir in my life. I was advised on multiple occasions to let it go and be considerate of his feelings. To make this easy for him. My self-worth was secondary to maintaining this relationship.

I found myself angry at all those people in my life, and as a result, some of them aren't in my life anymore.

I understand that we need to have other people in our lives who challenge us and our beliefs, but that's different from having to confront the negation of your very humanity. People like to pick me apart for daring to emote, express, and resist, to protect myself from the harm of those who see me as less than. They like to reduce my pain to something hormonal or irrational.

I've lost count of the myriad ways people will tell me to put my well-being and emotional and personal safety behind the needs of others, be they the men in my life, the white people in my life, the good of the family, the good of the company...the reasons are limitless. In this case, I am expected to swallow my S.O.'s abuse and pretend everything is fine...for their comfort. For their peace.

No.

My well-being demands that I not do that. Call it selfish if you want; I am always called selfish when I prioritize my emotional and physical needs. They aren't selfish for demanding that I risk my emotional well-being for their benefit, but I'm selfish for refusing to do so? Oh, well. I'll learn to live with it.

*****

Multiple people have asked me if I will go to my mother-in-law's funeral, and when I started writing this, I had no answer. I love my husband. I try to be there for him in any number of ways. And in the beginning of our relationship, I suppressed parts of myself for his comfort.

But being with him pushed me to grow in ways I never anticipated. His friends and family have forced me to engage with racist people on a level I'd never experienced before. It's complicated and difficult, but it taught me how egregious white people are when it comes to engaging in oppression. There is a level of denial I had to purge because I was seeing in real time how much of a fuck they didn't give. As a result, I am stronger, more confident, and better able to identify, address, and care for my needs.

Already, my S.O. is fielding emotional attacks from his family-- accusations of selfishness and attention-seeking for dropping everything to be with them and being chastised for not communicating enough or sharing too much with people other than family. His family is emotionally immature and manipulative on a good day--characteristics that are only exacerbated in times of crisis. He is terrible about asking for support and this situation with his mother's failing health exacerbates every part of him that he needs to continue developing. His pain and fear are palatable, and I don't believe his family will help him through this crisis.

My presence, or lack thereof, will be weaponized, as this is what they do. These are people who sat with my family at Xmas years ago, holed up in a corner, looking afraid to speak but when I was alone, would express their bigotry through seemingly innocent and inoffensive questions like "why are there so many Indian people in your neighborhood?" and "did you have a gay person at the wedding? They seemed kinda flamboyant." To them, I'm already this big, Black threat that they feel the need to manage and can't. And while my presence would soothe my S.O., it would cause so many other problems, where only my willingness to accept their abuse would keep shit from blowing up.

No.

I know society tells you that Black women are expendable, but I am not. This is the hill I choose to die on and while I hope we will work to find a workable solution for both of us, there are limits I will not compromise on.

I know that he needs me. I need him, too. And attending the funeral is an option. Not the viewing. Not the aftermath, but maybe the actual funeral. But anything where I need to socialize with his family?

No.

These people are dangerous to me and that is my line.

*****

My S.O. and I chose a complicated relationship that doesn't operate under the standards society dictates. We are not a social norm and that means that these situations will require complicated decisions. Untraditional choices. Non-linear pathways that he and I will have to create for ourselves. This is a situation where our needs are at cross-purposes, and we need to figure out how to be there for one another without putting the other in harm's way. We need to not punish ourselves for not looking like what's "normal."

We have to accept each other's needs and understand that sometimes, we cannot be there for each other in the way we envision. I continue to learn that as he works on addressing his anti-

Blackness and racism, and he needs to learn what it means for me to prioritize my self-love. Our needs are not the same.

Interracial relationships, specifically interracial relationships composed of Black and white partners, are complicated. They are intense work. Anti-Blackness is so commonplace as to be invisible without conscious effort to see and address it. I talk about it, I work through it, and I share my story because there is a lack of support for people in these relationships. People on the outside are cruel about this. I have been told repeatedly that I fucked up and should end the relationship; that this can never work; that I should have known what I was getting into...

Well, I didn't. I didn't understand the complexity of what this would be and how it would play out. I still don't know if we will last, but that's our decision to make. And in the meantime, I am learning. I'm learning what I need, what works for me, and what works for us.

Society has told me time and again that I am meant to be an emotional mule and a willing sacrifice. I'm telling society and anyone pushing that narrative to fuck off. I am more than everything you've said and fuck you if you have a problem with it.

This story first appeared at TheEstablishment.co, a multimedia site entirely run and funded by women, on February 6, 2018.

Our culture is inundated with images of Black women sacrificing themselves in every way imaginable for whatever greater good is in vogue. And when we collapse from the strain and die from the stress, people look around for the next martyr for the cause.

– TaLynn Kel, When Protecting Yourself from Racism is the "Selfish" Choice

Fandom

I have a love/hate relationship with fandom.

I love that it exists. I love that I can find people who share my enjoyment or criticism of a body of work; that we can have full discussions around themes and creative decisions and every aspect of a creative property. I love the ease with which I can now find these communities and I enjoy the relationships that can be found there. It was my love of cosplay that introduced me to a creative community that I may not have found without having engaged in this activity. Cosplay itself has become its own fandom, with people popping up and becoming cosplay celebrities and brands. It's amazing.

What I hate is the way people claim ownership of certain properties and make themselves the gatekeepers of it. I hate that, like many things in racist, patriarchal, heteronormative societies, there exists glass ceilings and barriers to entry. I hate that there are self-appointed "geek cred" evaluators, usually white men who claim their job is to maintain the purity and integrity of the culture so that "posers" don't ruin it for them.

Notice how scarily similar this rhetoric is to white supremacist propaganda? Yeah. There's a reason for that.

We saw their toxic brand of gatekeeping with GamerGate, where they repeatedly harassed and attacked a woman game creator because she received a favorable review of her game by a journalist she knew. Her ex-boyfriend claimed she slept with journalists to receive good reviews of her game, and white male cishet gamers went ballistic, exposing her personal information and threatening her life[40].

We saw this with the Hugo Awards. The Hugo Awards is a long-standing award for the best science fiction books and authors voted on by attendees of WorldCon, The World Science Fiction Convention. Due to an influx of "diverse" authors, in 2015, a right-wing group decided to control the finalists by heavily promoting writers they felt truly represented the core values of science fiction[41]. That these authors were all cishet white men was not lost on anyone. This "uprising" of cishet, white male "connoisseurs" of science fiction led to a huge discussion around what is considered to be "real" science fiction and who should be allowed to decide that. It also sparked discussion on the financial and informational barriers to access[42]. Until this controversy, I'd kind of heard of the Hugo Awards, but they had little bearing on whether I wanted to read a book because, as a fat, Black femme geek, I already knew that awards weren't for people like me. But it's a good discussion for people who believe the playing field is level and fair to investigate…especially as it directly reflects how politicians gain their office.

We saw it with Anita Sarkeesian, whose video series analyzing women in video games was met with such vitriol that a slew of YouTubers began creating videos calling her a liar. These videos

---

[40] Hathaway, Jay. "What Is Gamergate, and Why? An Explainer for Non-Geeks." Gawker, 10 Oct. 2014. Web. 19 Jan. 2018.

[41] Waldman, Katy. "How Sci-Fi's Hugo Awards Got Their Own Full-Blown Gamergate." Slate, 08 April 2015. Web. 19 Jan. 2018.

[42] Chu, Arthur. "Sci-fi's right-wing backlash: Never doubt that a small group of deranged trolls can ruin anything (even the Hugo Awards)." Salon, 06 April 2015. Web. 19 Jan. 2018.

became so popular that some of the creators earned income from slandering her and anyone they considered to be a Social Justice Warrior (SJW)[43].

These are the publicized examples. They happen throughout geek culture on many levels, from who is paid to be a guest at a con, to how many followers a cosplay has, to who and why someone is considered a "good" writer/cosplayer/artist/ representative of geek culture. And people who fall outside those criteria or challenge them are considered the enemy - as someone attempting to undermine everything that makes geek life and fandom special.

Guess what? It's the people who make fandom special. All the people. All the perspectives. Except white supremacist ones. Fuck those.

I love seeing the different ways people interpret creative properties. I love talking about it. The thing that white supremacy refuses to acknowledge is that we are shaped by our experiences and our experiences create and interpret everything – the white male gaze isn't the only gaze, nor is it the most important despite it being the only one those in power acknowledge.

Focusing on this one perspective has corroded popular culture. It's the main reason why we have all these shows and movies fascinated with how horrible white people can be. Movies like "Horrible Bosses," shows like "Despicable People" and other properties that either regurgitate past successes or mire themselves in the horrors of humanity while calling it art. I am fascinated and disgusted with white people's fixation on the atrocities they've

---

[43] Campbell, Colin. "Anita Sarkeesian's Astounding 'Garbage Human' Moment." Polygon, 27 June 2017. Web. 19 Jan. 2018.

committed through history and their fantasies about them. Sometimes it's a redemption narrative or it's about empathizing with a monster. They make cruelty both palatable and artistic and that is horrifying. Stop romanticizing your monsters; it's killing us.

And yet, despite this, fandom lets me be free. It helps me release a part of myself that I've had to lock down to conform to a society that ignores, resents, or hates my existence. It allows me to play with my creative, fun-loving side. And I'm not saying that it's all easy. I've dealt with negative reinforcement doing this, but my need to feel this kind of release motivated me to carve out spaces and find people who shared my joy. Cosplay is an art that needs an audience and while my audience is limited, it is supportive and nurturing. That matters more than recognition. I needed something that nourished my entirety. Cosplay and fandom became those things.

But, like with everything, fandom is problematic. I believe in acknowledging the bad and appreciating the good because in a society that doesn't love you, sometimes that's the best you are going to get.

*****

As a side note, I was really taken aback at the overall response to the racist Supergirl cosplayer. She stood out for me because I'd interacted with her before and when the story came out, people had all these instances of microaggressions. She couldn't be bothered to tell us apart. She never bothered to learn anybody's names despite hanging with them multiple time. To clear her name, she used private messages between her and one of my friend's teenage kids, as he basically begged her to say she wasn't racist. She exposed so much anti-Blackness and accepted racism in those around me that it changed many of my relationships. People who I'd trusted were no longer trustworthy, especially as they tried to find ways to rationalize the casual racism of their community. It was disheartening and especially annoying because my distance from many of those people was called racist and exclusionary rather than protective.

I was surprised by the number of Black people willing to give the white people around them passes for their racism without challenging them about it. Then again, I'm married to a white man who for a long time, refused to acknowledge his racism and still struggles to confront it. The difference is that I don't let it slide anymore. I can't. I also don't have the energy to vet every white person repeatedly to see if they are trying to be better than they have been. Instead, I assume they aren't and if they demonstrate differently, I'll figure it out then.

But for now, I have taken on the load I can manage, and it is more than enough.

As a Fat, Black Woman, Cosplay Has Tried to Make Me Invisible

I never considered myself a geek until I picked up a new hobby: costume play, aka cosplay. It's one of those things that happened organically. Someone took me to a geek convention, I saw people in costume, and not once did it occur to me *not* to dress up like them. Before I'd been there an hour, I had plans, ideas, hopes, and dreams for how to become a part of this world.

In short: I love cosplay. It is one of the highlights of my life, providing an outlet for my creativity, my problem-solving, my mild exhibitionism, and my need for expression.

I often try to capture my joy for cosplay through photos, of which I have many. And recently, when I did a cosplay photo shoot in my Asgardian Storm costume, I asked my significant other (S.O.) what he thought of one of my pictures. His response: "There's a little too much boob."

A little too much boob.

I looked at him, angry and offended, and said, "This is my body. That's just how it looks."

"I just think it detracts from the costume," he responded.

My S.O. loves my body. I know this. But for him to say that my body was a problem in the costume was *shaming*. It was judgment. It was him expressing that somehow my body was the problem in this costume that was designed with a top that is open-laced to the navel.

His comment brought back all the ways I'd experienced body criticism throughout my life. And it reminded me how, even in the cosplay community that has allowed me to be so free, I am still not immune from body shaming.

*****

Growing up, I was taught to be ashamed of my size and my breasts. I remember being in grade school, and my teacher loudly whispering during attendance that I needed a bra—and then my classmates talking behind my back when the molded-cup bra my mom then bought me made me look even more developed than I was. I remember being teased during gym class for how much my breasts bounced when I ran; I wore two bras to compensate and still faced comments like "you're going to give yourself a black eye" or "try not to get a concussion."

At the same time, I was told my body excited men. They felt entitled to inform me how I should dress, when I should smile, and how I should always try to make myself appealing for them. When I wore fitted clothes, people would tell me I looked "fuckable." When I wore baggy clothes to make my fuckability less pronounced, people told me I looked sloppy and should dress better.

My clothing was monitored and criticized by both men *and* women. I was told to look available, but not *too* available; approachable but not *too* comfortable...because comfortable meant I wasn't trying hard enough. I needed to show my body but not my skin; skin invited trouble.

I was shamed and policed for more than just the shape of my body. Because I am brown, I was told to stay indoors and avoid the sun because *heaven forbid* I get darker. I was told most sports weren't feminine and the ones on the approved list were subject to rules that moderated and tempered girls' aggression. I was taught that my bigger, browner body scared white women and that it was my responsibility to manage my effect on them.

I hated this. I still hate it. I've been groomed all my life to seek this body-related attention as an affirmation of my womanly worth—despite its apparent simultaneous lack of appeal.

Cosplay is ostensibly a community that accepts those, like me, who exist outside mainstream normative ideals. But in this community, I've simply found another arena where I need to manage body commodification and shaming, and in ways I didn't anticipate.

As a cosplayer, your audience, the people who enjoy cosplay, don't always see you as a person. They often see you as the embodiment of the fictional character you're portraying, and sometimes they impose their standards, their desires, and their interpretation of that character onto you. The cosplay stops being about you and instead becomes about you fitting into someone else's narrative about a character.

But I often *don't* fit that narrative. I don't/can't/won't physically resemble the character enough to satisfy a fan's embodiment of a beloved character—and so, I'm often rendered invisible.

This wasn't true when I first started. There were so few people dressing up that people were excited to see *anyone* adorned as their favorite character. As cosplay got more popular, though, there was an increasing number of people who actually looked like the characters—or who were willing to change their bodies enough to get as close to looking like the characters as humanly possible. And suddenly, *that* became the ideal.

Because I am a fat Black woman, I have worn costumes that are 95% accurate to the screen or comic book version of the character, but been dismissed and ridiculed. When I dressed as Cable, an X-Men character, people couldn't tell who I was because I was brown and obviously a woman. Because people associate brown skin and white hair with Storm, people kept asking if that's who I was; never mind my silver arm, illuminated eye, and extraneous yellow pouches, all characteristics of classic Cable.

At the same time, I've seen people who are slim or muscular or whatever the current illusion of attractive is wear a scaled-back version of the costume and be adored. They look "right" even if they aren't trying to be "right."

Since people like me don't really exist in comics, I can get a little closer if the character is masculine or an inhuman skin color. I recognize that this is both funny and fucked up—that my cosplay becomes more realistic for people the farther I step away from my identity.

This isn't to say marginalized people are never accepted in the cosplay world, but even this acceptance isn't what it should be. Just like the broader body positivity movement endorses certain bodies over others—the hourglass curvy, not the round curvy; the white bodies, not the brown ones; the cellulite-free bodies, not the ones with visible cellulite—true acceptance is modified.

When you look up Black women cosplayers, when you think about those you know, they are usually light-skinned and not fat. If they are darker skinned, they are thin and curvy. If they are fat, they are lighter skinned. I very rarely see dark-skinned, fat women cosplayers, and while I cannot say why that is, I can guess: Even in this community that built itself to accept the socially unaccepted, there remains misfit toys.

It's also worth noting that the cosplay community is hardly immune from the objectification of female bodies. I've experienced what it's like to have men try to make me responsible for their sexual desire, where I've been accused of teasing them and enticing them because of what I chose to wear. I know what it feels like to have strangers project their sexual fantasies onto me, to have them overwrite my humanity with their lust as they try to shape me into that fantasy. I've had them turn our interactions into the verbal equivalent of those fantasies, until they are not talking with me anymore and I'm just a placeholder for future jack-off material.

*****

I've always been aware that there are approved looks—socially approved beauty. And I've always known that I do not represent this. My brown skin alone rules me out of acceptability, but my broad nose, my full lips, my dark brown eyes, my fat body… all these things together firmly place me into the unapproved category. I see how some people are treated in the cosplay community, and as inclusive as it is, not everyone is visible. People like me are not visible.

Cosplay culture mimics societal "norms" in virtually every way, including body shaming and celebrating certain body types. And just like in "mainstream" culture, there are people who exist outside the accepted norm and who push back—and are still marginalized. Those of us who keep doing what we're doing, who keep occupying space in this hobby that actively tries to ignore us are pushing back. Every race, body, or gender nonconforming person who refuses to step aside is pushing back. Every person who has been told that they don't fit but they stay anyway is pushing back. We are making spaces for ourselves and when doors are shut in our faces, we cut another hole in the wall to make a new one.

Our bodies don't need to be tamed. They can be loved, cherished, and appreciated regardless of how they look or what they are capable of doing...including when they're dressed in a cosplay costume.

This story first appeared at TheEstablishment.co, a multimedia site entirely run and funded by women, on September 20, 2016.

I know what it feels like to have strangers project their sexual fantasies onto me, to have them overwrite my humanity with their lust as they try to shape me into that fantasy. I've had them turn our interactions into the verbal equivalent of those fantasies, until they are not talking with me anymore and I'm just a placeholder for future jack-off material.

– TaLynn Kel, as a Fat, Black Woman, Cosplay Has Tried to Make Me Invisible

Blackface Isn't a Compliment

Be it Halloween or a convention, anytime there is an opportunity to costume or cosplay, the issue of skin color arises—specifically, the brown skin of Black people. White people believe that they can paint it on and wash it off with impunity. I've heard every excuse possible, from the "it's harmless" to "my Black friend is okay with it" to "it's a sign of how much I love the character."

But regardless of how you wrap it in your head, blackface is not a compliment. It's a dehumanizing insult that people literally paint themselves in and try to hustle other people into believing. That anyone can look at the history of Black people in America—hell, the world[44]—and think that this is some kind of tribute only reflects how completely divorced they are from reality.

You see it in the cosplay community, any time a new brown-skinned character appears on the scene. White people and non-Black people of color promote the lie that skin-darkening is an attempt at authenticity. "It's an inherent part of the character," they say. "You should feel honored," they say.

Why? Why should I feel honored? Do you think that you are doing me or any other Black person a favor? Why would you think that? What is it about wearing my skin color that makes you think you are doing something nice? Especially when so many Black people have spoken about how fucking insulting it is? Every year there are posts, essays, videos, podcasts talking about how terrible blackface is, and every year there's a new crop of costumers crying victim when Black people tell them it's wrong.

---

44 Blaque, Kat. "Are Zwarte Pieten Racist?" YouTube, 19 Oct. 2014. Web. 27 Sept. 2016.

If you really want to honor me or any Black person, how about listening when we say that culture isn't a costume[45], blackface isn't okay[46], and it certainly isn't a compliment. And then how about you stop doing that shit.

When you take a person's characteristics and shrink them down to their skin color, you are promoting a dangerous way of thinking about people. This is a technique that has been used to dehumanize and destroy Black people for hundreds of years. You may claim to associate brown skin with strength of character, but historically it's been used to say Black people are animals, criminals, primitive, and in need of strong discipline. To this day, white people interpret brown skin as dangerous and threatening. That is one of the reasons why police are so quick to use excessive violence to "subdue" us instead of just talking to us. Any movement we make is deemed threatening and they feel justified in using physical force to suppress it. This is a very real interpretation of my skin color, something over which I had no control.

It doesn't matter that you see my brown skin as strength. It doesn't matter if you see it as resilience. Strength and resilience are indeed traits I possess, but they're traits that I've had to develop to compensate for the racist environment I live in. It doesn't matter that you think my skin is beautiful. It doesn't matter how many positive descriptors you load onto my Blackness—it doesn't validate the dehumanizing aspect of it. This act of reducing my worth to my skin color is how stereotypes are made and doing it erases the complexity of human identity. It limits me to some finite list of

---

[45] Blaque, Kat. "Cultures are Not Costumes" YouTube, 08 Oct. 2014. Web. 27 Sept. 2016.

[46] Blaque, Kat. "Veds 28: What Is Blackface?" YouTube, 29 Sept. 2014. Web. 27 Sept. 2016.

characteristics that in many cases I've had to protect myself from—
like the oversexed Jezebel stereotype that follows Black girls and
women around, coloring their friendships and relationships
throughout life and the angry Black woman stereotype that
negatively affects how I'm regarded in the workplace[47].

Assigning specific behaviors and characteristics to skin color makes
it easy for people to project their idea of what they think I am on
me. They create the me they think I should be instead of actually
getting to know who I am. I've gone to clubs and had white people
approach me demanding that I show them how to dance because
"everybody knows Black people can dance." (For the record, I love
dancing, but I'm terrible at it.) I've had men assume I was available
because I was at the bar having drinks. I've had co-workers assume
I'm violent because I was angry about something.

It is annoying and aggravating to constantly inform people to
squash their assumptions. I've lost the expectation that new people
will actually try to know me instead of projecting whatever their
expectations of Black women are onto me. I'm not a caricature, and
I'm not a costume to be put on—or a voice to be affected, so please
don't yell "yaaaaass girlfriend!" and then make strong eye contact
for some affirmation that we are in the secret Black girl club. I don't
fucking talk like that and I sure as hell don't appreciate either the
projection or the mimicry.

These stereotypes are boring and trite, but more than that, they're
dangerous. Just ask 17- year old Trayvon Martin[48], 13-year old Tyre

---

[47] Kel, TaLynn. "The Face that Paused a Thousand Meetings." Breaking Normal, 28
April 2016. Web. 27 Sept. 2016.

[48] Biography.com Editors. "Trayvon Martin Biography." The Biography.com Website,
09 Feb. 2016. Web. 27 Sept. 2016.

King[49], and 12-year old Tamir Rice[50]—all murdered because of the assumptions someone's overactive imagination projected on their skin.

This is what we Black people live with. We live with the knowledge that our skin, a superficial physical characteristic we were born with, has been tainted by white people. Marred by white people with power. Disparaged by white people who work to punish us for existing. Growing up, we learn that the people around us, the pale ones who burn in the sun, actively and passively suppress us, oppress us, and benefit from mistreating us. We learn that you lie in your heads and hearts about us, and then lie to our faces[51] when you say we're all human and equal.

American history does not agree with you and we are living in its toxic present. A present where white people continue to make dehumanization a social norm.

You wouldn't skin someone and wear their skin. So, ask yourself, what are you actually trying to do when you feel the need to darken your skin in order to costume as your favorite Black person or character? What are you saying when you claim that darkening your skin makes you feel closer to them, like you are embodying them? It's like you're trying to symbolically absorb them into you and

---

[49] Josefczyk, Aaron. "Community Gathers to Mourn 13-Year-Ole Tyre King Who Was Killed by Cops." The Huffington Post, 26 Sept. 2016. Web. 27 Sept. 2016.

[50] Williams, Joseph P. "Tamir Rice Shooting: Not Just a Tragedy." U.S. News and World Reports, 29 Dec. 2015. Web. 27 Sept. 2016.

[51] Kel, TaLynn. "White People, You Have A Lying Problem." The Establishment. 07 July 2016. Web. 27 Sept. 2016.

replace them. You are trying to be them and that isn't admiration. It's psychological cannibalism and it's sickening.

Is this type of behavior the modern-day descendant of colonialism? Is this 4constant cannibalism[52] of other people, other cultures, until you absorb them at every level and become them feeding the inherited need to conquer, consume, and destroy?

I don't know. What I do know is that absorbing us won't make you into a better person. It doesn't imbue you with the strengths you admire. It just feeds your sickness and masks your rot a little longer.

This story first appeared at TheEstablishment.co, a multimedia site entirely run and funded by women, on October 24, 2016.

---

[52] Kel, TaLynn. "When White People Consume Blackness for Personal Gain." The Establishment. 29 June 2016. Web. 27 Sept. 2016.

You may claim to associate brown skin with strength of character, but historically it's been used to say Black people are animals, criminals, primitive, and in need of strong discipline.

– TaLynn Kel, Blackface Isn't a Compliment

When Inclusion Becomes Erasure

No person is just one thing. We have a multitude of identities that define us and are often weaponized against us. As a woman, I'm told I'm too emotional in my decision-making. As a Black woman, I'm told that I'm too angry and aggressive with a perpetual victim mindset. As a fat, Black woman I'm told I take up too much space and should learn my place in this world, which is either unseen or behind a lot of other people. But I make myself seen while giving the finger to all these people trying to dictate who I should be…that is, when I remember to notice them. I've been hearing nay-sayers for so long that they've become white noise…not that I miss it when it's gone, but still. It's the ever-present buzz that constantly seeks to steer me out of the way.

So, when I see people and organizations promoting inclusion, my inner skeptic steps up to see what's actually going on. Inclusion is a challenging thing to do because to do it, you must consciously define groups and then purposefully seek out members of that group, not as tokens but to provide a platform to elevate their voices. These identities are so nuanced that representation of everyone feels impossible, but every bit helps. And to do that, you have to keep pushing to include as much diverse experienced people in your events.

Which is reason one why the BLERD IS THE WORD panel was so disappointing.

To provide a little background, a convention called BlerDCon will open its inaugural doors this summer. As of today, I'm a panelist at the convention where I'll be presenting COSPLAY IN NON-CANON BODIES and ANTI-BLACKNESS IN FANDOM. My providing content for a convention doesn't exempt them from scrutiny, though, which brings us to where we are today.

I attended BLERD IS THE WORD with zero expectations. I had no idea what to expect from this panel, so when I saw the panel consisted of three Black men, I wasn't bothered. That is, until they started speaking. The panel was about BlerDCon, a convention designed specifically for marginalized and underrepresented fans and cosplayers. The goal of the convention is to be inclusive. Which made it an interesting choice not to have any Black women on the stage.

The speaker began by defining the word "Blerd." For the uninitiated, Blerd is a mash-up of Black nerd. Blerd is a word I've come to love, because, well, I am a Black nerd. I love that this word speaks to the unique experiences of Black people in nerd/geek culture, cuz it's different. It's specific. And while Black people are not a monolith, the discrimination and racism we face is global.Considering how little choice we have in choosing our identity, it's awesome to see it prioritized in our fandoms and nerd/geek lives.

So, you can imagine my disgust when the speaker stated that anyone can be a Blerd. Anyone.

Full stop.

He said that being a Blerd wasn't just for Black people. That it includes everyone…anyone who has nerd/geek interests. Blerd is universal. Yes, he did. He sure did say that. Yup.

As you can see, I'm still a little fucked up by the tone-deafness of that statement. I know what he was trying to say. I know his goal was to ensure everyone felt welcome at BlerDCon. But here's the thing. Everyone isn't going to feel welcome at a Black-centered convention. And they shouldn't, because if they believe and support white supremacy, anything Black-centered is atrocious to them. And here's the thing — BlerDCon's core audience is Black. That's why you chose the fucking name. How the hell you going to have a panel directed at your core audience and then erase them from the narrative?You didn't have to name the convention Blerd anything if you wanted it to include everyone. But, you know, gotta make sure the white people are comfortable with Black folks to "succeed" right?

I was not the only one who had a strong reaction to that statement. A wave of discontent moved through the audience, too, but as the panelists weren't taking questions at the moment, we moved past it. That is, until we reached the topic of whitewashing. Now, I'll admit, whitewashing is a challenging topic, mainly because the film and television industry barely bother to create Black characters or hire Black or POC writers, producers, or filmmakers. That lack is felt throughout the industry in america. Without fail, in virtually every Black nerd group I'm in, there are Black people who defend this environment. They pull out the "create your own" argument. They talk about times where Black people and POCs were cast in roles that were assumed to be white. I am so tired of this conversation...you have no idea. And people's perplexity about it takes me out because we know what it is. We know it's white supremacy flexing its power to remind us, Black people and POCs, that we ain't shit. We KNOW this. So, when Black people start talking about how these are financial decisions, I get exhausted. How many fucking shitty movies do we need to see white people lose money on, only to turn around and make more before we understand that the money is just another excuse to justify their racism? The money is irrelevant. They make the movies they want to make, and they don't want brown folks in them, except as expendable scenery.

This shit ain't that hard to understand.

Yet, when the conversation turned to Ghost in the Shell, it was all the same shit. One panelist brought up the point that they took the movie to Japan andasked "actual Japanese" people what they thought. Like the Asian-American people who don't see themselves represented on the screen at all and watch as every opportunity for a lead role is given to a white person don't have final say in how fucked up this practice is. Like he/we have the right to speak for that community when they have done an amazing job speaking for themselves and their response was a resounding "that's some fucked up shit." They sat on stage and tried to legitimize racist white bullshit during their Black-centered panel, and that shit was unacceptable.

This was when I couldn't stay silent anymore. I'd listened to them "all lives matter" the word Blerd, heard them struggle to be universal when none of the Black people in the room wanted that. I listened to their tone-deaf take on inclusion and their assumption that they were doing it right and decided to point out the fallacies in their monologues.

It did not go well.

I need to be clear here. My issues arose with only two of the three panelists. Barr Foxx, who is a friend of mine, was included on the panel last minute and learned the content at the same time we, the audience, did. The other two...well...here's how that shit went.

One panelist took the condescending route. He tried to infer I didn't know what I was talking about, tried to lead me down a path of thinking to his conclusion, and refused to listen to anything I said. He centered his opinion in the Ghost in the Shell discussion and completely erased the Asian American community who'd been the most vocal about it. At one point, he stated he approved of their argument, as though his approval was relevant or necessary. And, I was told later because I missed this, he called me "sweetie," the most patronizing of the agree to disagree endearments. The other panelist just kind of let it roll but then later referred to me as "sister girl" as he praised the idea that he created a space where we could discuss these issues. As I am neither his sister or a girl, it just added fuel to the fire. But even I know a futile argument when I see it, so I ejected because, basically, the discussion was trash. Their points were trash. The panel was trash. And sadly, Black people are so hungry for inclusive spaces, they thought it was fine. Ok, not really. Several Black women approached me afterwards and thanked me for speaking up because they were on some bullshit.

I really felt bad for Barr Foxx, though. I don't think he expected to experience so much casual sexism and anti-Blackness from his co-panelists, much less expected to represent a convention where everyone can be a Blerd, regardless of race.

Straight up fuckery.

And I know it wasn't just me. I know that many people struggled with the messaging we were receiving from the most vocal of the panelists. It was just amazing to hear the creator of a Black convention work to minimize the Blackness of it, especially in a room full of Black people. Seriously, there was ONE white person in the room, something the panelists actually called attention to because heaven forbid we ignore the white person in the room.

Ungh.

All this is to say that I'm worried. I'm worried that the inclusion BlerDCon is promising is a lie. I'm worried that it's going to be casually sexist because the people running the convention can't see their sexism. I'm concerned that there aren't enough women involved in the decisions making aspects of the convention. And I'm wondering if "Blerd" and "inclusion" are just buzzwords to appeal to a certain demographic.

Maybe I'm wrong and I hope that I am. We'll see.

Laterz.

Everyone isn't going to feel welcome at a Black-centered convention. And they shouldn't, because if they believe and support white supremacy, anything Black-centered is atrocious to them.

– TaLynn Kel, When Inclusion Becomes Erasure

On Cosplay: My Humanity Is Not Optional

I should have known the conversation would to go to shit when she described me as "bodacious" in her opening. The word by itself isn't a big deal, but it set off my radar for incoming, fat-focused fuckery. "Bodacious" is a specific way of referring to fat people; it's a signal that my fatness is an important aspect of how they see me. Other words that do the same thing are voluptuous, rubenesque, fluffy, curvy…they are all meant to be complimentary descriptions of my fatness. And it's a microaggression because we live in a fat-phobic society that openly discriminates against and marginalizes fat people.

Because this woman was a stranger and I didn't have any experience to draw on, I let her first comment slide. Next, she asked me to join in a group cosplay. I assumed it was for a character I'd done before but it wasn't. She wanted to cosplay a group of Black women from a specific cartoon. Four of the women are varying heights and slim. The fifth member is short and round. Guess who she wanted me to cosplay?

The reality is that I am a fat, Black woman who cosplays[53] and because media panders to white men, there are not a lot of characters out there who look like me. And while that's important, I didn't start cosplaying because I wanted to dress like characters who resemble me. I wanted to dress as characters who were either fun or spoke to me. My very first cosplay was Dark Phoenix, and I chose that cosplay because I was fighting my own self-destruction and I

---

[53] Kel, TaLynn. "As a Fat, Black Woman, Cosplay Has Tried to Make Me Invisible" renamed "The Cosplay Community Has Tried to Make Me Invisible Because I'm a Fat, Black Woman." The Establishment, 20 Sept. 2016. Web. 17. Jan. 2018.

---

often felt like I was failing. Dark Phoenix's story spoke to that part of my personality and that part of my life. I cosplay characters because I see parts of them in me. And every time I've participated in a group cosplay, the choice of character has always been mine.

So, to be asked to play a character because I'm a fat Black woman and the character is a fat Black woman is a new experience for me.

My reaction wasn't positive. I sat back and reflected on it for a while. Then I asked why they asked me to cosplay this character and they confirmed my assumption. In fact, they were confused that I questioned it. Clearly, I'm fine with being fat so why would I have a problem cosplaying a fat character?

And you know, I could live with it if many of the fat, Black women characters weren't dehumanized into a punchline or a desexualized mammie figure. I'd feel better about it if the pop culture representations of my physicality were articulated into fully actualized people. Instead, they are the tropiest tropes that ever troped and it's an insult to ask me to cosplay that with no consideration to whether I relate to that character in any way. She had no other justification for the ask except that I'm fat, so I should be ok with being asked and since I could, and did, say no, it shouldn't have been a big deal. Then came the accusations of insecurity and how I'm being ridiculous because I "look just like the character."

Lawd, save me from these superficial, limited perspective people who like to flatten my depth into one easy thing. Save me from these people who value the superficial over the humane. Save me from these people who, when challenged by my humanity, say "you just don't like yourself, that's why you don't want to cosplay someone who looks like you."

Sigh.

She fat-splained why I cosplay characters who don't look like me…because again, for her it's all about the look. Fuck any of the many reasons people do this. Hell, most people don't look like the characters. It's not about that. It's about the challenge of artistically capturing that aspect of them using cosplay. That very act itself is at the core of why many people do it. Which is not to say that some don't do it cuz they look like a character. I mean, I know a white guy who has cosplayed every white superhero out there, they're all that bland and interchangeable, just like him.

That she, a Black cosplayer, cannot see how her ask is fucked up. She, who is part of a group of people that's always told not to cosplay cuz they don't look like the character. But you know, accuracy. Cuz accurate cosplay of fictional people that are envisioned by the artists who drew them that day is always the goal.

So, I said no. I'm not going to be assigned a cosplay. It rubbed me the wrong way to be steered in that direction so I'm out. And she's okay with that because it's really important that I have her approval of my feelings. *eye roll*

If she had provided any context for picking me other than the superficial, I might have been able to roll with it. Might. Maybe. Ok, probably not cuz it would have felt like a lie. She sees my fat and not me, that much is clear. And in her head, that's all I am. Except I'm not and I won't tolerate someone trying to make me into something so limited. And while that probably wasn't her conscious intent, but it was her conscious impact. So much so that she questioned my discomfort with it. And for a moment I wondered if what I was feeling was wrong, but feelings are not wrong — they are indicators that something else is.

It's not easy living in a culture that only values your beauty while embodying the very things that society says are ugly. It's not easy divorcing my self-worth from how others judge me. It's not easy embracing and loving who I am and doing things I enjoy that make people see me, knowing that these acts will also cause people to attack me for having the audacity to want to be seen. For feeling as though I have the right to be seen. For demanding I be seen.

I can't stop people from seeing me how they choose to see me but I do have the power to eject it from my life. Yes, I'm a fat, Black, cosplaying woman and I love who I am. But I choose who and how I cosplay with the entirety of who I am, and I don't take requests. Especially not superficial ones.

The reality is that I am a fat, Black woman who cosplays and because media panders to white men, there are not a lot of characters out there who look like me. And while that's important, I didn't start cosplaying because I wanted to dress like characters who resemble me. I wanted to dress as characters who were either fun or spoke to me.

– TaLynn Kel, On Cosplay: My Humanity Is Not Optional

On Logan and the Death of Black People in Films

Here there be spoilers.

I finally saw *Logan* last night.

It was a brutally violent film. You got to see characters who'd been defined by their strengths as weak, a weakness that compounded their issues as people. You got to see the vulnerability of characters whose superhero personas erased the day-to0day minutia of being a human being. It was a stark reminder that our legends, our larger than life heroes are really people whose stories have been condensed into bullshit for others to admire. LOGAN reminds us that people are complicated and fucked up, and sometimes we don't even know why.

Overall, I enjoyed the movie except for one deeply hurtful thing — the casual anti-Blackness of the movie. There were four Black people with speaking roles in the movie. Three of them are brutally murdered, closeups given of their maimed bodies as they were left dead for giving hospitality to strangers. I knew not to get too attached to them. I knew that any character connected to Logan, Professor X, and X-23 was dangerous, but there was a small hope that maybe they'd get away, mostly unscathed.

It was the common lie I tell myself when Black people are in movies. And it is almost always proven a lie.

I got to watch this kind family become victims of their kindness. We saw they had their struggles — maintaining a farm in an area that had been bought out by corporate interests. They had a cute son who was willing to drop out of school to travel the country with his parents. People who were willing to open their home to strangers in need. I wanted to like them. I wanted to see people I'd grown up living next to in them. And I knew that I couldn't let myself care because they were going to be killed.

I had to forcefully distance myself from my love of Black people because I knew that I was going to see them killed.

Representation Matters

I'm not going to lie, I am very tired of having to say the phrase "Representation Matters". I'm tired of hearing this phrase and I'm tired of the constant need to remind people that representation is much more than having Black people in a movie. It's about the roles we play, the characterizations we see, the lives we have portrayed on-screen. It's about seeing people who look like us, our friends, our families living lives on screen and not getting murdered to move a plot forward every time. It's about seeing Black joy and Black love and Black humanity in a way that is owned by the characters instead of exploited by the white protagonist in their quest. It's about being able to see Black people on screen without having to watch them criminalized, sacrificed, or slaughtered because they needed a plot device and it's cool to make it the Black person.

I remember the first time it really hit home for me...that was *Terminator 2: Judgement Day (T2)*. I saw that movie in the theater with my dad — he's the one who introduced me to sci-fi. In the movie, the creator of Skynet was played by Joe Morton, currently known as Olivia Pope's father, Eli, in Shonda Rimes TV show, *Scandal*. Back then, he played Dr. Miles Bennet Dyson, the creator of the end of humanity. As you can see, we're already off to a bad start. Except his character was kind. Curious. An explorer. He wanted to change the world and had no idea that the AI he developed using technology from the first Terminator would be ultimately responsible for humanity's war against machines. He had a family.

They were all super likable people and he reminded me of my dad. I felt myself connect to this character who reminded me of the wonderful man sitting next to me in the theater and then I got to watch him die.

It wasn't an easy death. In many ways, my father's actual death mirrored it. And while *T2* was just a movie, I got to experience the loss of someone I connected with on a basic level. Even though the connection wasn't real, it still felt real because that's how the human brain works — when we see things, they become memories for us, virtually indistinguishable from our actual memories. And that's why when we watch Black people die again and again in television shows in movies, we learn to distance ourselves from their humanity. We learn to see that violence as not real violence and then when real violence occurs, we're numb because that's how we've taught ourselves to survive the visual representations of the casual brutality enacted on Black people. We learn to close our eyes, mute the pain, and keep trying to live.

And every time we leave a piece of our empathy behind because living in that pain is living in pain. Constantly. And I can't keep moving forward with my heart in a never-ending ache. I don't know many people who can.

My options are to hurt or to numb; I'm tired of hurting and I need to feel so I can care.

I still get emotional when I think of that movie. And as awesome as the special effects are in *T2*, effects still used to this day, I cannot watch that scene again, especially now that my father is gone. It creates an ache and a longing that paralyzes me and now is not the time to be still. But it's real. And I know I am not alone in feeling this.

In some ways, that's great writing and it wouldn't be so bad if there were so many representations of Black people on the screen to choose from, but there aren't. There are tropes[54], clichés, and stereotypes[55]. In *T2*, Joe Morton's character was the sacrificial Negro, the Black man who gives his life for the white protagonist, something that's been seen in productions like *The Core, The Walking Dead, The Green Mile*, and, most recently, *Logan*.

I don't want to see Black people die in these white narratives anymore. I don't want to see people who look like me be destroyed over and over and over again. People have talked about the trauma of seeing Black people murdered by police[56] in the news[57]—just because it's "only a movie" doesn't make it less traumatic because that's how our brain works. The more we see certain types of images, the better we remember them. Seeing repeated images of Black people being killed, real or fabricated, are stored in our memories and we can't tell the difference[58].

Because that is how our brains work and I do not want to be indifferent to the death of Black people. I don't want to be indifferent to the loss of people who look like me. Ever.

---

[54] TV Tropes.Org. "Black Index." TCTropes.Org. Web. 17 Jan. 2018.

[55] Valerie Complex. "Will It Get Better for Black People in the Horror Genre?" Black Girl Nerds, 15 July 2015. Web. 17 Jan. 2018.

[56] Ross, Indigo. "Trauma Porn: Hyper-Consumption of Black Death and Pain." Odyssey, 12 July 2016. Web. 17 Jan. 2018.

[57] Downs, Kenya. "When Black Death Goes Viral, It Can Trigger PTSD-like Trauma." PBS News Hour, 22 July 2016. Web. 17 Jan. 2018.

[58] Costandi, Mo. "A Physiological Marker for False Memories." The Guardian, 27 Jan. 2012. Web. 17 Jan. 2018.

...when we see things, they become memories for us, virtually indistinguishable from our actual memories. And that's why when we watch Black people die again and again in television shows in movies, we learn to distance ourselves from their humanity.

– TaLynn Kel, On Logan and the Death of Black People in Films

At the Intersection of Blackness & Nerdom

Being Black in amerikkka is scary.

It's scary because white people are violent and dangerous as fuck. No bullshit cuz we've seen what they are capable of and how quickly they will default to killing anything they perceive as a threat, a list that includes my skin, my voice, my independence. White people have honed the skill of brutally murdering competition over hundreds of years, wielding a scythe of silence among those who would speak against them. Only now to watch their façade of civility crumble under the all-seeing eye of social media and information sharing.

Now they cling to the lies of their public relations teams and pretend their rot is still hidden.

It is my fear that has often kept me silent and complicit. I fight my fear to be seen and heard constantly. I know what happens to Black people who are seen as with Malcolm X and Martin Luther King, Jr. I know what happens when too many Black people are visibly independent and self-sufficient as with Black Wall Street and the Philadelphia MOVE bombing. We know what happens to Black people who fight for liberation like the Black Panther Party or dare to think they are equal to white people, as with Sandra Bland, Korrin Gaines, and Charleena Lyles. I've seen time and time again what happens to Black people in this country for daring to feel free.

Black freedom equals death.

But still, we try. We push for civil rights. We push for equity and equality. We fight for our friends, neighbors, children, strangers. We push back on white supremacy and patriarchy and ableism and sizeism, and sexuality and all the systems and structures that diminish us even when they cost us financially, socially, and eventually kill us, exactly as they were designed to do.

And one of the ways we push back is through the creation of Black spaces, including Black nerd spaces. Which brings us to BlerDCon.

Full transparency, I knew of BlerDCon before there was BlerDCon. Its creator, Hilton George reached out to a friend of mine about a year and a half ago to discuss the possibility of a Black nerd convention. My friends and I were invited to talk about the things we like about conventions and what he could do to make this into a real thing. He gathered information from us, told us that we'd be part of it. After the initial conversation, I tried to link him up with Jamie Broadnax of Black Girl Nerds because I knew BGN was talking about a Blerd convention online. That was when I learned that he's already purchased the domain and obtained the social media handles for this event.

As you may have already figured out, they were unable to come to terms on working together, so now we have BlerDCon, run by Hilton George and his team, and Universal FanCon, created and managed by Black Girl Nerds and The Black Geeks.

From the beginning, BlerDCon was problematic. The con was marketed as "exclusively inclusive" which sounded great 18 months ago, but since then, the conversation on racism and inclusion grew more nuanced in the public eye. Instead of continuing to center whiteness in our work and day-to-day operations, we saw Black people actively enforcing Black-only spaces[59]. And while there was

---

[59] Ziyad, Hari. "BLM Philly Did Not 'Ban White People from Its Meetings' but Created Necessary 'Black Only Spaces.'" AfroPunk, 04, April 2017. Web. 17 Jan. 2017.

backlash, the need for these spaces[60] became more and more obvious and attainable.

Sometimes we forget that the right to congregate was illegal. That this was forbidden in the slave codes and Jim Crowe laws. We forget that Black protests are met by police in riot gear, while pussy hats protests get photo ops with cops. We forget, or are never taught, that Black centered existence is something impermissible in white supremacy and that is circumvented by quietly congregating in spaces of white indifference. But creating a Black space amid geek culture, a notoriously white, patriarchal space? That is defiance. That is creating your own space. Naming an event "BlerDCon" means standing in the face of white geekdom and saying "Fuck you. We're here and fuck you for trying to erase us." And BlerDCon sounded beautiful...until you read the subtext of the convention: "exclusively inclusive."

Linguistically, "BlerDCon: Exclusively Inclusive" states that the event is exclusively inclusive of all Black nerd identities — be them gender non-conforming, differently abled, varied sexualities...all Black marginalized identities. And that is how Black people interested in the event read it. But that's not how the creators marketed the event. I get it — we live in a white supremacist, capitalist system which tells us that centering whiteness is the norm and the only way to succeed. As a convention needs money to function, how can one make money on an event that doesn't include whiteness?

Popular media would suggest this isn't possible, but we've seen it. I've seen it. All it takes is commitment and a good product to change it. Unfortunately, BlerDCon doesn't have that commitment

---

[60] Glover, Cameron. "No, Black-Only Safe Spaces Are Not Racist." Wear Your Voice, 31, May 2017. Web. 17. Jan. 2017.

to Blackness, as evidenced by Hilton's "anyone can be a Blerd" comment[61] at MomoCon this year. In 2015, you may have been able to get away with that. In 2017, you need to be Black and proud or sit the fuck down. Even though we still live in a time where demanding Black-only spaces is deemed radical and punished by white people...punished by laws enforcing white supremacy, we're still creating and re-creating our spaces. We're still defining ourselves without using the lens of our oppression. We are learning to let ourselves be carefree and joyous, despite being bombarded with messaging telling us we aren't allowed.

BlerDCon should be the big "fuck you" to white male nerd supremacy but this "all lives matter" approach is undermining that message. It's a shame because it was a good event. Marketing aside, I really enjoyed BlerDCon. The cosplay was fierce, many of the artists and vendors were Black, and the panels were both timely and relevant. And while I didn't attend many of the panels, the ones I did attend were run by and focused on Black people. The panelists created spaces for Black people to talk about our experiences without worrying about offending white people. Almost every Black person I spoke with said they found the convention to be cathartic and what they needed to celebrate their Black nerdiness. That is quite an accomplishment.

Black joy and Black love should not be a side-effect of this convention; it should be the intent. That it's not makes me sad because it is so clearly desired and needed. But if the organizers won't say BlerDCon is a Black nerd con and instead insist on promoting it as an all-nerd con, then this convention is not a safe space for Black nerds. It will be a watered-down, hybrid convention

---

61 Kel, TaLynn. "When Inclusion Becomes Erasure." Breaking Normal, 30 May 2017. Web. 17 Jan. 2017.

that continues to pander to white supremacy at the expense of Blerds. And the organizers will justify the harm done to the Blerd community as the price of this "Black space" being allowed to exist. And it will continue to dismiss the concerns of Blerds who still felt marginalized in a space that they thought was designed with them as the priority.

BlerDCon doesn't have to be this way. We deserve a space for us, by us, that's not afraid to BE us.

Just as an FYI — There are more Black-focused conventions. Some of them feel like I'm not Black enough to attend but then I go and have a great time. Here's a short list of the ones I know:

Atlanta Science Fiction and Fantasy Expo (ASFE), OnyxCon, East Coast Black Age of Comics Convention (ECBACC), MECCACon, Sol-Con, Blacktasticon, and Blerd City Con.

We forget that Black protests are met by police in riot gear, while pussy hats protests get photo ops with cops. We forget, or are never taught, that Black centered existence is something impermissible in white supremacy and that is circumvented by quietly congregating in spaces of white indifference.

- TaLynn Kel, At the Intersection of Blackness & Nerdom

Protecting Becky at All Costs — Peak White Feminism in Wonder Woman

SPOILERS AHEAD. YOU'VE BEEN WARNED.

Full disclosure: I enjoyed *Wonder Woman*. I've also grown up in the racist shitstorm that is Amerikkka so white supremacy is the air I breathe, the food I eat, the water in which I bathe, and the bed upon which I sleep. It's so entrenched in my life that I do white supremacist shit and have to constantly check myself about it. So, it's pretty natural for me to watch something with shitty messaging and not completely reject everything about it. Being a Black woman who is constantly told she doesn't matter kinda trains you to parse things out of necessity.

It is my ability to parse that allowed me to enjoy the movie despite there being a moment where the movie breaks for me. It was when, during her struggle with Ares, Diana was faced with the choice of giving in to her rage and destroying humanity or choosing love and hope. Now, that choice isn't a problem for me; I think we make that choice multiple times every day of our lives.

Dr. Poison, played by Elena Anaya, is a character who took joy in her work. She loved making lethal concoctions and testing them on people. She had no issue with murder and often seemed to take a perverse pleasure in ensuring the deaths of those she experimented upon. Dr. Poison had no conscious. She knew her creations would murder hundreds, if not thousands, of people. She exhibited no remorse.

Dr. Poison was a sociopathic murderer who needed to die. Instead, the preservation of her life was the pivotal moment for Diana to choose to save humanity rather than destroy them, regardless of how deserving they are. This choice sends the message that to forgive the worst of us, to love the ugliest of us is what makes us good people.

Well, fuck that.

There is a problem with showing the active decision to spare a cruel killer. For that killer to be a white woman, the most underestimated agent of racism[62], is white supremacist propaganda. It begs the question asked by Kinitra Brooks, "what Becky gotta do to get murked?[63]" Seriously.

How the fuck did the writers, director, and producer decide that sparing the life of a ruthless murderer, a white woman, was a good idea? How does this cruel mass killer get a second chance from Diana? Why would anyone support that type of message?

I will give one possible pass. Perhaps Diana didn't know who Dr. Poison was. But she recognized General Ludendorff was so I'm guessing she had enough intel to know who the main players were. This brings us back to her decision to spare the evil white woman and protect her from her choices. I ask again, why?

My guess: Peak. White. Feminism.

The toxic white feminism this choice represented probably wasn't intentional, but the decision to save Dr. Poison was. They didn't have to do it this way. We could have seen Dr. Poison escape during the fighting. She could have crept away under the guise of night. There was no need for Diana to confront Dr. Poison and choose to

---

[62] Storey, Kate. "Inside the Lives of White Supremacist Women." Marie Claire, 10 Jan. 2017. Web. 17 Jan. 2018.

[63] Brooks, Kinitra. "What Becky Gotta Do to Get Murked? White Womanhood in Jordan Peele's Get Out." Very Smart Brothers, 03 March 2017. Web. 17 Jan. 2018.

save her. That act is an insidious choice made by the people behind the scenes.

The reason this stands out so sharply for me is because of how often we, Black people and POCs, are encouraged to be lenient when white women's transgressions are revealed. How we are conditioned to look at white women as above wrongdoing when we have clear examples of them actively participating in racist acts[64] that can and have led to Black people's, Black children's deaths[65].

We've seen articles trying to explain/justify white women's support of that Cheeto in the oval office[66]. I've seen articles painting his wife as a victim of him[67] instead of an active participant in their relationship. White women are shielded from the consequences of their racism and when there aren't any heroes there to shield them, they shed their white tears[68].

It is this constant picture of white women being deserving of special consideration and extra protection that makes Diana's choice to let Dr. Poison live irresponsible. Especially as it was a plot device used to define Diana's "goodness." Forgiveness is not a tool that demonstrates one's inherent goodness; it's a tool to keep monsters

---

[64] Jionde, Elexus. "Racist White Women: An American Legacy." Intelexual Media, 8 March, 2017. Web. 17 Jan. 2018.

[65] Workneh, Lilly. "Emmett Till's Accuser Admits She Lied About Claims That Led To His Murder." Huffington Post, 27 Jan. 2017. 17 Jan. 2018.

[66] Roberts, Laura Morgan; Ely, Robin J. "Why Did So Many White Women Vote for Donald Trump?" Fortune, 18 Nov. 2016. Web. 17 Jan. 2018.

[67] Kuntzman, Gersh. "Donald Trump is still abusing women — with his wife Melania the latest victim." New York Daily News, 18 Oct. 2016. Web. 17 Jan. 2018.

[68] Patton, Stacey. "White Women, Please Don't Expect Me to Wipe Away Your Tears." Dame, 15 Dec. 2014. Web. 17 Jan. 2018.

unchecked[69]. In this case, it was used to empower Diana and that is a very dangerous, subversive message to send.

We live in a world with many monsters. They look like our world leaders, police, teachers, and families. And our society protects them[70], much to our collective detriment. We live in a society where people believe their own lies[71] and cannot recognize the rot within themselves. Watching Wonder Woman tell herself that sparing the life of a heinous murderer made her a good person was the reinforcement of all the lies this country tells itself to feel like heroes instead of violent, racist, mass murdering colonizers[72].

I did enjoy *Wonder Woman*. I liked the action and it was good to see a woman live the life she chose despite the men around her trying to control her actions. And yes, there were issues with inclusion and representation, as well as how it shrugged off indigenous genocide.

But for me, the stand-out message will always be how Wonder Woman protected Becky despite Becky's malevolence.

This essay was originally published on Black Girl Nerds on June 8, 2017.

---

[69] Kel, TaLynn. "Demanding Black Forgiveness Is Just Another Way to Control Us." The Establishment. 10 Aug. 2016. Web. 17 Jan. 2018.

[70] Kel, TaLynn. "American, Stop Protecting Your Monsters." The Establishment, 10 Oct. 2016. Web. 17 Jan. 2018.

[71] Kel, TaLynn. "White People, You Have a Lying Problem." The Establishment. 07 July 2016. Web. 17 Jan. 2018.

[72] Kel, TaLynn. "Violence is the White Normal." Breaking Normal, 26 June 2017. Web. 17 Jan. 2017.

The reason this stands out so sharply for me is because of how often we, Black people and POCs, are encouraged to be lenient when white women's transgressions are revealed. How we are conditioned to look at white women as above wrongdoing when we have clear examples of them actively participating in racist acts that can and have led to Black people's, Black children's deaths.

- TaLynn Kel, Protecting Becky at All Costs: Peak White Feminism in *Wonder Woman*

I Don't Fuck with the Mainstream Cosplay and Geek Scene

I don't fuck with the mainstream cosplay and geek scene. Not one bit. I don't join their groups. I don't follow their social media. I don't read their magazines. And I don't submit my pictures. I don't pitch essays to them. The most that I participate in any of it is going to some conventions, and when I go, it's usually with the intent to research or do a presentation that will address racism in some way. Sometimes, all it takes is my presence in the room to initiate that dialogue. Other than that, I do not fuck with mainstream cosplay and geek scene, because it's too racist.

That scene is racist in every fucking way. It's incidentally racist. Intentionally racist. Subconsciously racist. Overtly racist. The scene uses every tool in its arsenal to ensure it is white dominated, white supremacist, and anti-Black as fuck and I am not here for it. The scene has an idealized perception of what it wants to be and it is white and mostly eurocentric. Even in the body positivity groups, the ideal look is pale skin, often blond and blue-eyed, and hourglass shape...just a fatter one.

When you see Black people in these cosplay groups, they are usually racially ambiguous. You very rarely see dark brown-skinned women and when you do, they fit every other mainstream standard of attractiveness, and by mainstream, I mean popular white standard. And despite this, they get racist comments like "this character isn't supposed to be burnt" or "stop n*ggerfying cosplay." I've seen Black cosplayers catch so much hell for daring to cosplay a character who isn't Black, and I've also seen communities split about defending the cosplayers.

And this isn't limited to cosplay. I've seen it in gaming, modeling, comics, movies, books…the moment white people are not centered in something, they turn hostile. And usually the moderators and administrators protect hate speech and eject those fighting racism. They defend hate speech as "free speech" and call Blackface "cosplay accuracy." I used to participate in online arguments with white geeks until I learned that these folks weren't interested in my perspective. They were just trying to wear me out. And it worked. I left those spaces and they control them.

Why would I participate in groups that are fine with not just denigrating me, but protecting the offenders while punishing me for defending myself? The answer is, I don't. I don't participate in that shit because I already know the deal. Instead, I focus on spaces that center Blackness and are invested in protecting me. And when I venture into hostile areas, I do so by choice, and spend much of my time conducting periodic threat assessments because, again, I know the deal. It's exhausting and frustrating but that's how you survive white geek spaces — by protecting yourself when you refuse to be quiet, inoffensive, and out of the way.

But now, with the open warfare declared by white supremacists who have made clear that they are at war with Black people, non-Black People of Color, undocumented POCs, any brown person in a turban, Jewish people, and non-christians, I'm noticing white people who in the past wouldn't say shit, actually speak up. And while a part of me is glad to see a greater number of white people finally pushing back on racism, I'm pissed that it took putting known members of the KKK in government positions for them to grow a backbone and have some fucking empathy.

I'm angry that people in my local cosplay community regularly associated with a white supremacist and didn't know she was because she talked to Black people. I'm angry that white people are debating whether nazi cosplay should be banned from conventions. I'm angry that despite numerous, glaring signs of white supremacy, white people still spend a shit-ton of time making excuses for themselves and their friends; that they refuse to acknowledge obvious racism. Instead they explain it away, as we are watching yet again with PewDiPie's racist ass. Like we're seeing with those white teens in New Hampshire who fucking lynched a Black child. Like we're seeing in New Jersey with those white people committing welfare fraud. Like we're seeing all the damn time because whiteness protects whiteness.

So, no, I don't trust white spaces. I don't trust white people. I've spent my entire life learning how to live with them, diminishing myself so I don't accidentally intimidate them. Speaking softer, or not at all. Navigating hostile spaces and swallowing my ego and pride in the face of overwhelming incompetence time and time again because my Blackness somehow reduces me in their eyes.

But I refuse to sacrifice the joy and comfort I find in this hobby by forcing my way into spaces that don't want me. We've been building our own and it's been wonderful. That is where I feel safest. That is where I want to be. I'll support Black people who has the tolerance to continue pushing into these hostile, white dominated spaces, provided they don't practice anti-Blackness, because this is a multifaceted war with many fronts. I've chosen where I'll fight my battles cuz every battle won is an opportunity for someone else to win more.

Where's your battleground?

I'm angry that people in my local cosplay community regularly associated with a white supremacist and didn't know she was because she talked to Black people. I'm angry that white people are debating whether nazi cosplay should be banned from conventions.

- TaLynn Kel, I Don't Fuck with the Mainstream Cosplay and Geek Scene

The Terror of the Now

I'm trying to function in the terror of the now. The now that actively seeks my destruction and the destruction of those like me. The now that preys on brown children and brown bodies, blaming us for our victimization as whiteness feeds on our fear and intentionally manufactured vulnerability. The now that screams to me with violence and rage, warning me of what's to come while providing me with no sanctuary.

I'm trying to live in the terror of the now, telling myself my fears are exaggerated. That my worries are unwarranted. That my anxieties are superfluous. I live in this sea of wrathful whiteness and tell myself it's fine, quelling my survival instincts that are telling me to flee.

I'm drowning in the terror of the now, slowly sinking into my own demise. Comforting myself in the warmth of the hatred. Soothing myself in the claws of white rage. Feeling the lull of the nothingness of death.

*****

I haven't been writing.

Not all of it has been bad. I was working, had a few big projects, got sick, and then two conventions, OnyxCon and DragonCon. Both events were great in different ways and I'll have some work coming out as a result, but I'm also exhausted, physically and mentally, because the attacks and bullshit just keep coming.

White people are exhausting me, my significant other (S.O.)
included. I am tired of being around white people trying to figure
out how much of me is going to set them off. I've written about
how white people are racist landmines[73], which they are and I'm
tired of constantly being on the alert for the more dangerous ones.
I'm also tired of them and their goddamn white guilt that they keep
looking to me to absolve them of. I want them to be better people
but fuck...is it my job? Is it my fucking unpaid job to nurture white
folks through their racist bullshit?

I think not.

And yet, I found myself in this weird position of expecting to have
to do just that because two weeks before DragonCon, it came out
that one of the more well-known cosplayers was at the
Charlottesville march[74], marching with the white supremacists. That
incident sent ripples through a group of people I know pretty well.
Geek spaces are predominantly white, and sometimes the Black
people in those spaces cater a bit too much to whiteness for my
comfort, so when it turned out that this woman was a white
supremacist, I heard everything from outright denial, to people
deciding that it didn't matter. Black people deciding that it didn't
matter. This led to some self-reflection, some knowledge that I'd
been letting my S.O. coast a bit, and the realization that DragonCon
could potentially be a hot ass mess. I was not looking forward to it.

In fact, I was scared.

---

[73] Kel, TaLynn. "White People are Racist Landmines." Breaking Normal, 21 May
2017. Web. 17 Jan. 2018.

[74] Johnston, Rich. "The Supergirl Cosplayer Who Went to Charlottesville – Guess
Whose Side She Was On." Bleeding Cool, 18 Aug. 2017. Web. 17 Jan. 2018.

Fortunately, I had OnyxCon the weekend prior. And despite being somewhat ill, I went and met so many talented Black creators and supporters. It was fucking amazing. That room was filled with talented people and while all the art wasn't my taste, I could not deny the talent. I met people doing fan art, creating comics, writing booking about pride in our 4C hair & physical differences...I met novelists, graphic artists, and filmmakers. It was an amazing experience filled with nothing but love and respect. My only complaints were that the room was a little small and I didn't feel well. Other than that, it was an amazing event for meeting and supporting independent artists. And, most importantly, it felt safe. I just wish I'd felt better and had more time because I wanted to interview EVERYONE in the room. Unfortunately, I ended up spending the 2nd day of the event in bed.

OnyxCon reminded me that there is a huge community of Black geeks and creators in Atlanta, not to mention the many that descend on the city to participate in DragonCon. And this year, several groups created safe spaces for Black people interested in celebrating ourselves at the convention. The spaces weren't advertised as such. They never are. They are just spaces that center Blackness and that's really all it takes. It's also why events like BlerDCon become so disappointing when the creators work to de-center Blackness[75]. We want spaces where loving ourselves in the norm, not a fucking burden.

---

[75] Kel, TaLynn. "When Inclusion Becomes Erasure." Breaking Normal, 30 May 2017. Web. 17 Jan. 2018.

I spent DragonCon immersed in Blackness[76] and I loved it. I mean, sure, the event is predominantly white. And sure, plenty of fuckery goes down. I'm sure you heard about those two women who were hit by chairs thrown off the 10th floor of the Marriott[77]. Every year someone does some fuckshit, like they are trying to get the event canceled. Thankfully, both women survived despite stitches and hospitalization. I hate the fuckers who did that.

And here we are post DragonCon where I learned that DACA[78], Title IX, reproductive rights, and brown people continue to be under direct attack while hurricanes are headed in every fucking direction, including mine. Good times.

Real talk, when I heard about the hurricanes I thought, "dying wouldn't be too bad," to which my S.O. stared at me real hard for a long time before contradicting me. He's wrong, though. There comes a point where it all feels like too much and the will to survive just fades away. I live a comfortable life...some would even say blessed and I feel that way. I just returned from a weekend full of great shit and still I feel exhausted by fuckery of whiteness. I can't imagine if shit was harder for me. I don't know if I'd try to make it.

---

[76] Barnes, Mo. "Black Heroes Matter: Black Geeks Rise at DragonCon 2017." Rollingout, 05 Sept. 2017. Web. 17 Jan. 2018.

[77] Eldridge, Ellen. "Two Women at DragonCon Hit by Chairs Thrown from Hotel Balcony." Atlanta Journal Constitution, 04 Sept. 2017. Web. 17 Jan. 2018.

[78] Dickerson, Caitlin. "For DACA Recipients, Losing Protection and Work Permits Is Just the Start." The New York Times, 07 Sept. 2017. Web. 17 Jan. 2018.

And right now, living feels more like surviving the racist apocalypse and everyday it feels more like a mistake instead of a goal. But every morning I wake up and as long as that keeps happening, I'll try to pretend that hope is real, change is possible, and the future can be better. Otherwise, I wouldn't bother trying anymore.

The terror of the now is real and it didn't take a zombie apocalypse to make me hate survival.

Geek spaces are predominantly white, and sometimes the Black people in those spaces cater a bit too much to whiteness for my comfort, so when it turned out that this woman was a white supremacist, I heard everything from outright denial, to people deciding that it didn't matter. Black people deciding that it didn't matter.

- TaLynn Kel, The Terror of the Now

America's Whiteness Problem is Part of Your Fandom

Hey, white people. Yeah, all of you. Your fandoms are racist.

No, don't argue. This isn't a question. I'm telling you that your fandoms are racist because your shows are racist and the show identity you want to preserve is rooted in white supremacy and Black erasure.

Dr. Who, the show that reluctantly casts Black women only to ignore and marginalize them[79]? The show who booted Pearl Mackie before her episodes even aired[80], and when reported upon, never mentioned her Blackness, just that her character is gay. Stop pretending you don't see color and that her treatment had nothing to do with her race. We know her Blackness mattered.

How about the gaming fandoms with their openly racist players and streamers? We currently have PewDiePie apologizing for casually using the N-word again[81] and too many people defending him[82]. He was defended when Disney dropped him[83], and he's being

---

[79] White, D.S. "Is Doctor Who's Black Companion Really Traveling Back In Time, This Time?" Black Girl Nerds, 11 May 2017. Web. 17 Jan. 2018.

[80] Duncan, Amy. "New Doctor Who Sidekick Pearl Mackie 'Given the Boot after Just One Series.'" Metro, 03 April 2017. Web. 17 Jan. 2018.

[81] Ohlheiser, Abby. "PewDiePie Said the N-Word on YouTube. The Internet's Most Famous Gamer is Out of Excuses." The Washington Post, 12 Sept. 2018.

[82] Hernandez, Patricia. "YouTubers Worry About Blowback from New PewDiePie Controversy." Kotaku, 11 Sept. 2017. 17 Jan. 2018.

[83] Winkler, Rolfe; Nicas, Jack; and Fritz, Ben. "Disney Severs Ties with YouTube Star PewDiePie After Anti-Semitic Posts." The Wall Street Journal, 12 Feb. 2017. Web. 17 Jan. 2018.

defended as another developer seeks to ban him[84]. He's trash but he's white so he "deserves" another chance, right? No. He doesn't. Stop protecting racists.

The racism in cosplay is off the rails. From the Overwatch cosplayer who was attacked online for having the audacity to cosplay D.Va[85] to cosplay Blackface[86], and how being Black is used to exclude you from cosplay photo shoots[87], the racism and its effects are felt everywhere. Then, when we form our own cosplay communities and conventions, suddenly we're the ones being racist for wanting to feel safe in our hobby. You can't win.

And this isn't limited to con participation. When the organizers of conventions are all white, inclusion stops being an option. Look at the controversy with the all-white leadership of GeekGirlCon[88], where several members chose to quit and publicly accuse the organization of "reverse racism," sexism, and fraud rather than include anti-racism content. They felt the content was too offensive and then were offended at their allyship being called into question.

GeekGirlCon is an obvious example of racist leadership. I attend conventions, mostly in the southeast and have found that the more

[84] Hernandez, Patricia. "Indie Dev Calls for Copyright Strikes Against Pewdiepie After He Says N-Word on Stream." Kotaku, 10 Sept. 2017. 17 Jan. 2018.

[85] Khosaravi, Rye. "Racist Reaction to Black D.Va Cosplayer Shows the Struggles of Being a Nerd of Color." Mic, 8, June 2017. Web. 17 Jan. 2018.

[86] Doll, DeLa. "Blackface Is Ugly, And I'm Being Harassed: A Tale of Cosplay and Cosplayers Gone Wrong." Huffington Post, 07, Sept. 2016. Web. 17 Jan. 2018.

[87] "The World of Black Cosplay: Discrimination, Rejection, Invisibility of the Black Cosplaying Community." The Columbia Chronicle, 1, Mar. 2015. Web. 17 Jan. 2018.

[88] Faroughm, Amanda. "GeekGirlCon 2017 Controversy: Tensions Boil Over and Leads Key Organization Staff Members to Quit." Mic, 14 Aug. 2017. Web. 17 Jan. 2018.

my panel centers Blackness, the less likely it is to be approved by "mainstream" conventions. For example, DragonCon, a huge convention here in Atlanta refused several panels that talked about racism, discrimination, and diversity in fandom, citing lack of interest. One of the reasons why BlerDCon remained attractive despite their leanings toward erasure[89], was the focus on Black experiences in fandom. Much of the content was led by Black creators in a way I'd never experienced before, something I haven't seen at larger, "mainstream" conventions and I believe lack of diversity in the leadership creates this lack, as comics have historically been racist[90].

The status quo of the comics industry is to pander to white, cisgender, heterosexual men. This decision is so hardwired into geek culture that the hint of characters that don't center them causes screams of "social justice warrior" and "PC police" to reverberate across the forums of reddit. The norm is white male creators all the time, writing Black characters[91], women characters, every character. This decision impacts the entire industry, from what movies are made[92] to what toys are sold[93].

---

[89] Kel, TaLynn. "When Inclusion Becomes Erasure." Breaking Normal, 30 May 2017. Web. 17 Jan. 2017.

[90] "'Good Shall Triumph over Evil': The Comic Book Code of 1954." History Matters: The U.S. Survey Course on the Web. Web. 17. Jan. 2018.

[91] Kel, TaLynn. "Black Characters and Non-Black Writers: An Imperfect Union." Black Girl Nerds, 21 June 2017. Web. 17 Jan. 2018.

[92] Trumbore, Dave. "Scarlett Johansson on Black Widow: 'The Character Is Right for a Standalone.'" Collider, 13, Feb. 2017. Web. 17 Jan. 2018.

[93] Davis, Lauren. "Paul Dini: Superhero Cartoon Execs Don't Want Largely Female Audiences." Io9, 15 Dec. 2013. Web. 17 Jan. 2018.

And the racism never ceases: there's whitewashing in movies[94] and television shows, racist depictions of comic characters[95], and rampant anti-Blackness[96]. Fandom is a shit-show of epic proportions for Black people. And yet, here we are, fully invested in participating in this medium that has told us repeatedly it does not want us there.

Actually, it's the white people who say they don't want us there. And they keep saying it. Sometimes they say it explicitly, as when white supremacist Supergirl marched in Charlottesville, Virginia[97] with the would-be Nazis. To this day, she claims that she's not racist[98] and was only marching with her husband, who is much more honest about his feelings. Her friends claim they had no idea, but white supremacist language is so normal for white people…well, it's just normal. The fact that the red flag for many people was her participating in that march is telling.

I keep being reminded white people don't care. At least, they don't until they get caught. Then they want to prove to everyone[99] that

---

[94] Rose, Steve. "Ghost in the Shell's Whitewashing: Does Hollywood Have an Asian Problem?" The Guardian, 21 Mar. 2017. 17 Jan. 2018.

[95] Hoffman, C.P. "Guardians of the Galaxy Vol 2 Turned Mantis into the Butt of a Joke." CBR.com, 11 May 2017. Web. 17 Jan. 2018.

[96] Kel, TaLynn. "On "Logan" and the Tropes of Black Folks." Black Girl Nerds, 18, April 2017. Web. 17 Jan. 2018.

[97] Johnston, Rich. "The Supergirl Cosplayer Who Went to Charlottesville – Guess Whose Side She Was On." Bleeding Cool, 18 Aug. 2017. Web. 17 Jan. 2018.

[98] Johnston, Rich. "We Talk to The Supergirl Cosplayer "Along for The Ride" at the White Nationalist Rally in Charlottesville." Bleeding Cool, 19 Aug. 2017. Web. 20 Jan. 2018.

[99] McKenzie, Mia. "How to Tell the Difference Between Real Solidarity and 'Ally Theater.'" Black Girl Dangerous, 04 Nov. 2015. Web. 17 Jan. 2018.

---

they aren't racist. That even though they have racist friends, they are different. FYI — you're not[100]. Then they harass the fuck out of their Black "friends" for some way to atone for the evils of whiteness, because Google requires too much effort and words are confusing. In the meantime, they are still engaging in conversations on how making Johnny Storm a Black man is racist[101] and that Black Panther doesn't have enough white people in it[102].

Whiteness begets whiteness. And heaven forbid anything center Blackness or exclude whiteness in any way. Cuz white supremacy is the law of the land and if you forget, they got some tiki torches to remind you. Or they can just make up a new white character like they did with the *Aladdin* movie[103] because, again, can't have shit in amerikkka without white people. Except crime, which gets redefined when white people do it[104]. And drug abuse, which again gets reframed as an epidemic that deserves compassion[105], not harsher drug laws and sentencing. The only thing that gets to be as Black as possible is prison. White people seem okay with that.

[100] Witt, Laura. "No, You Can't Be Friends with a White Supremacist and Not Be One Yourself." Wear Your Voice, 06 June 2017. 17 Jan. 2018.

[101] Berlatsky, Noah. "The Incoherent Backlashes to Black Actors Playing 'White' Superheroes." The Atlantic, 20 Feb. 2014. Web. 17 Jan. 2018.

[102] Wallace, Edward. "As Expected, there are Idiots Who Find the Black Panther Trailer Racist." Fortress, 15 June 2017. Web. 17 Jan. 2018.

[103] "Disney Creates a New Character Just to Cast a White Actor in Latest Aladdin Film." The New Arab, 08 Sept. 2017. Web. 17 Jan. 2018.

[104] Judge, Monique. "White People Commit Welfare Fraud, State Creates Amnesty Program so They Won't Go to Jail." The Root, 11 Sept. 2017. Web. 17 Jan. 2018.

[105] Mechanic, Jesse. "When A Drug Epidemic Hit White America, Addiction Became A Disease." Huffington Post, 10 July 2017. Web. 17 Jan. 2018.

Amerikkka has a fucking whiteness problem and it's killing this country. It's killing us with its lies and its refusal to correct itself. We now have the least qualified administration in history grabbing brown people off the streets and detaining them indefinitely before shipping them to parts unknown. We have laws being enacted on LGBTQIA rights and freedoms. We have non-Black People of Color (NBPOCs) having their citizenship questioned at will and Black people being murdered by white men[106] who cannot accept their own mediocrity.

And still white people struggle to tell their shitty comic-con friend that they said some racist shit. They still won't eject racist people from their circles. They still interact with their racist relatives and try to explain how some fucked up remark was actually harmless. They still support the police. And they still protect whiteness at the cost of Black people's and NBPOC's lives.

So, don't question me when I opt out of your fandom gatherings, your watch parties, your cosplay events, or whatever fan event you're planning. I can't trust you. Unless you are willing to confront and actively dismantle white supremacy, your whiteness put me in danger. And when you take a moment and realize that you live in a homogeneous echo chamber of bullshit, maybe then you'll realize you haven't been doing the work to make this country better. Maybe then you'll realize you are the problem and actually do something to change it.

---

[106] Kunzelman, Michael. "White Man Arrested in Slayings of 2 Black Men in Louisiana." Chicago Tribune, 19 Sept. 2017. Web. 17 Jan. 2018.

The status quo of the comics industry is to pander to white, cisgender, heterosexual men. This decision is so hardwired into geek culture that the hint of characters that don't center them causes screams of "social justice warrior" and "PC police" to reverberate across the forums of reddit. The norm is white male creators all the time, writing Black characters , women characters, every character.

- TaLynn Kel, America's Whiteness Problem is Part of Your Fandom

Is *Thor: Ragnarok* a Subversive Takedown of White Supremacy?

Spoilers ahead! You've been warned.

Full disclosure: Despite the almost overwhelming physical appeal of Chris Hemsworth as Thor, I dislike the Thor movies. The first had potential, but that unnecessarily compressed timeline killed it dead. *Thor 2* was just a vehicle to introduce the Infinity Stone of Reality, turning the characters into a senseless backdrop to achieve that goal. It was wretched, and I don't care if I never see it again.

But the trailers for *Thor: Ragnarok* were promising. The film wouldn't be set in Asgard. Hulk was there. Mjölnir was destroyed. Valkyrie was Black. And the trailers were funny — really funny. Not to mention how bad-ass Hela seemed to be. I mean, she shattered Mjölnir and it wasn't a dream sequence. I was in.

Happily, I found the film to be as fun as advertised. More importantly — and surprisingly — it also contained an extraordinary, eviscerating message about colonialism and white supremacy.

I will freely admit that I am tired of seeing powerful white men wielding power they do not deserve and earned through violence. That narrative is played out, yet it is the crux of the Marvel cinematic universe. In *Thor: Ragnorak,* this trope is challenged by Hela — the first-born of Odin and sister of Thor and Loki — when she returns from exile to reclaim her spot atop the throne and calls out Asgard's ill-gained riches and powers in the process. As Hela points out in one particularly stunning scene, the spectacular gold of the Asgardian Palace was bought through brutal conquest and war. Before becoming ostensibly "peaceful," Odin used his own daughter as his executioner, mercilessly taking lives to achieve his place in the kingdom. The he stashed the murdered bodies in an underground vault, never to be spoken of again.

If that sounds familiar, perhaps you know the history of colonialism, including in the United States, where we tout our exceptionalism while ignoring the violence it was built upon. All of which makes the film's ending — Asgard and Hela are completely destroyed by the fire-demon Surtur, the lies of perceived superiority left in ashes — particularly satisfying.

But it's one line in particular that I keep returning to:

"Proud to have it, ashamed of how he got it." (I remembered this later as *"Proud of where you are; ashamed of how you got there."*)

When Hela uttered these words about Odin's rise to dominance, I froze in my seat. This sentence, spoken as she destroyed the veneer of Asgard and shattered its image of itself, was so much truth. This sentiment is at the core of American exceptionalism, this pride in being American without acknowledging the horrors committed to become this nation people are proud of. (One could say we have buried the dead bodies in our own underground vault.)

Just last week, I watched white people on Twitter argue about equating Robert E. Lee to George Washington and Thomas Jefferson. The original tweeter was actually not trying to call all these men monsters but was using the framework to humanize Lee. Still, his tweet sparked outrage among proud Americans arguing that Lee was much worse than Washington and Jefferson.

The truth is, though, that they were *all* violent, capitalistic hypocrites who profited off human suffering — monsters who used dishonorable tactics to emancipate themselves from a dishonorable ruler while lying about the humanity and suffering of people they chose to own and treat as property. All of them committed treason. All of them exploited people for financial gain. All of them owned people. Yes, I know Jefferson's role in abolishing slavery, but he still owned slaves[107], some of them his blood relatives, refused to free them, and believed Black people were less human.

Yet despite Washington's and Jefferson's active engagement in the horrific, emotional, and physical violence of slavery, they are considered heroes. There is nothing that erases the horror of their choices from their histories. There is nothing that erases the barbarity of slavery from the fabric of America. Yet the keepers of history have tried time and time again to downplay the brutality of colonialism[108]; how it decimated indigenous people, empowered European imperialists, and created America. It is still argued that Washington and Lincoln are "good," if problematic, white men.

"Proud to have it, ashamed of how he got it."

Hela's words spoke to the crux of the American identity. For hundreds of years, this country brutalized people[109], created and maintained a racial hierarchy used to justify this brutality[110], and then denied its existence. Our history books are sanitized to remove

---

[107] "Thomas Jefferson: A Film by Ken Burns." PBS, Public Broadcasting Service, 1997. Web. 20 Jan. 2018.

[108] Robinson, Nathan L. "A Quick Reminder of Why Colonialism was Bad." Current Affairs, 14 Sept. 2017. Web. 17 Jan. 2018.

[109] "Atrocities Against Native Americans." United End to Genocide, 2016. Web. 17 Jan. 2018.

[110] Rogers, David; Bowman, Moira. "A History: The Construction of Race and Racism." Racial Equity Tools. Web. 17 Jan. 2018.

the gory history of colonists[111] and how they tortured and murdered people at will[112], seeing their violence as intellectual superiority. Americans view the willingness of colonists to kill those in their way as proof that they deserve to lead; that it makes them strong. Yet they deny the shape violence has given our current reality. They deny that violence gave these people the power and access they still wield today. They lie and lie and lie and can no longer discern what is true[113].

"Proud to have it, ashamed of how he got it."

The acceptance and denial of this violence is the foundation upon which we stand today. The lover's embrace of white supremacy at all costs — specifically the embrace of white, male, cisgender, heterosexual, able-bodied whiteness — remains our modus operandi. It's how white male rapists can admit to and be found guilty of rape but still be protected from consequences like imprisonment[114]. It is how white men can kill Black people[115],

---

[111] Thompson, Tracy. "The South still lies about the Civil War." Salon, 16 March 2013. Web. 17 Jan. 2018.

[112] Nazaryan, Alexander "California Slaughter: The State-Sanctioned Genocide of Native Americans." Newsweek, 17 Aug. 2016. Web. 17 Jan. 2018.

[113] Kel, TaLynn. "White People, You Have a Lying Problem." The Establishment. 07 July 2016. Web. 17 Jan. 2018.

[114] Levenson, Eric. "Judge Sentences Man Who Raped Sister to Probation, Citing 'Stigma.'" CNN, 24 May, 2017. Web. 17 Jan. 2018.

[115] Robles, Frances; Stewart, Nikita. "Dylann Roof's Past Reveals Trouble at Home and School." The New York Times, 16 July 2015. Web. 17 Jan. 2018.

children[116], church-goers[117], and still not be labeled terrorists. It is how they can inflict violence on a massive scale, and still be left unharmed by police — and how they can then be diagnosed with mental illness[118], pathologized and treated rather than punished. It is how they can march and kill in the name of whiteness and still be humanized. White people in America are comfortable with violence because their violence maintains their power. Violence *is* their power. Many of the nicest white people I know carry guns because they accept the violence of their culture and believe they need to protect themselves from it, all the while not quite sure why there's so much of it in this country.

"Proud to have it, ashamed of how he got it."

So much patriotism masking American violence. So much American pride harboring inhumane behavior. So much blood flowing freely within this country — sanctioned violence, glorified violence, artistic violence. A country full of vicious monsters convinced they are saviors. Just as Asgard presented itself as the "benevolent" ruler of the Nine Realms, saturated with the blood of all that was conquered, America asserts its "dominance" through worldwide violence under the mask of democracy. The United States is a violently racist thunderdome, where only white people and their agents of white supremacy are armed.

---

[116] "Remembering the Sandy Hook Elementary School Shooting Victims." Daily News, 2017. Web. 17 Jan. 2018.

[117] Yan, Holly; Stapleton, AnneClaire. "Authorities: Texas Church Shooter Had Three Gunshot Wounds." CNN 07 Nov. 2017. Web. 17 Jan. 2018.

[118] Farrington, Dana. "Planned Parenthood Shooter Found Incompetent To Stand Trial." NPR, 11 May 2016. Web. 17 Jan. 2018.

"Proud to have it, ashamed of how he got it."

And then there's Hela, Odin's first-born, the gloriously violent tool used to unite the Nine Realms under Asgard's rule. Is it an accident that a white woman was the tool for Asgard's rise to power, a tool later hidden so well that no one remembered her? Is it coincidence that Hela sought to re-establish Asgard as the violent, conquering, imperialistic power of old, and that her reappearance was the impetus for the complete destruction of Asgard?

Maybe.

Or maybe *Thor: Ragnarok* is a deliberately subversive commentary on our current state of affairs — our battle with the increasing popularity of white supremacy. A nod to how the safety and protection of white women was used as a rallying cry[119] to unite racists under the banner of the KKK. An acknowledgement of the weaponization of white womanhood[120] to encourage savage violence against Black people.

Maybe, just maybe, this Asgard really did need to burn.

This story first appeared at TheEstablishment.co, a multimedia site entirely run and funded by women, on November 9, 2017.

---

[119] Bouie, Jamelle. "The Deadly History of 'They're Raping Our Women.'" Slate, 18, June 2015. Web. 17 Jan. 2018.

[120] Gilmore, Stephanie. "On Using White Womanhood to Justify Racism and White Terrorism." Mic, 25 June 2015. Web. 17 Jan. 2018.

Yet the keepers of history have tried time and time again to downplay the brutality of colonialism; how it decimated indigenous people, empowered European imperialists, and created America. It is still argued that Washington and Lincoln are "good," if problematic, white men.

- TaLynn Kel, Is 'Thor: Ragnarok' A Subversive Takedown of White Supremacy?

Your Fandom Is Racist and So Are You

Two weeks before my annual cosplay extravaganza known as DragonCon, my Facebook notifications began blowing up. Within an hour, I had more than 40 notifications about an article published on *Bleeding Cool* about a popular cosplayer[121] who'd marched with the white supremacists in the Charlottesville "heritage" protests. Curious, I read the article and then went back to my day, entirely unsurprised. Just like water is wet, white people are racist, and racism in cosplay culture has been normalized and capitalized on for years.

At least, this was my perspective. But the white and white-adjacent people on my friendlist were having fits, acting like this was an anomaly. They demanded people unfriend the white supremacist Supergirl or else. Suddenly — despite years of rarely if ever acknowledging, challenging, or confronting racism in the cosplay community — these people wouldn't tolerate white supremacists.

Meanwhile, me and other Black cosplayers wondered how this was going to affect our experience at the convention. We wondered if the woman who marched was going to go to DragonCon (she didn't). We wondered if her defenders would say or do anything (some uncomfortable, and frankly, white sympathizing conversations ensued, but they were not enough to cause disruption).

---

[121] Johnston, Rich. "The Supergirl Cosplayer Who Went to Charlottesville — Guess Whose Side She Was On." Bleeding Cool, 18 Aug. 2017. Web. 17 Jan. 2018.

Once again, we had to navigate an event openly hostile to our participation, and to seek out spaces that felt safe[122]. Once again, we had to consider the reality that true safety in any fandom is a lie.

*****

It is well-known that euro-centric media is anti-Black and white supremacist; that it is rooted in erasing Black people from history, literature, science, pretty much everything. So, it shouldn't be a shock that the fandoms built around these properties are racist, too.

Take, for example, comic books, the source of a huge portion of popular culture and fan events today. For a long time, they were only publicly written by white men, and in 1954, their racism was enshrined in the propaganda-laden Comics Code[123]. The code didn't specifically say that Black people couldn't be included in comics, but it did require the exaltation of police, judges, government officials, and respected institutions, and condemned all criminal activity, which at the time included things like a Black person using a "whites only" water fountain. Comics were written during the Civil Rights Movement, a time when Black people were arrested for daring to seek equality in the eyes of the law, something many white people to this day are fighting against, as evidenced by the current white supremacist commander in chief.

Sixty-three years later, and Black people are still fighting for civil rights and representation in media. And, as part of this same racist

---

[122] Kel, TaLynn. "The Terror of the Now." Breaking Normal, 08 Sept. 2017. Web. 17 Jan. 2018.

[123] "'Good Shall Triumph over Evil': The Comic Book Code of 1954." History Matters: The U.S. Survey Course on the Web. Web. 17. Jan. 2018.

---

ecosystem, we have racist fans fighting to keep their fandoms as white and male as possible.

There are countless examples of fans working to protect comics' all-white-men legacy, from Trekkies threatening to boycott a new Star Trek series[124] because the protagonist is a Black woman and the captain is an Asian woman, to people pushing back against Tessa Thompson being cast as Valkyrie[125], or Idris Elba as Heimdall[126].

Quite simply, racism is built into cosplay because cosplay is rooted in racist intellectual properties[127]. Everything from the lack of Black women characters to the criticisms and outright rejection Black people experience while trying to participate in fandom illuminates this issue. We watch shows about futures that have no Black people and fantasize about alternative histories that somehow have no Black people. Worlds with dwarves, trolls, orcs, wizards, dragons, unicorns, and all types of mythical creatures and possibilities somehow still manage to have no Black people.

And then, in turn, this racist legacy is enshrined by fan culture, which tells us we don't belong[128] — on the ludicrous grounds of

---

[124] Reed, Brad. "'White genocide in space': Racist Fans Seethe at Diversity in New 'Star Trek' Series." Raw Story, 24 May 2017. Web. 17 Jan. 2018.

[125] Simon, Rachel. "'Thor: Ragnarok' Star Tessa Thompson Knows the Color Of Valkyrie's Skin Is The Least Important Thing About Her." Bustle, 07 Sept. 2017. Web. 17 Jan. 2018.

[126] Westbrook, Logan. "Black Thor Actor Talks About Racist Comic Book Fans." The Escapist, 04 May 2011. Web. 17 Jan. 2018.

[127] "The World of Black Cosplay: Discrimination, Rejection, Invisibility of the Black Cosplaying Community." The Columbia Chronicle, 1, Mar. 2015. Web. 17 Jan. 2018.

[128] Khosaravi, Rye. "Racist Reaction to Black D.Va Cosplayer Shows the Struggles of Being a Nerd of Color." Mic, 8, June 2017. Web. 17 Jan. 2018.

"reverse racism" — when we deign to include ourselves in these fantastical narratives meant to excite the imagination.

This is how the vicious cycle continues, and fictional realms remain firmly the domains of white people.

As a fat, Black cosplayer[129], I'm very much aware of the lack of characters who resemble me. I know that when I cosplay, it will be my version of that character, because there aren't any characters who physically match my skin, my body type, my hair, *me*. Even when strides are ostensibly made, I am left out; when Valiant Comics released *Faith*, their fat woman superhero, she was a white, blue-eyed blond.

Just as mass media is a product of the whiteness that's had a stranglehold on America for hundreds of years, so is geek culture and everything spawned from it — conventions, watch parties, movie franchises, hobbies, fandoms.

And just as with everything else, the unbearable whiteness of fandom won't change without tangible effort by white people committed to changing it. Racism is a conscious choice that's become the white noise of American culture, and addressing it takes conscious effort to disrupt how white people see the world.

I'm not talking about performative shit — like what happened with Geek Girl Con[130], a supposedly inclusive organization that saw several members leave en masse when their white allyship was

---

[129] Kel, TaLynn. "As a Fat, Black Woman, Cosplay Has Tried to Make Me Invisible" renamed "The Cosplay Community has Tried to Make Me Invisible Because I'm a Fat, Black Woman." The Establishment, 20 Sept. 2016. Web. 17. Jan. 2018.

[130] Faroughm, Amanda. "GeekGirlCon 2017 Controversy: Tensions Boil Over and Leads Key Organization Staff Members to Quit." Mic, 14 Aug. 2017. Web. 17 Jan. 2018.

questioned, and they were asked to actually do anti-racism work. Actual change requires actual effort — the kind that hurts white feelings and triggers white guilt. Unless and until that happens, not only will we continue to be erased from our cultural contributions, we will continue to be erased from society.

The reaction to the cosplayer who marched in Charlottesville indicated some change is happening on this front. But while white people seem ready to discuss the topic of white supremacy, which they skirted in the past, this isn't enough. The same people who publicly expressed outrage over the racist cosplayer, after all, have by and large failed to question their own racism.

I want to participate more frequently in different fandoms, but I'm finding it harder and harder to ignore the misogynoir in most media content. I am tired of either not seeing Black women or seeing them abused and hypersexualized. I'm tired of only being seen when some white character needs a sacrifice, so they can find their shitty humanity. And I sure as hell don't want to be surrounded by folks too willfully ignorant to even recognize what's going on, who are tired of hearing about inclusion and diversity because, like, can't we just enjoy shit anymore?

It's never just a show, or comic book, or a game. Someone wrote that shit. Someone else edited it. Someone else reviewed it. Still more people offered criticism and finally approved it. Then the director and producer reviewed it and made more adjustments. So, by the time something reaches the masses, many people have contributed to that final product — and when that product is racist as hell, maybe fan culture shouldn't work to vehemently defend and uphold its racism.

Fighting white supremacy in fandom, in culture, in society, in politics, in everything is hard, and it takes commitment from white people to reflect on their privilege. It takes the effort of addressing and analyzing how that privilege impacts everything they think and know. It means making intention efforts to include Black and NBPOC voices in decision-making, if not outright having them be the decision-makers. It requires the willingness of white people to be wrong, especially when working with Black people. To improve quality of life for everyone, you must listen to the voices of those who historically haven't been heard. And you need to be willing to step back and let go.

Always strive to be better than you have been and make this world a better place for everyone.

This story first appeared at TheEstablishment.co, a multimedia site entirely run and funded by women, on December 8, 2017.

We watch shows about futures that have no Black people and fantasize about alternative histories that somehow have no Black people. Worlds with dwarves, trolls, orcs, wizards, dragons, unicorns, and all types of mythical creatures and possibilities somehow still manage to have no Black people.

- TaLynn Kel, Your Fandom Is Racist and So Are You

Misogynoir

First, thank you to Moya Bailey[131] for creating this word. Thank you to Black women feminists, thinkers, activists, and scholars for helping develop this language that centers our experience in this racist patriarchal, oppressive society. Thank you for helping us shape our identity in a structure that was designed to deny us one. Thank you for carving out spaces where we could address our needs and work towards building a better future for ourselves, one that can include the most marginalized populations.

Thank you for helping me free myself from the prison I've been taught I deserved.

*****

I keep trying to articulate how misogynoir manifests in my life. It's challenging in many ways but mostly because it literally is my day-to-day life. It is the judgement I experience for daring to be sexual. It is the shame I'm subjected to for choosing not to be. It is the criticism of my walk, my talk, my skills, and how I use them, whether I choose to use them. It is the various ways I'm told to be silent and to submit to everyone else's expertise, despite knowing that we are all figuring this out and fucking this up together.

---

[131] Bailey, Moya. "They Aren't Talking about Me." The Crunk Feminist Collective, 14 March 2010. Web. 27 Jan. 2018.

Misogynoir is the seemingly endless instruction on how to be a better woman, Black person, human. It is being forced to separate my identity for the comfort of others. It is the denial that I am more than one label and I am oppressed in more than one way. It is the knowledge that no matter when, where, and how I say this, it will be interpreted as self-victimization and lies instead of my reality.

My life, my truth is something that has been denied language for entirely too long. It is something that, once able to be articulated, is deemed unreliable and self-serving...as though that isn't something people are. Protecting myself is painted as selfishness. Giving myself is self-serving martyrization. My actions are always suspect; my knowledge untrustworthy; and my accomplishments false.

It is constantly being told that you cannot trust yourself because people, Black women, are liars and cheats, and frauds.

Every choice we make is subject to scrutiny and belittlement - from how I wear my hair, to who I choose to fuck, my decisions are not my own. They reflect a deficient morality that society says is inherent to who I am. My indifference, rage, vulnerability, and pain are weaponized against me; tools to remind me that I belong at the end of the line and need to be grateful to be allowed in this line at all.

As I write this, we're watching this play out with the comedian, Monique. She was offered a low amount of money for a Netflix special and instead of taking it, she made a stand and asked people to stand with her against Netflix. But, unlike the protests of Black men and white women, Monique has faced nothing but ridicule, vitriol, and derision of her accomplishments and her talent. Virtually everything I've read about her since exposing Netflix's offer has been people talking about how they don't like her or that she doesn't deserve higher pay. Even the think pieces defending her right to create a conversation around how Black women are routinely and deliberately paid less and penalized for speaking about it, all begin with the caveat of "I don't like Monique but…"

"You don't have to like Monique…"

"Whether or not you like Monique…"

"Regardless of whether you think Monique is talented…"

Is this how we're doing this? Like really? Are people really erasing her from the discussion of pay inequity while she is experiencing and calling attention to it? I say this with full struggle in my heart because I've had to deal with this in some fashion since I decided to start building a business. I've had people, usually men, try to advise me on how to do it better, how to make myself more palatable to the public. Men who have never tried to do what I'm doing, yet somehow feel qualified to advise me.

I've had people, usually men and white people, second guess my moves.

I've had people, usually men and white people, tell me I'm being dramatic and confrontational when I command my space and the respect I deserve.

I have found that when I don't back down, when I don't defer, when I step up, lean in, and own my space, I accused of being egotistical and difficult to work with. As long as I project the idea that I'm less than what I am, people try to mentor and guide me, regardless of whether I want their guidance. Yet, the moment I stand and say, "I got this," I am arrogant and problematic.

I have learned that the best way to receive support and assistance is to pretend I know less than I do and appear to dither over decisions. Then people will step in and offer help – sometimes guidance, sometimes resources, regardless of whether they've done it before. As long as I let them think I'm clueless, everything is okay, because they know better than me, even with no experience.

My life consists of moments where people tell me how I'm doing life wrong. People who have never walked in my shoes. People who don't know what it's like to navigate the world with brown skin and a femme appearance. They tell me what they think I should be. They advise me on how to be more pleasing for them and when I reject their shitty, self-serving advice, I'm difficult and stubborn. I'm a problem.

I'm always a problem when people can't control me. And their inability to control me doesn't mean I'm out of control. It just means I'm out of their control and they don't like it.

It's such a funny thing, working through this. Just thinking about how much language is constructed to box me in and limit my choices is eye-opening. People are constantly asking me what my S.O. thinks of my work because they are trying to gauge whether I have his consent, as though his consent is necessary for me to do anything. And when I say I don't need his consent, I feel the social pressure to assure everyone that I care about him, when really, he's the only one who needs to be comfortable with our relationship. I have to fight myself to explain how I'm a good person, even though I don't owe anyone that explanation.

It's hard. It's hard to deprogram myself. It's hard realizing that I have to question my impulses and motives, and that I have to sit with emotional discomfort as I work to figure this shit out. I'm still understanding that I need to question everyone's motives when they talk to me. I must be suspicious. I have to poke their words and see what racism and sexism falls out – not IF it's there but how it's manifesting. It's my job to figure out how their words are designed to keep me in my place and then decide whether to ignore it or nullify it and keep moving forward.

Misogynoir is so easy to engage in; it is the status quo. It's harder to avoid it, it feels almost impossible because you have to look at everything, unpack it, be introspective, follow the money, share the resources, and learn to trust and listen to people you've been conditioned to mistrust and ignore. You need to let go of your assumptions and really listen to people. You must engage in the environment and people in ways you haven't before. You have to accept that what you know isn't true for many people and shake your fucking foundation until it turns to rubble because we've been taught lies and live in a society that perpetuates them.

But first, you gotta admit that you're a liar and bust your ass to stop doing it. And then you need to trust that Black women, femmes, and gender non-conforming people know themselves and their needs better than you think they do.

It seems like everyone really struggles with that part. Sometimes, even I do. But instead of assuming I know, I sit back and listen and think and trust my feelings about what's happening. And if I'm not sure, I take some time to think about it because it's complicated and I need time to sort it out.

And if I, a person who experiences misogynoir constantly, need time to sort it out, you do, too.

The most difficult part of sorting through this has been learning the ways I've stifled myself in response to the negative reactions and social punishment from others. I constantly struggle with this – with recognizing and unlearning the ways that I've been taught to make myself smaller and less noticeable. The only thing that's saved me is my stubbornness, and that's because if I hadn't been stubborn, if I hadn't prioritized my need to survive, I might have decided to opt out of this life. But I didn't. And now I'm here, able to better recognize the ways I've been convinced to place my needs second to everyone else's. Now I am better able to recognize silencing techniques used against me. I can see the ways I've been taught that self-sabotage is ethical. I can now see how my need for financial security is weaponized against me. I am learning the ways that my humanity is maligned and mistreated, framed as weakness, and I'm learning how to fight that messaging in myself so that I can treat myself as a fully actualized human.

I'm learning to stop questioning my humanity and to embrace myself and my needs.

It's a struggle because it does permeate every aspect of my thinking and being. It manifests in so many different ways, from my difficulty in valuing my work, to my belief that I should be completely independent and self-sufficient. That I don't need care or help.

Being a Black woman is constantly being reminded that your place is meant to be behind everyone else. And nobody is shy about reminding you of that. It's being shamed for expressing joy and being punished for expressing pain. It is being denied the baseline humanity of emotional response, having every aspect of yourself weaponized against you. It is knowing that needing help is grounds for it to be denied.

I question my value constantly and push myself to prove my worth to myself and others. I find value in my success and despite learning from my failures, I believe they lessen my worth in the eyes of others. I fight to believe I have the right to exist and I feel undeserving of goodwill, fortune, and gifts. I believe self-sacrifice is necessary for me to matter.

None of this is true. In fact, all of it is rooted in misogynoir.

These essays explore the various ways I've learned to see and unpack misogynoir in my life. It is an ongoing process with real consequences that negatively impact the lives of Black women, femmes, and gender non-conforming people every day. But learning to see it is a step closer to learning how to protect yourself from it, and to stop doing it.

Maybe, one day our society will grow out of this, but everyone has to do the work that right now too few people are willing to admit is needed.

The Face That Paused a Thousand Meetings

Once again, my face stopped the meeting. Halted it completely because someone felt insecure about it.

I wish I could say this wasn't a common occurrence, but it is. I have stopped meetings at every position I've held in the past ten years. It's getting to be impressive, despite being unintentional. I've been told that my smile makes me look guilty, my frown is frightening, my expressionless face is intimidating, my shifting in my seat is discouraging, my avoidance of eye contact as disrespectful, and my laugh is disdainful.

And while I am sure that at some point, all these things are true, it hasn't escaped my notice that these descriptors usually come from managers during and after team meetings…usually when they want to discuss some other way I've somehow challenged their authority or made them feel less authoritative. This happened so often that a couple of years ago, I started warning people about the faces I make when I'm thinking about what's being said. At the time, I felt like I was heading a confrontation off before it became a problem. Turns out I was just apologizing for being myself and this year I've decided that shit was unacceptable.

No more apologies. That I felt like I had to explain and apologize for my face to avoid trouble is fucking ridiculous to me, but I did. I did it because I like paying my bills – ok that's not true. But I do like being able to meet my needs and have a bit of fun with my income and I didn't want that to stop. So, every time someone gave me some "helpful feedback" on how I'm perceived, I internalized it and tried to adjust.

I sat in meetings with my head in my notebook, avoided eye contact, schooled my face into a non-expression, sat very still, didn't speak, didn't ask questions, filtered my suggestions through better liked co-workers...and found that regardless of whatever technique I employed, they still had a problem with me. I was too assertive, not assertive enough. I looked devious or bored. I didn't offer enough feedback, or I was too critical. My laugh was too loud or I seemed like I didn't want to be there. The list of things my body language communicated to them[132] was negative and endless.

Eventually I realized that it didn't fucking matter what I did. Their problem with me was ME. Not actually me, personally, but something about my physicality[133] caused them to see every part of me negatively, regardless of what I did. These people were never going to like ME.

For a while, I internalized that message. I figured I was unlikable...until I noticed that I made a lot of cool acquaintances and some friends every place I worked. People I spent time with outside of the office. Some of these people are still in my life a decade later. If I was so unlikable, how the fuck was I making friends all over the place?

It's no secret that Black people face a lot of racism in the workplace. Black women also have to deal with the Angry Black Woman stereotype[134], where we can't ever express anything that isn't positive without fear of retaliation. I had to realize that this response to me wasn't that I wasn't good enough – it was that I was

---

[132] Hobson, Janell. "Angry or Complicated? Misrecognizing Black Women." Ms. Blog, 22 Sept. 2014. Web. 28 April 2016.

[133] Yancy, George. "Walking While Black in the 'White Gaze.'" The New York Times, 01 Sept. 2013. Web. 28 April 2016.

[134] Conger, Cristen. "How the 'Angry Black Woman' Stereotype Tries to Control Black Women." Everyday Feminism, 03 March 2016. Web. 28 April 2016.

a threat to their perceived superiority. Thing is, I am good at a lot of things I try, and when I'm not, I'm comfortable admitting it. That level of self-confidence triggered a negative response in a lot of people and until I humbled myself (by apologizing or some such bullshit) they felt compelled to do it for me.

That means that in every work environment, I had some boss who tried to take me down a peg and put me in the place they felt comfortable with me. As you can guess from the first paragraph, that shit didn't go well. And the older I get, the less of this bullshit I'm willing to entertain.

Yesterday, a young Black woman colleague approached me about her office experiences. She's fresh out of school and facing her first wave of racist microaggressions[135] in the workplace. I feel for her. Truly. You don't realize the dumb shit people are going to ask you or say in front of you until it happens. And when it does, you think, "Am I making something out of nothing?" Yet, you will continue to hear and be asked things that will put your race front and center in the discussion. People will be openly disdainful and if you confront it, you will be punished. These people will not think they are racist. They will think shit like, "I have Black people on my team. I'm liberal as hell!" when in reality, they are spouting silly ass white supremacist bullshit frequently and enforcing that shit at every opportunity.

My advice to her was, "white people do racist shit all the time and don't think it's racist. They will hold positions of power over you in the workplace and will enact these things both consciously and unconsciously. Your role is to define what you need from this

---

[135] Boylorn, R. "Working While Black: 10 Racial Microaggressions Experienced in the Workplace." Crunk Feminist Collective, 11 Nov. 2014. Web. 28 April 2016.

situation and decide how much you can push back while still getting what you need. Your job is to build coping mechanisms for dealing with this. They can be as simple as calling a friend, or visiting your therapist. Sometimes, you'll have to quit. But don't do that if it's going to fuck you up financially. If that's the case, make them fire you because as long as you follow the correct steps, you can collect unemployment for a little while."

I feel bad telling someone to dim her shine and not rock the boat, but she doesn't have the financial support to leave her job at this time. She can work on creating that support but until then I suggested she figure out how to maintain her independence without sacrificing her self-worth, and that is a difficult dance. You will always take damage and you will always need time to heal.

I wish I knew a better way but this is the reality I see and experience. And while creating your own business, one where you don't have to face the same attempts to disempower you, you will still face this when you deal with white people. You will be told that you won't be trusted because of how you look[136]. You will be told that you will always seem less than white people. You will be perceived as violent despite never doing anything to warrant that perception. People will ask you about "Black" things and be surprised when you refuse to answer. Your contributions will be ignored or dismissed, often publicly, and then implemented in the background – and you will not receive credit for them. Then, when you point out your contribution, you will be viewed as narcissistic.

---

[136] Woodard, Monique. "The White Elephant In The Room." 13 April 2016. Web. 28 April 2016.

This is what I face. This is just one of the struggles[137] we as Black women face in the workplace.

Needless to say, I hate meetings. It's hard to keep a semi-smile on your face while listening to people say ridiculous, irrelevant shit for an hour. It's difficult trying to suppress your curiosity and interest in the goings on of the company because your every utterance that isn't "that's great! Love it!" are seen as criticism. Or your problem-solving skills are looked at as a burden, not an asset. As I said, it's not an easy space to occupy. I've failed several times and I will likely fail again. Until I get my independence from this environment, I'll fail and rebound like I always have.

[137] Johnson, Maisha Z. "6 Struggles of Being Unapologetically Black in a Professional Environment." Everyday Feminism, 04 Nov. 2014. Web. 28 April 2016.

That means that in every work environment, I had some boss who tried to take me down a peg and put me in the place they felt comfortable with me.

– TaLynn Kel, The Face That Paused a Thousand Meetings

Leslie Jones Embodies the Least Protected Blackness of All

This essay originally published on the week that she was viciously and relentlessly attacked by racists on Twitter. It was so cruel and dehumanizing, yet unsurprising because white men on the internet seem to relish being bottom feeders.

This was my response.

*****

It all started with the idea to remake a classic and beloved movie—*Ghostbusters*.

And, as it's 2016, why not make the cast all women? Shouldn't be a big deal, right? Women are equal—we can vote, have jobs, own property…it really *shouldn't* have mattered. But it did. It mattered so much that sexists led a charge to tank the movie[138], simply for starring women.

After its release, the movie got middle of the road reviews[139] and did okay financially[140]. But that wasn't enough[141] for all the anti-Ghostbuster trolls. Nope. They needed to punish someone for the film being made. And the target they chose was Leslie Jones.

---

[138] Cox, Carolyn. "The Ghostbusters Trailer Backlash Shows Men Believe in the Power of Representation (But Only When It Applies to Them)." The Mary Sue, 01 May 2016. Web. 23 Aug. 2016.

[139] Ghostbusters (2016). Rotten Tomatoes, 2016. Web. 23 Aug. 2016.

[140] Ghostbusters (2016). Box Office Mojo, 2016. Web. 23 Aug. 2016.

[141] Riedel, Sam. "Why Busting 'Ghostbusters' Reboot Myths May No Longer Matter." The Establishment, 19 Aug 2016. Web. 23 Aug. 2016.

They called her names, went on a now-infamous racist and sexist insult-spree that temporarily drove her from Twitter[142], and yesterday we found out that someone hacked her account and leaked nude photos of her (I refuse to link to any of that).

Do you know why they keep attacking Leslie? They keep attacking her because she's a Black woman and think this makes her a "safe" target. I mean, why *wouldn't* they think that? Historically, Black women have been cruelly and viciously attacked by white people. We have been victimized, brutalized, and vehemently attacked by men of *every* race. We have been belittled, ridiculed, and mocked at every turn.

And historically, we haven't been defended, protected, or appreciated. These attacks happen and the only people who demand justice are Black women. Not Black men, not white anyone. Not any other group. We stand up for ourselves and are consumed and regurgitated as stereotypes in the process: Angry Black woman. Belligerent Black woman. Loud Black woman. Sassy Black woman. Strong Black woman. Invulnerable Black woman. Tired Black woman.

This angry, belligerent, loud, sassy, strong, invulnerable, tired Black woman faces constant and consistent misogynoir[143]. Like my peers, we are always fighting against physical and emotional abuse dealt to us by a culture that tells us that we are nothing. That we are not privy to the rights of white people or men. That we are not loved.

---

[142] For Harriet. "Leslie Jones Quits Twitter After Spending a Day Battling Racist Twitter." For Harriet, 19, July 2016. Web. 23 Aug. 2016.

[143] Bristol, Keir. "On Moya Bailey, Misogynoir, and Why Both Are Important." The Visibility Project, 27 May, 2014. Web. 23 Aug. 2016.

That we are not equal. That the only protection we have is in the community we build for ourselves.

And even within that community there is internalized racism in the form of colorism[144]. There is this idea that only the lightest of us deserve humanity and empathy. The darkest of us are treated as an embarrassment, as someone who shouldn't be seen. The darkest of us are treated as an embarrassment, as people who shouldn't be seen. Even when Black people are front and center, we are the ones who remain hidden.

Leslie, in all her beauty and strength, embodies the least protected Blackness of all.

Her pain is our pain when our nudes are leaked and people pretend it's a fucking compliment that anyone wants to see us naked[145].

It is our pain when we are physically assaulted and raped[146] and people assume we invited it either with our aggressive personalities or hypersexual bodies.

---

144 LaSha. "We Need to Talk About Leslie Jones and Colorism in Our Community." Ebony, 12 Aug 2016. Web. 23 Aug. 2016.

145 Lennard, Natasha. "'Why are black women less attractive?' asks Psychology Today." Salon, 17 May 2011. Web. 23 Aug. 2016.

146 Leicht, Angelica. "Suspects Arrested, Charged in #Jadapose Rape Case." Houston Press, 17 Oct. 2014. Web. 23 Aug. 2016.

It is our pain when we are misgendered as an insult[147] and that misgendering permits people to ignore our abuse[148].

It is our pain when we are taught that calling the police on a Black male abuser is a bigger sin than being abused[149].

It is our pain when a Black man harasses or rapes a Black woman[150] and moves on with minimal impact to his career[151] while we are attacked for speaking out against the rapist[152].

It is our pain that survives in a world designed to beat us down — and it is our resilience that demands that we still rise.

We are the fastest growing group of entrepreneurs[153] and are earning degrees at a higher rate[154] than any other group in the United States. We are beacons of style and innovation. From our

---

[147] Roberts, Monica. "Misgendering Attacks On A Black Woman's Femininity Aren't Funny." TransGriot, 02 June 2015. Web. 23 Aug. 2016.

[148] Cooper, Brittney. "The world only has ugliness for black women. That's why Serena Williams is so important." Salon, 15 July 2015. Web. 23 Aug. 2016.

[149] Azalia, Loy. "My struggle to protect black men when they've been my abuser." Blavity, August 2016. Web. 23 Aug. 2016.

[150] Blay, Zeba. "'Confirmation' And The Silencing Of Black Women To Shield Black Men." Huffington Post, 15 April 2016. Web. 23 Aug. 2016.

[151] Drayton, Tiffanie. "On Nate Parker's College Rape Case & Why Black Women Should Not Watch 'Birth of a Nation.'" Clutch, Aug. 2016. Web. 23 Aug. 2016.

[152] Shackelford, Ashleigh. "Stop Excusing Black Men's Violence – Like Nate Parker's – for the Sake of Black Liberation." Wear Your Voice Magazine, 16 Aug. 2016. Web. 23 Aug. 2016.

[153] Haimerl, Amy. "The fastest-growing group of entrepreneurs in America." Fortune, 29 June 2015. Web. 23 Aug. 2016.

[154] Davis, Rachaell. "New Study Shows Black Women Are Among The Most Educated Group In The United States." Essence, 07 June 2016. Web. 23 Aug. 2016.

hairstyles[155], to our bodies[156], from our original content[157] to our political movements[158], white people revisit their colonialist roots by appropriating every fucking thing we do[159] and then trying to destroy us when we fight back.

And still we fight. And still we shine. Black Girl Magic[160] is real.

This shit that's happening to Leslie Jones is yet another manifestation of white supremacy and its utter disregard and disrespect for Black women. It is a travesty of the highest order.

If I could say anything to Leslie Jones, it would be this:

Dear Leslie,

I'm sorry that you are experiencing this. I am enraged on your behalf. All you did was your job and as a result, you are facing outrageous and illegal attacks upon your person, your privacy, and your wellbeing. I'm not going to bullshit you by saying that this is going to be easy. It's not. It's fucking horrendous and I hope you are

---

[155] Kinks, Klassy. "White Hair Blog Claims Bantu Knots Were "Inspired" By Marc Jacobs, Black Twitter Goes Nuts." Black Girl Long Hair, 27 May 2015. Web. 23 Aug. 2016.

[156] Wellington, Elizabeth. "When Black Girls Get Criticized and White Girls Get Celebrated." For Harriet, Oct. 2014. Web. 23 Aug. 2016.

[157] Phillips, Kady. "Blavity Exclusive: Akilah Obviously on BuzzFeed and #StopBuzzThieves." Blavity, Aug. 2016. Web. 23 Aug. 2016.

[158] Bowerman, Mary. "Is White Lives Matter a movement or white supremacist group?" USAToday, 22 Aug. 2016. Web. 23 Aug. 2016.

[159] Kel, TaLynn. "When White People Consume Blackness For Personal Gain." The Establishment, 29 June 2016. Web. 23 Aug. 2016.

[160] Wilson, Julee. "The Meaning Of #BlackGirlMagic, And How You Can Get Some of It." Huffington Post, 12 Jan. 2016. Web. 23 Aug. 2016.

able to find these criminals and fuck their lives up. This will not make you stronger. It will make you acutely aware of just how vulnerable you are, but your vulnerability is not the problem. The problem is these entitled fucks who feel like they have the right to abuse anyone they choose. I hope they pay with everything they are because they have revoked their humanity.

You did not deserve this and they deserve to suffer.

Let me know how I can help.

TaLynn

This story first appeared at TheEstablishment.co, a multimedia site entirely run and funded by women, on August 25, 2016.

These attacks happen and the only people who demand justice are Black women. Not Black men, not white anyone. Not any other group. We stand up for ourselves and are consumed and regurgitated as stereotypes in the process: Angry Black woman. Belligerent Black woman. Loud Black woman. Sassy Black woman. Strong Black woman. Invulnerable Black woman. Tired Black woman.

– TaLynn Kel, Leslie Jones is the Least Protected Blackness of Us All

On Sex: My Humanity is Not Optional

While watching Saturday morning cartoons, I reached for his hand, seeking the comfort of physical touch. He pulled away sharply and said, "Why can't you wait for me to show you affection? Why are you always demanding it first? Damn! Give a man a chance to want you."

I turned away, blinking back tears, my breath entering and exiting my body too fast. I stared at the ground, working to slow my breath and erase the spots that had begun appearing in my vision. We were sitting on his roommate's couch watching some asinine cartoon in which I had no interest. I was trying to be open to his interests because everyone told me that I was too focused on myself.

"That's why you're single," they told me. "You don't know how to compromise. You always put yourself first. When you want to be with a guy, you're going to need to put him first and let him know he's the most important person. You gotta let him pace the relationship."

I crossed my arms while my breathing evened out. Once I felt like I was in better control, I pretended to watch the show. The unoriginal nonsense designed to get children to buy shitty, cheap toys. The writers didn't even bother with a plot and I was to sit there and endure that shit with some fucker who looked at hold my hand as an imposition after spending hours of my pussy enveloping his dick.

I stood up, grabbed my shit and left. There was nothing left to say.

****

Throughout my 20s, I recreated this scenario in many forms — one-night stands, friends with benefits, casual on-going engagements. And every time I became better at learning the various ways I felt like an invisible shit after fucking someone so that I could enact it on someone else. I created arbitrary rules, promised sexual escapades that I would only enact if they arrived at the destination precisely at a specific time. One minute early or late and the deal was off. I learned to make men crawl, begging for an opportunity to touch me, lick me, fuck me. And I took immense pleasure in watching their confusion as I stripped layer after layer of their autonomy and humanity away. They hurt me, constantly, and I became skilled at giving it all back to them while making them cum during their humiliation. I used shame, disinterest, disdain, dismissal…I wouldn't offer them a glass of water. I refused every veneer of courtesy and stripped encounters down to the necessary mechanics of attaining my orgasm and their degradation. I embraced the monster that patriarchy made.

Because love doesn't defeat monsters. Only other monsters can do that.

How did I learn to be that monster? I learned from other monsters…from men who told me I was invisible unless I dressed to please them. From women who taught me to hide my intelligence, opinions, and personality in favor of modeling them for the specific interests of some guy. I learned from the conversations of men who talked about the characteristics they found unattractive — the qualities I loved about myself. I learned that my body was valued, not my mind. My usefulness to them was prized, nothing more. I learned how to see myself as a thing and then, when the pain of being nothing became overwhelming, I taught them how it felt to be everything I'd learned to be.

They didn't like it.

In retrospect, I was lucky that I'd never incited violence in anyone. I felt like I screened them appropriately. I picked most of them up online and screened them for weeks on end. I learned how to make them hungry, how to tease and give just enough to keep them interested. I didn't need to pull them all, and I didn't. Many men walked away, suspicious that all was not what it seemed — that I wasn't what I seemed. But I had enough men, enough to be monstrous and cruel to make up for the many ways I'd been dismissed in my life.

I won't lie and pretend it didn't make me feel powerful. Heterosexual relationships with cisgendered, heterosexual men are weighted to give men significant power. Every fucking date I went on was a balancing act to maintain my autonomy without driving them away. I failed constantly. I learned that men don't like humanity with their women. They just want the fun, moist, penetrable bits.

Men who claim to respect me tell me shit like this all the time. They tell me that I'm sexy but just so difficult. Too strong. Too hard to control. They make disparaging comments questioning my significant other's masculinity at being with me. At his lack of dominance over me. They find the idea of breaking me, making me conform to their idea of womanhood sexy. There is a colossal disconnect between what they think they sexually desire and their actual stimulation by my intellect. It makes me hate them a little bit, these men who cannot wrap their heads around a relationship with a woman that isn't sexual. I struggle to respect them and wonder why I should.

Over time, I changed. Grew. Learned not to care about the opinions of others so much. Learned to weigh their comments, interest, desire and disregard them. I interact with men giving no fucks as to whether they think I'm flirting or teasing; their interest is none of my business, unless I perceive a threat. I center and focus on my needs in those interactions. My priority is myself.

I've had people ask if I worry about leading guys on. The answer is no. Again, their interest is none of my business and if some guy is hanging around in hopes that one day something more will happen, he's fucked up and that's his problem. It only becomes my problem if they become a threat, which is something I have no control over. I am a card-carrying member of the "I don't give a fuck about your lust" club. Keep that shit to yourself.

It took years to stop being the monster. Years of learning about myself and recognizing what behaviors elicited that response from me. Years of learning how to interact with men without needing to hurt them. Years of managing my emotional well-being and shaping myself into the person I want to be and learning the qualities I needed in the person I could be with. I never thought I'd find that, had actively stopped looking. I just wanted to live without causing and enduring the psychological power struggle that is heterosexual relationships. I wanted the freedom to be me without any pressure to change into someone's idea of a partner. Weirdly, that relationship fell into my lap. That isn't to say we don't have problems — racism is a huge shit-show we're constantly working through, but he has always supported me and encouraged my endeavors — even the ones that bother him. He doesn't try to make me less than who I am and doesn't mind disappearing in my glow.

He embraces my humanity and my womanhood. One doesn't compromise the other and he's never asked me to sacrifice my

humanity for his hard-on. It's sad when that's the criteria for a
healthy relationship.

I learned that my body was valued, not my mind. My usefulness to them was prized, nothing more. I learned how to see myself as a thing and then, when the pain of being nothing became overwhelming, I taught them how it felt to be everything I'd learned to be.

– TaLynn Kel, On Sex: My Humanity is Not Optional

Men Are Shitty Friends

Sometimes it's really fucked up being friends with men.

In some ways, it's easier. They rarely press you about your feelings. It's easy to keep things superficial, until they try to fuck you. And for some reason, many of them try to fuck you despite constantly denying their intent, even going so far to accuse you of being over-confident.

It gets hard when they casually and hypocritically dismiss your opinions. When they argue with you on what's sexist, when they have little to no experience in dealing with sexism. It's hard when your every response and opinion is deemed as overreacting and being sensitive.

It's hard to realize they don't respect you and constantly twist reality to support the illusion that they do.

I've called many men my friends, but I'm realizing that I hold male friends to a different standard, a lower one. The same respect they give me, actually. Why would I respect someone who doesn't respect me? They entertain me. They amuse me. Sometimes they help with shit, but having real conversations about our experiences? Why bother with that when they spend the entire conversation telling me that my thoughts aren't worth shit and don't matter. When they "agree to disagree" and refuse to acknowledge their blind spots. When they literally say that I'm creating a problem where there isn't one, all because they cannot see it. When they essentially call me a liar.

They get angry when I mirror their behavior. I've had men try to check me in conversation when all I did was talk to them the way they talk to me. Funny how they don't like receiving the same respect they give.

Interestingly, I don't have fights with my S.O. about sexism because when I tell him something is sexist, he doesn't fucking argue with me about it. He asks me how and we talk about it and then we keep it moving. It's not an argument; it's a discussion. It's not dismissive; it's dialogue. And it doesn't make me angry — it makes me happy. Side note — he had to learn to do this when we talk about racism[161].

Yet, other men? Other men tell me that the issues I have are pathological. They tell me that all I do is point out problems. They conveniently ignore or forget when I agree or like some shit but constantly have an issue when I don't like things or find them problematic. When I point out the issues with a movie, a book, a television show, a song, an artist, etc., I'm told that I look for problems. I'm told that I'm making problems where there are none. I'm told that I'm being angry, bitter, and judgmental.

I'm told I'm the problem, not what I'm critiquing.

Then they take that and make it into a general characteristic about me — not quite a flaw, but this thing that I do. "She's just super critical." And then they use that characteristic to silence me.

"Don't pay any attention to her, she's just angry."

"She thinks there are problems with everything. Don't worry about it."

"TaLynn doesn't like anything."

---

[161] Kel, TaLynn. "My Husband's Unconscious Racism Nearly Destroyed Our Marriage." The Establishment, 05 May. 2016. Web. 17 Jan. 2018.

This happens so frequently, so casually, that when I point it out, I'm told I'm overreacting and being dramatic. Because I can't have a legitimate issue. Nope. I'm just a troublemaker.

When I was younger, I'd let this slide. I'd tell myself it wasn't a big deal and try to maintain a friendship with that person. Now, I say fuck it and cut my losses. I don't need to fuck with people who don't respect my experiences and thoughts. I can accept disagreement. I cannot accept dismissal. I won't. I deserved to be listened to. I deserve to be respected. And I deserve to be believed.

What I don't deserve is to be told that my thoughts are not worth considering.

I don't deserve is to be lied to.

I don't deserve to be bothered by your lust when I've made it clear I'm not interested in fucking you.

And I sure as fuck don't need you telling me what I think or what you believe I "really mean." Listen to the words I'm actually saying and stop trying to change that shit to fit your reality. I know what the fuck I mean, and I know what the fuck I want. I also know how to articulate that shit and if you have questions, ask them.

What you are gonna do is stop trying to override my opinion or manipulate me into being who you think I'm supposed to be and accuse me of being difficult when you can't shift me.

What you're gonna do is accept who I am and give me the same respect you want from me.

If you can't, you don't have to be in my life. In fact, it's better if you aren't.

I don't need to fuck with people who don't respect my experiences and thoughts. I can accept disagreement. I cannot accept dismissal. I won't. I deserved to be listened to. I deserve to be respected. And I deserve to be believed.

– TaLynn Kel, Men Are Shitty Friends

You Are Not in the Fight for Equality if You Protect Your Privilege

You are not in the fight for equality if you protect your privilege.

You are not in the fight for equality if you protect your privilege.

You are not in the fight for equality if you protect your privilege.

Recently, I entered discussions with men in my life about women-centered, safe spaces. At least, I tried to talk about them and the need for them. Instead, we ended up talking about how I take things to extremes and how men get sexually assaulted, too so I need to acknowledge that.

eye roll

What I learned from these conversations is that one, knowing someone is derailing the conversation doesn't necessarily prevent it and two, it's hard to get men to admit their privilege. Using a mix of tone policing, false equity, and shitty attempts to discredit me by talking around the topic, I exposed a base level of sexism that I'd chosen not to challenge because I like having these men in my life. But now, I'm reaching a point where I'm wondering how to navigate this because, like with racism, this shit is everywhere and it's toxic. I haven't met the man who doesn't default to this bullshit, and frankly, I'm tired of dealing with them.

So many men think they are not sexist. They think they are liberal and inclusive. Yet, the moment their male privilege is challenged, they expose that they are trash who don't understand on a basic level how sexism works. It leaves me fucking frustrated and exhausted because they know they have male privilege and yet they vehemently protect themselves by trying to talk around the issue and victimize themselves. I'm still trying to process this shit cuz damn.

Men ain't shit. Even the "good" ones.

*****

Privilege is an interesting concept. I can't say everyone has privilege, because so much of it is circumstantial, but what I can say is that privilege is not a stagnant thing. It shifts based on environment, proximity, and circumstances.

I know I have privilege. I am intelligent by white people's standards and educated in a white supremacist system that, while toxic, holds value in white spaces. I was born in the United States and have the documentation to prove it. I have an ivy league degree that I only recently finished paying for, 20 years after the fact. I am cisgender and heterosexual. I do not live check to check at the moment, but that can always change. I'm able to be openly affectionate with my Significant Other (S.O.) in many of the places we visit and I'm free to use the bathroom without fear of harassment. I do not need to worry about access to buildings, or whether sidewalks are wide enough for my mobility assistance devices. My health issues are manageable, and I am insured through my employer. I have worries but these are not them. These are my privileges.

*****

My S.O. is a white cisgender, heterosexual male born in the U.S. with documentation to prove it. He has an advanced degree and can work virtually anywhere he chooses. He shares many of my privileges, except he has the "bonus" of being white and male in a country that prioritizes that above all else. He is catered to in virtually every arena, except in the spaces where I've decided that he has no voice. He cannot speak to me about oppression because he is not oppressed. And sometimes he doesn't understand that.

I have a Black male friend whose privilege is his maleness, not his skin color. You'd think being a member of an oppressed group would make you more aware and sensitive to the oppression experienced by others, but that isn't so. Instead, you find them engaging in the very actions they advocate against for themselves. It is always amazing to me that so many Black men engage in misogynoir[162], especially as our struggle is their struggle, too.

Yet, when confronted with sexism and sexual abuse performed by men, both these liberal men, one white and the other Black, got defensive. When you talk about the rampant physical abuse and rape culture experienced by women, these men, instead of listening and discussing the contributing factors, leaped into the "not all men" rhetoric and start trying to deflect or dismiss the issues. They each became more concerned with proving that maleness is harmless and blameless. They prioritized their male identity and privilege over women's oppression and it is ugly.

I pushed back. I explained. I gave examples. And every step of the way, I was stonewalled, either with accusations of extremism, tone policing, or outright dismissal. I was accused repeatedly of saying all

---

[162] Kirabo, Sincere. "Why Black Men Participate in Misogynoir – And 3 Ways We Can Fight Against It." Everyday Feminism, 17 Oct. 2016. Web. 17 Jan. 2018.

men despite written evidence that I never did. They actively tried to silence me, and eventually, I wrote them off as irredeemable.

Except I am married to one of them.

Sexism has never been a big part of my marriage. I excel in many areas and often outperform my S.O., so while it's come up, it has never been an issue. We've bumped heads on some of the Gamergate stuff, which made me realize he was getting his information from shitty sources, which then resulted in my providing alternate sources for information. Sources that he now uses, not exclusively, but regularly. There was mild awkwardness when I told him I wasn't ever going to take his name, but that only happened when other people asked us about it. Cuz they ask and those in-laws I don't speak to still send mail to Mrs. (S.O.'s last name) because passive aggressive shit is an Olympic sport for them.

pause to experience the rage passive aggressiveness ignites

Anyway, I can understand forgetting that you have some privileges. I can understand how easy it is to take your "normal" for granted. What I do not understand is defending it, especially when you constantly see evidence of how it hurts others. I don't understand how you can read about almost 200,000 known untested rape kits in the U.S.[163] and not see there's a big fucking problem when it comes to addressing and prosecuting rape in this country. I don't understand how you can read cases where men receive reduced sentences for raping infants[164] and not be outraged by how your

---

[163] "Where the Backlog Exists and What's Happening to End It." End the Backlog. Web. 17 Jan. 2018.

[164] Phillip, Abby. "Man Who Sexually Abused 3-Year-Old Girl-Didn't 'Intend to Harm' His Victim California Judge Rules." 07 April, 2015. Web. 17 Jan. 2018.

privilege protects them. I don't understand how I can provide a list of sexual assaults performed by men[165], most of which remain unpunished, and despite this, you still feel an overwhelming need to protect men.

He's fucked up. Seriously fucked up. I need him to seriously re-evaluate his morality and priorities.

It's becoming impossible to process how this man who does everything he can to comfort and care for me, can and will express ridiculous shit about men's rights. This is a man who doesn't sexualize women, who encourages my work, even when it hurts him, who will get up at 3am to make me tea when I'm sick and comforts me without trying to suppress my emotions. This is a man who has always stood next to me or behind me, encouraging me to pursue my dreams. And yet, he devolved into some shitty men's rights rhetoric because he felt threatened by something I said. I watched him become someone I don't like and wouldn't willingly fuck with.

So, I told him that he is still babystepping out of his privilege and fuck that. Do better. Remedial anti-oppression class is over. It's time for him to step up or I'm not going to do this anymore. That he could sit there and defend some oppressive nonsense means that he's not working hard enough to fix his shit. There are no more resets on this — either he's in this fight or he's my enemy.

This fight...it's not just for women, or Black people, or POCs, or LGBTQIA+...it's for EVERYONE. We are fighting to eradicate a poison that is decimating the world. White supremacy is an empathy

---

[165] Kel, TaLynn. "American, Stop Protecting Your Monsters." The Establishment, 10 Oct. 2016. Web. 17 Jan. 2018.

snatcher. It destroys your humanity and encourages you to corrode from the inside to gain the illusion of power and independence. It's a lie that creates false hierarchies of humanity and it creates divisions among people that lead to mass murder and genocide. White supremacy is a monster that is never sated, never satisfied. It is a soul sucking abyss that will never be filled.

We don't have to be these people. But to change, we have to stop defending our privilege. When we defend privilege, we support oppression. When we defend privilege, we encourage tyranny. When we argue in defense of our privilege, we are advocating for violence against those who lack that privilege. When we defend our privilege, we are the monsters.

This isn't debatable. This isn't something you can parse out and only partially be a monster. It is all or nothing.

You are either my friend or my enemy. I've told you my criteria. You decide which one you're going to be.

When you talk about the rampant physical abuse and rape culture experienced by women, these men, instead of listening and discussing the contributing factors, leaped into the "not all men" rhetoric and start trying to deflect or dismiss the issues. They each became more concerned with proving that maleness is harmless and blameless. They prioritized their male identity and privilege over women's oppression and it is ugly.

– TaLynn Kel, You Are Not in the Fight for Equality if You Protect Your Privilege

When It Comes to Free Speech, the 'Whites Only' Is Silent

There's a reason why the authors of the Declaration of Independence could write "all men are created equal" while owning Black people and silencing women. It's the same reason why, yesterday, a Black woman professor from Princeton University, Keeanga-Yamahtta Taylor, decided to **cancel talks in Seattle and San Diego**[166], after receiving death threats for giving a commencement speech calling he-who-shall-not-be-named a "racist, sexist megalomaniac" who "has fulfilled the campaign promises of a campaign organized and built upon racism, corporatism, and militarism."

American society is so racist and misogynistic that it has convinced itself that attacking and threatening a Black woman for criticizing the words and actions of an abuser is the moral high ground. That silencing the voices of those who can see that the Emperor has no clothes is the proper thing to do. And that free speech should protect those who seek to hurt the marginalized, but not the marginalized themselves.

And here's the thing: What Professor Taylor faced is considered the norm in this country and has been since the U.S. was first colonized. In the Gamergate[167] and sexist-white-straight-man-bullshit online communities, these kinds of threats are standard. Online advocates

---

[166] Bernard, Sara. "Princeton Professor Cancels Seattle Talk Following Deluge of Racist Threats." Seattle Weekly, 31 May 2017. Web. 17 Jan. 2018.

[167] Lieu, Johnny. "Prominent GamerGate Target Details Disturbing Harassment, All These Years Later." Mashable, 28 Feb. 2017. Web. 17 Jan 2018.

and activists[168] face them all the time for discussing history. For acknowledging demographics. For discussing shitty-ass cultural norms. The brotherhood of white maleness and its disciples firmly embrace violence against anyone who speaks against them.

And the really scary part? Their disciples are everywhere. They are in the schools, teaching our children[169]. They are in the hospitals refusing Black people care[170]. They are in the police forces[171], criminalizing Blackness[172]. In the restaurants, demanding the right to refuse to serve Black people and other people of color (POCs)[173]. They are the lawyers claiming to defend us while quietly encouraging us to plea bargain behind closed doors[174]. They are the judges handing down extreme sentences at will[175] and the

---

[168] Jones, Feminista. "We Have Had to Defend Ourselves Against Online Threats." 03 Aug. 2016. Web. 17 Jan. 2018.

[169] Klein, Rebecca. "Texas Teacher Fired After Disturbingly Racist Post in Response to Pool Party Incident." Huffington Post, 11 June 2015. Web. 20 Jan. 2018.

[170] "US: Black Woman Forcibly Removed from Hospital Dies 2 Hours Later." Telesur, 25 Dec. 2015. Web. 17 Jan. 2018.

[171] Oppel, Richard A.; Stolberg, Sheryl ay; Apuzzo, Matt. "Justice Department to Release Blistering Report of Racial Bias by Baltimore Police." The New York Times, 09 Aug. 2016. Web. 17 Jan. 2018.

[172] Lee, Vic. "Department of Justice Report Cites Bias by San Francisco Police." ABC 7 News, 12, Oct. 2016. Web. 17 Jan. 2018.

[173] Lazarus, Jeremy. "Black Patrons Turned Away from Fan Restaurant." Richmond Free Press, 04 Nov. 2016. Web. 17 Jan. 2018.

[174] Demby, Gene. "Study Reveals Worse Outcomes for Black and Latino Defendants." NPR Code Switch, 17 July 2014. Web. 17 Jan. 2018.

[175] Harriot, Michael. "Black Man Found Not Guilty of Crime, Still Sentenced to 7 Years in Prison." The Root, 23 May 2017. Web. 17 Jan. 2018.

politicians deciding which people deserve clean water and housing[176].

They are the white women who protect patriarchy[177] through supporting dangerous leaders and inciting brutal violence over their assumed "purity." They are the non-Black POCs who think aligning with whiteness will protect them[178]. They are the Black people[179] who think the same ill-informed nonsense.

We are past the time of sirens and warning bells. We are fully in the fuckshit of the downward spiral. Now it's just a matter of when and how it all falls apart. If the argument is whether I'm human and deserve human rights — and it is — then this is the only way things can go.

Professor Taylor canceling her talks is all the more troubling when you consider the state of free speech in this country. Leaders in the progressive community have devoted themselves to defending those who openly disparage and threaten the marginalized. According to the ACLU, white nationalists like Richard Spencer[180] and anti-trans incendiaries like Milo Yiannopoulos can openly spew hate because of free speech protections under the First

---

[176] Covert, Bryce. "Race Best Predicts Whether You Live Near Pollution." The Nation, 18 Feb. 2016. Web. 17 Jan. 2018.

[177] Chira, Susan. "'You Focus on the Good': Women Who Voted for Trump, in Their Own Words." The New York Times, 14 Jan. 2017. Web. 17 Jan 2018.

[178] Chang, David; Lozano, Alicia Victoria; Gutierrez, Gabe. "Family of Syrians Deported from Philadelphia Supported Donald Trump." NBC Philadelphia, 31 Jan. 2017. Web. 17 Jan. 2018.

[179] Kel, TaLynn. "To the Black Women Who Align Themselves with White Supremacy." The Establishment, 27, Feb 2017. Web. 17 Jan. 2018.

[180] McLaughlin, Eliott C. "War on Campus." CNN, 1, May 2017. Web. 17 Jan. 2018.

Amendment[181]. Even when this speech could very likely lead to violence against Black people or trans people or other groups that have been historically oppressed, it is apparently worth vigorously protecting[182].

But a Black woman criticizing the leader of the free world? We aren't meant to be heard, and to insist upon it can literally lead to our death. (Some of the 50 e-mails Taylor received in the wake of her commencement speech threatened murder.)

I would have canceled if I were Professor Taylor, too.

Right now, in this country, we have white people fighting for the right to refuse to deal with Black people and POCs[183]. We have people whose paid responsibility is to protect, serve, heal, and provide, fighting to exclude people[184] they think don't deserve the same amenities as them. We have an Attorney General, appointed by the man Professor Taylor cannot speak out against, turning his back on police brutality[185], and launching a crusade against Black people and POCs.

---

[181] Interview. "The ACLU Explains Why They're Supporting the Rights Of Milo Yiannopoulos." NPR, 12 Feb. 2017. Web. 17 Jan. 2018.

[182] Stone, Geoffrey R. "Richard Spencer's Right to Speak at Auburn." The New York Times, 18 April 2017. Web. 17 Jan. 2018.

[183] Markus, Bethania Palma. "Fresno bar kicks out two black women — and it turns out they are attorneys for the ACLU." Raw Story, 24 March 2016. Web. 17 Jan. 2018.

[184] Kutner, Jenny. "Kentucky Fire Chief Refuses to Help Black Family after Traffic Accident: "We Ain't Taking No N–gers Here." Salon, 20 Nov. 2014. Web. 17 Jan. 2018.

[185] Serwer, Adam. "Jeff Sessions's Blind Eye." The Atlantic, 05 April 2017. Web. 17 Jan. 2018.

I've always worried about my safety, but this environment helps me realize how much of my safety has been an illusion[186]. It has reinforced every negative thing I'd been taught to think about white people when it comes to my well-being. And on top of all that, I worry that if I'm physically assaulted by some white person and the police are called, that officer may choose not to get involved, or may side with my assailant.

White people don't value Black lives. We know this. And this country is filled with white people who I'm forced to give the benefit of the doubt to on a daily basis. But guess what? I have enough of a survival instinct to say, "fuck it" when I need to. And I commend Professor Taylor for exercising that right. In a statement after canceling her talks, she said:

"I will not be silent. We have to change this dynamic and begin to build a massive movement against racism, sexism, and bigotry in this country. I remain undaunted in my commitment to that project."

Did the haters win? Nope. Because she is still alive and has the ability to speak her truth. That is not something that can be said for a lot of Black people.

This story first appeared at TheEstablishment.co, a multimedia site entirely run and funded by women, on June 2, 2017.

---

[186] Okeowo, Alexis. "Hate on the Rise After Trump's Election." The New Yorker, 17 Nov. 2016. Web. 17 Jan. 2018.

American society is so racist and misogynistic that it has convinced itself that attacking and threatening a Black woman for criticizing the words and actions of an abuser is the moral high ground. That silencing the voices of those who can see that the Emperor has no clothes is the proper thing to do. And that free speech should protect those who seek to hurt the marginalized, but not the marginalized themselves.

– TaLynn Kel, When It Comes to Free Speech, the 'Whites Only' Is Silent

The Hate We Receive: On Colorism & Anti-Blackness Among Black People

When I was a child, having dark skin was a flaw. Dark skin was considered ugly. I can remember slinging insults that were nothing more than describing how dark a person's skin was. It was cruel, and now that I know the damage I was doing, I am ashamed.

At the time, I had two best friends, B and K. B was on the lighter end of the brown spectrum. Sometimes people referred to her as redbone. Her hair was a softer texture, her eyes were a lighter brown, and everyone thought she was gorgeous. Boys constantly asked me to help them get close to her. Men, boys, and white people were generally nicer to her, all because she had light brown skin.

K, on the other hand, caught hell all the time. The boys would call her names and throw rocks at her. She had more issues in school and was thought to be a troublemaker. Ironically, B was the one who was sneakiest and a much better liar than both of us, yet K was the one people singled out to blame. Sometimes K and B would fight — K could see that people treated B nicer than her all the time, but K couldn't lash out at them. B was accessible. Over time, they became less close; at the time, I thought K was jealous, but honestly, I'd get tired of being mistreated in such close proximity to someone who wasn't. And in a society where attractiveness is currency, it doesn't make sense to stay near someone who would always be perceived as more attractive for the superficial reason of lighter skin. To survive, she distanced herself from someone whose presence invited attention from those who would assault her and this was her normal.

B had her own issues. Having sexual attention from boys and men foisted on her before she was 10 years old is some nonsense. Having to learn to avoid and escape sexual predators was challenging. We all had to, but her lighter skin, hair, & eyes made her highly sought after and she was put into dangerous situations and forced to make adult choices. I know they affected her and her life is finding joy in managing the fallout. To survive, she had to learn to manipulate those drawn by her looks and this was her normal.

Regardless, we had two girls, both sexually objectified and terrorized by men — B was pursued as a sexual conquest while K was a verbal punching bag and it was all based on the perceived attractiveness of their skin color. And this is what I think of when I hear Rickey Smiley[187] say hateful things about Black women. This is the very dynamic we see in all media — Casting Gurl Wonder wrote a Twitter thread discussing how casting agents specifically request racially ambiguous women for Black roles. We see it when dark skin performers like Leslie Jones[188] are attacked by racists. We see it when Black women are removed from our own narratives[189] and replaced by women of color who are not Black.

---

[187] Ways, Kays. "Rickey Smiley Dragged for Disgusting Joke About Dark Skin Women." Lisa A La Mode, 29, April 2017. Web. 17 Jan. 2018.

[188] Kel, TaLynn. "Leslie Jones Embodies the Least Protected Blackness of All." The Establishment, 25 April 2016. Web. 17 Jan. 2018.

[189] Kwateng-Clark, Danielle. "'Guerilla' Director John Ridley Says Black Women Are Erased from His Series Because He's 'In A Mixed-Race Relationship.'" Essence, 10 April 2017. Web. 17 Jan. 2018.

We are constantly erased from our stories[190], from our history, from media, and from any representation of daily life. We are constantly told we are ugly. Sick. Unworthy of respect or love. The features we're told are ugly become beautiful when grafted on paler bodies. Our hairstyles ridiculed until they are adopted by whiteness. We get it — the darker our skin, the less deserving we are of human treatment.

You'd think that people who shared our range of hues would understand. You'd think that Black men would understand and relate to this issue. Instead we see them experience pleasure and obtain success in exploiting this anti-Blackness toward Black women and femmes. We watch them participate in the negative perception of Black women and profit from it. And the ones who can't eke out a living by beating the drum of misogynoir settle for the emotional orgasm they receive from being the oppressor instead of the oppressed. They capitalize on ridiculing our looks, our bodies, our ways of speaking. We are blamed for the ills of the world whether we choose to have children, need public assistance, or are financially independent. We are found wanting regardless of how we wear our hair, makeup, clothing. Somehow, we consistently find ourselves subjected to criticism, ridicule, dismissal, and erasure.

I'm not sure when I realized I'd never be good enough and stopped trying. I'm not sure I ever really did. I do know I go through periods where I seek outside validation...then I realize that validation is fleeting and a form of control I don't need or want. But what I'm talking about isn't only about me. The only space I have in this conversation is how I'm "average" Black. I'm the Black woman who is the troublemaker next to the light-skinned Black woman and the

---

[190] Pennington, Tonya. "Why Black Women in History Deserve to Have Their Stories Told." Black Girl Nerds, 19 April 2017. Web. 17 Jan. 2018.

"good one" next to the dark-skinned Black woman. And yes, this happens. My worth and attractiveness is dependent on who I'm around and when I'm around white people, I'm just that Black woman who is to be silenced or ignored.

But, again, it's not just about me. It's about watching assholes like Charlamagne the shithead interact with loud, ignorant, belligerent white women and then say Black women should aspire to be like her[191]...because a thin, blond white woman makes the "angry Black woman" trope palatable. I guess it's because the Black was removed. It's about Black men like Gilbert Arenas[192] straight up saying that dark-skinned women aren't attractive. And it's about shitty jokes like the one Rickey Smiley made about a dark-skinned Black woman. The message is everywhere and its messengers are disappointing on every level.

It's fucked up watching this continue to play out over and over again. It's fucked up knowing that Black women and femmes are being hurt and killed because we're considered easy targets who are punished when we protect ourselves[193]. It's fucked up knowing that the only people who care about Black women and femmes are other Black women and femmes.

---

[191] Scott, Sydney. "Charlamagne Tha God Is Problematic Once More, Says Black Women Should Use Their Voice Like Tomi Lahren." 07 Dec. 2016. Web. 17 Jan. 2018.

[192] "Gilbert Arenas Says Lupita Nyong'o 'Ain't Cute' in Tirade about Dark-Skinned Women." The Grio, 14 April 2017. Web. 17 Jan. 2018.

[193] Andrews, Masai. "The UAlbany Bus Incident Is Repeating History." Huffington Post, 01 May 2017. Web. 17 Jan 2018.

But it does make it a lot easier to stop caring about the people who don't care about us.

We are constantly erased from our stories, from our history, from media, and from any representation of daily life. We are constantly told we are ugly. Sick. Unworthy of respect or love. The features we're told are ugly become beautiful when grafted on paler bodies. Our hairstyles ridiculed until they are adopted by whiteness. We get it — the darker our skin, the less deserving we are of human treatment.

– TaLynn Kel, The Hate We Receive: On Colorism & Anti-Blackness Among Black People

You May Never Understand the Truth of Me

I love writing. It helps me sort through ideas, organize my thoughts, and gives voice to emotions in ways that I wouldn't necessarily take the time to voice without an audience. While one does not require an audience to write, having an audience brings a greater significance to the act.

I love writing. For reasons tangible and not, it's something I have always felt compelled to do. But there comes a point when you have to ask yourself why you're writing. Is it for attention? To educate? Because you have a story to tell? Because you have something you need to share? Is it a job? Is it more about your audience or about you?

Sometimes I don't like to answer those questions because it makes me feel as though I'm compromising myself for money. And let's be real, we live in a capitalist society that requires money to survive. I'm not rich so sometimes it's about the money.

Lately, I've been trying different ways of expressing myself, sometimes with my writing, sometimes with video, and as always with cosplay. My writing is the closest to my core. It is the least externally manipulated aspect of me. It is my internal self, using only my filter...at least my personal posts are. The essays that have been published on other sites, while they are my voice, are edited. Sometimes the essays are changed to educate readers, specifically white readers. Sometimes this is problematic as fuck; other times, not so much because I intended to educate white readers. But those problematic times stick in my throat.

I'm having that moment now. I was asked to revise an essay, which is the right of any publication. I've started and stopped several times. The original essay needs some cleaning up, but I like it. I like the rhythm and cadence of it. I'm still smoothing it out, but it speaks in a way I appreciate. Being asked to revise it so that it could become more universal and include some statistics disturbed me for a couple of reasons...

It made me feel as though my writing only has value if it's teaching something. I mean, I get it. Publications have an audience that has specific expectations. When I want to read something lyrical and creative, I read literature magazines. When I want something technical, I read subject matter specific magazines. Sometimes my writing sits on a line between audiences and the editor needs to nudge me towards the genre that centers their primary audience. And while it makes sense for them to do that, this time it bothered me.

Sometimes I struggle with how people, community, and society try to make me fit into various categories that makes me comfortable for them. It happens with the -isms in my life, as well as the activities I engage in. My writing, cosplay, and public health activities don't always fit into social justice, geek fun, or my professional life. Sometimes I'm too abstract. Sometimes I'm too carefree. Sometimes I'm too irreverent, whimsical, confrontational, analytical, or grounded. And sometimes all these things manifest in an essay or a cosplay, because I am all these things all the time. They are never separate and they are always me. Being asked to revise me to suit you is challenging and limiting. I don't like it and I don't like that I understand why people encourage it.

I also struggle with being asked to prove my experiences. Whether it's through being asked to include statistics and data to substantiate my experiences or asked to share more examples of my abuses and trauma, it is troubling. It speaks directly to the marginalization of Black women's voices, my voice because if I cannot provide enough evidence of something that is deeply coded and openly denied, then my experience is deemed invalid. As it is, we are often told our experiences are false; that we are misinterpreting some well-intended act. It places the burden of proof of someone else's fuckery on me, and silences me if I cannot find some additional, external validation. Often, I'm counseled against being vague or too general in my essays, when sometimes that's the experience. Instead, I am encouraged to provide examples and evidence that I am not alone. It contributes to a feeling of not being believed, a common and intentionally manufactured feeling when talking about oppression with your oppressors.

I'm still questioning myself about this. The request was made so kind and timidly, that I am still asking myself if I'm overreacting. The answer to that question is no; I'm just reacting. I learned long ago that when something makes me feel weird, look at it and try to figure out what's really happening. Our emotions are a tool that helps us identify danger or pain, long before we are able to consciously identify it. I gently interrogate myself; ask if this is ego or something more. Because I rarely receive feedback asking me to clean up my writing, I am not used to certain types of criticism. But when a response to my work causes a strong emotional reaction, I pause to assess why and in this case, it's because I'm seeing a pattern in how my work is rejected, causing me to question the value of my writing.

I know my writing has been weaponized by white people against other white people. I've seen it used as evidence of a Black experience to which white people cannot relate. I've seen it misinterpreted, misconstrued, and misread, particularly by those who wish to discredit me. I also know that my writing has helped people, and that it helps articulate a complicated situation that Black women in my situation are blamed for…because we chose to marry a white man. But that experience, and how I shared that experience, is not all that I am. Nor is my rage. Or my disappointment. Or my joy.

I am many, many things and I communicate that in numerous ways: spoken, written, even visually, as seen with my cosplay. And while I do engage in activism, that isn't always by choice. Often, my refusal to hide, my desire to be seen and heard, and my insistence on participating in a space that has told me I'm not welcome is perceived as activism. My willingness to speak about tough topics, my comfort in being me is interpreted as resistance. I call it living my life, but you know how identity politics work — if your politicized identity is visible, you don't get to choose what it is. Just like you don't always choose what resistance looks like. For me, resistance looks like daring to exist and live my fat, Black, geek life unapologetically, i.e. everyday existence.

What I will say is that if you find yourself in the role of gatekeeper and are working with marginalized populations, think about how that informs your expectations. Think about how your perceptions and expectations shape your criticism, editing, and feedback. Ask yourself if you are projecting what you want to see onto their work and whether that is appropriate. In return, I'll seek out venues more in-line with my voice and my intent. Or I'll self-publish, where I have the 100% control over my content. That way, when my whimsy is rooted in uncomfortable truths, instead of having to explain and clarify my experience for an unfamiliar audience or be asked to conform, I can publish and let my writing reflect the truth of me; a truth that you may never understand.

As it is, we are often told our experiences are false; that we are misinterpreting some well-intended act. It places the burden of proof of someone else's fuckery on me, and silences me if I cannot find some additional, external validation.

– TaLynn Kel, You May Never Understand the Truth of Me

I'm Ashamed to Fight for My Financial Survival

When I was a child, I watched shows about evil rich people; people who'd been corrupted by their greed. Or sad, lonely, rich children who would trade all their money for their parent's love. I was taught to sympathize with people who had money, be afraid of money corrupting me, while figuring out how to make money to survive. It was acceptable to earn money doing service, but only through established institutions who earned a percentage. Expecting payment for services wasn't respectable unless it was somehow governed and managed.

I learned that needing money was ugly. That it made you less than human. I learned that this manufactured tool needed to survive in our society made me dirty. My desire for it, my need for the things it afforded me...all that was subhuman, and I should be ashamed of that need.

I learned that I am always for sale. That my body, my time, my intellect, and my creativity are all on an auction block, their worth determined by nameless, faceless people, diminished by my skin, my size, my abilities... I am a compilation of parts and skills whose worth is defined by everyone but me. And when I am with a man, it proves that I can be bought — be it with flowers, dinner, cash, a ring — in some way that man met my price be it for the night or for all the years ahead of me. Because I am for sale.

Dinner and a movie was a respectable price for an evening of my time, pre-Netflix and chill. I should be proud that a man wanted to date me. I was taught to take pride in being bought. Unless we had sex. Then I should be ashamed of being for sale. You see, there are layers to this shit but it all comes down to understanding that white male cis-het society sets my price, not me. If I set a price and sell myself, I'm worthless but if the system does it, it's respectable. Prostitution for survival is bad. Marriage for survival is respectable. My identities set my price, and being a fat, Black, woman of a certain age lowers my value, which is also determined by who's buying. Like I said, this shit has layers.

As a woman, I'm expected to care for people without pay. Everyone is entitled to my caring, nurturing, and encouragement. When I deny them this, suddenly I'm a problem and should I seek payment for my services, I'm crude. Strangers on the street have asked "when you gonna cook for me" as though that is a good introduction. As though my labor is my value. My appeal is never about me, but rather what I can do for you.

I learned it was noble to be poor...as long as your poverty was invisible. As long as you didn't ask for aid. No welfare. No food stamps. No begging. No subsidized anything. Needing help was shameful. There was only joy in giving, never taking. How many of us have seen a viral video of a homeless person sharing their belongings or giving back a handout? How many of us have been told that enlightenment comes from giving away all that you have? How often have we extolled the virtues of those choosing to live without?

And how often have we sought to punish those who don't have that choice?

It's amazing to me that not only did that narrative fly, but it still does. It is impacting my life right now. People offer to support my work and I tell them not to. My S.O. had to push me into setting up a Patreon account. I still struggle to figure out whether anything I do has value. I give away the vast majority of my writing. I still seek out "respectable" employment, as I cannot figure out my worth. I'm afraid to charge for my work, which is a damn problem, especially as I do not have "respectable" employment at the moment.

I deliver content constantly, content that it costs me time and money to make, yet I can't figure out how to comfortably break even. I have plans for future projects and I have no idea how much I should value my time. It's frustrating to constantly fight myself about my worthiness because I still see money, and needing money, as shameful. I tell myself that I am not for sale, then I have to determine my hourly worth because that's the society we live in and that's how we survive.

Fuck you, poor little rich boy. Maybe money can't buy happiness, but it can buy you peace of mind to sleep, eat, and take care of yourself. Poverty isn't romantic or noble, but I have bought into that messaging to my detriment for years. YEARS! I find myself having to fight shame about wanting to comfortably pay my bills. Ain't that some shit? I'm ashamed of my need for income and any difficulty I have in finding someone to pay me.

I don't have an entrepreneurial spirit because I'm ashamed to demand the thing that makes it possible — money. I just take what people are willing to pay me and if that's nothing, then I get nothing.

That is not how we survive. That is not how we live. And it is definitely not how we thrive in a capitalistic society that is comfortable exploiting everyone to get and stay rich. And I don't actually have to exploit anyone to make a living.

Instead, I've been focusing on creating content — my writing, cosplay photos, creator videos...and I promote custom art on t-shirts. All the art is commissioned from independent artists. I also sell cosplay prints and my first book...things that I hope bring value to those who purchase them.

But it's work. Constant work. Between meeting with my friend and producer, photoshoots, utilizing conventions as interview spaces and panel discussions; it's bigger than I thought and it's a financial drain. I love it, but I need to figure out how to value it...how to value me.

I've seen people have the audacity to sell shit I've made by accident. I have seen people sell skills they don't have. Yet I struggle with myself to sell shit that's actually good.

We all suspect why that is, but I'll leave it for another essay.

Thank you for your support. Truly.

* * * * *

The easiest way to give support is to follow my social media and subscribe to my mailing list. Here is the list of options. There are a couple of links to give money, too.

Website: www.talynnkel.com

Facebook: www.facebook.com/talynnkel

Twitter: www.twitter.com/talynnkel

Instagram: www.instagram.com/talynnkel

Medium: https://medium.com/@TaLynnKel

Tumblr: https://www.tumblr.com/blog/talynn

Patreon: https://www.patreon.com/talynnkel

As a woman, I'm expected to care for people without pay. Everyone is entitled to my caring, nurturing, and encouragement. When I deny them this, suddenly I'm a problem and should I seek payment for my services, I'm crude.

– TaLynn Kel, I'm Ashamed to Fight for My Financial Survival

White Male Patriarchy Says I'm Disposable — Until White People Need Us to Save Them from Themselves

As I sit here, reflecting on the Senate race in Alabama, wondering how a credibly accused child molester and open homophobe and racist was ever seen as an acceptable candidate — and how he only lost because Black voters and organizers[194] worked tirelessly to ensure he did — I'm reminded of my childhood. Of how I've always been taught, and always known, that Black people must do so much and benefit so little.

When I was a kid, my father would say things like, "Your teachers are going to underestimate you. Prove them wrong." Or "They are going to look for reasons to punish you. Don't give them any." Or "They are going to assume the worst about you. Be the best, instead." And "Sometimes your best will still be seen as less than their worst. Be your best anyway."

That was a lot of pressure for elementary school. Looking back, I see why he said these things. When I was in first grade, my teacher didn't realize for half the year that not only could I read, but I was reading at a middle school level. Instead of acknowledging this, my teacher called me a troublemaker. My mom routinely came to school for "discipline" reasons due to my boredom. Once my mom understood what was happening, she had me moved to a teacher who not only understood that I was capable but used my capability as a resource in her class, assigning me the task of helping other students with their reading. I know I wasn't the only Black child labeled a troublemaker; I just happened to have a parent with the bandwidth to challenge that presumption. Those other kids were

---

194 Newkirk, Vann R. "African American Voters Made Doug Jones a U.S. Senator in Alabama." The Atlantic, 12 Dec. 2017. Web. 17 Jan. 2018.

diminished and marginalized by a teacher who couldn't be bothered to engage with her Black students; their future was defined by a white woman's assumptions.

By middle school, I was the only Black child in the accelerated program. Twenty-nine white children and me. I've always found it peculiar that no other Black students were in that class with me, especially as many of the students in that class should not have been there, and by the next year were gone. Not that it was a great experience. My questions were interpreted as insubordinate. My high-test scores were evidence of cheating. My boredom with school was seen as a sign of disrespect. Over the years, I learned to still my fidgeting, mask my impatience, and stop asking questions, only to then be accused of not caring about my education. And when I behaved like the other kids in my class, I was forcibly reminded of my real status by my father.

"You don't get to mess up," he'd say. "You don't get to do what everybody else does. You have to remember that when something goes missing, they will accuse you. When something is broken, you are their first suspect. Those people out there aren't interested in your mistakes. When you screw up, you lose your chance."

And when I forgot his lesson, the world reminded me of it, be it through re-tests when I earned perfect scores, or questions about the sources of my paper topics, or punishments for things outside of my control, like the time I lost my badge as a safety monitor for not preventing a fight from breaking out. Once, I was expected to take a test after returning from an educational trip — the teacher explained that despite spending the week in DC learning about the government, he couldn't give me a week to learn the new material. That test brought down my grade, but my request for a few extra days was dismissed as asking for "special treatment" — and who was I to expect that?

Discrepancies like this happened throughout elementary school. Middle school. High school. Being in the accelerated program did provide me some protections; my proximity to what was thought to be the smartest examples of whiteness meant that I did receive the benefit of the doubt at times. I spoke like them. I excelled in their studies. I'd shown them that I could do what they do and do it well. But they always saw my Blackness as something to be watched. Studied. Anticipated. They waited for an opportunity to prove I was irredeemable — just like those other Black people. Blood always shows...or in this case, skin. For years, they waited for the opening to throw me away.

I went to parties where my Blackness was shouted out. "Come meet my BLACK friend," they'd say. When I balked they said I was too sensitive, and when I pushed they stopped inviting me. Disposable.

I was always on the outside. My absence, unnoticed. It is no surprise that when I stopped associating with them altogether, life moved on, the loss unimportant to all of us. I made new friends, gained new white people from forced proximity, and continued to learn that our friendships would never be deep, never be meaningful, and never last. I knew that if I couldn't keep them comfortable in their whiteness, I would be disposed of. I learned not to care because by then, they were disposable, too.

But that was 20 years ago, and racism was talked about differently then. I grew up in the generation of kids raised by Black people who lived through the Civil Rights protests. Black people who now had opportunities that had been barred from them. My father taught me to do my best, stay quiet, and excel. Give them no reason to see you as disposable. Make yourself indispensable. Overcompensate. When they steal your work, learn to let it go. When they lie, protect yourself, just not at their expense. When they harm you, learn how to manage it without accusing them of anything. Do not make waves. Do not call them racist. Do not call them sexist. Smile, pretend everything is great, and then come home and let everything out. And always remember, they don't want you there, so do everything you can to avoid giving them a reason to dispose of you. They will never let you belong.

We see this in all ways, all the time. From seemingly small incidents like being ignored at work[195] to large ones like the lack of reporting on police violence against Black women[196], we see the humanity of Black women being dismissed and discarded in favor of whiteness. We see it every time a Black girl is viciously attacked by police or school security or the neighborhood watch, and white supremacy races in to "justify" that abuse. White people and people who support white supremacy justified Korryn Gaines' murder[197]. They justify attacking Black teenage girls[198]. They justify inhumane treatment of Black women because we aren't supposed to matter, so for them, we don't.

[195] ByBlacks.com. "The Harsh Reality of Being a Black Woman in the Workplace." Huffington Post, 24 April 2017. Web. 19 Jan. 2018.

[196] Jeffreys, Zenobia. "Why Police Violence Against Women of Color Stays Hidden." Yes Magazine, 10 Aug. 2017. Web. 18 Jan. 2018.

[197] Raser, Tess. "Twenty-Three Years of Resisting Police Brutality: The Life and Death of Korryn Gaines." Truthout, 19 July 2017. Web. 19 Jan. 2018.

[198] Finn, Jessica. "Black 5ft 2in Teenage Girl Weighing 115lbs Tells of Horrific Ordeal as Police Confronted Her at Gunpoint and Punched Her in the Mouth When They Mistook Her for a 170lb Bald 5ft 10in Male Suspect." Daily Mail, 12 July 2017. Web. 20 Jan. 2018.

Which brings me back to Alabama.

Over the last few months, we watched white supremacy work overtime to disenfranchise voters[199] and advocate for a known racist[200] and alleged sexual abuser[201] to take public office. And now that the election is over — and we see from the exit polls[202] that Black women played a pivotal role in electing Doug Jones, the first Democrat Alabama senator in 25 years[203] — we must, in typical fashion, watch as white supremacy skews the narrative to minimize and erase the impact and importance of Black women.

"They saved us," white people say[204], erasing our personal motives and structuring the narrative to prioritize whiteness. As usual with white supremacy, our votes aren't being viewed as designed to save us — they're being viewed as designed to save white people. To save the country.

And meanwhile, this country we saved? It will inevitably continue to turn its back on us. "This is not just a question about African

---

[199] Levy, Pema. "Reports of Voter Suppression Tactics Pour in From Alabama Election." Mother Jones, 12 Dec. 2017. Web. 19 Jan. 2019.

[200] Kaczynski, Andrew. "Roy Moore in 2011: Getting rid of amendments after 10th would 'eliminate many problems.'" CNN, 11 Dec. 2017. Web 19 Jan. 2018.

[201] Paiella, Gabriella. "Fifth Woman Accuses Roy Moore of Sexually Assaulting Her When She Was a Teenager (Update)." The Cut, 13 Nov. 2017. Web. 19 Jan. 2018.

[202] Burlij, Terence. "The 7 Most Revealing Findings in the Alabama Exit Polls." CNN 13 Dec. 2017. Web. 19 Jan. 2018.

[203] Clark, Dartunorro. "Meet Doug Jones, Alabama's First Democratic Senator in 25 Years." NBCNews, 13 Dec 2017. Web. 19 Jan. 2018.

[204] Lockhart, P.R. "The Alabama Election is the Latest Example of the Political Power of Black Women." Vox, 13 Dec. 2017. Web. 19 Jan. 2018.

American voters," Doug Jones said[205]. "This election is about everybody in the state." But somehow, that American "everybody" seems to rarely, if ever, include Black women.

We live in America, a country that was built on the exploitation and casual murder of Black people, and which has continuously blamed us for our struggles. For Black women in America, there are no good options. Very rarely are we able to choose someone who understands and represents us, and when we do, we are met with extreme prejudice and dismissal[206], regardless of qualifications and achievements.

And so, we are forced to support candidates who advocate locking us up, who call Black men "super predators[207]," who pass legislation to destroy our economic capabilities[208], and who profit off the suffering of Black and Indigenous People of Color (BIPOC)[209]. We do not make these decisions because we believe in these candidates. We do it out of pure pragmatism, because the choices are just that dismal.

Black women's votes save so many people, yet our interests are the first to be discarded and ignored. Consider that, in the case of the Alabama election and so many others, we had to step up in spite of

---

[205] Fang, Marina. "Black Women Played a Big Part In Doug Jones' Surprise Victory In Alabama." Huffington Post, 13 Dec. 2017. Web. 20 Jan. 2018.

[206] Landers, Jackson. "When Shirley Chisholm Ran for President, Few Would Say: 'I'm With Her.'" Snithsonian.com, 25 April 2016. Web. 19 Jan. 2018.

[207] C-SPAN. "1996: Hillary Clinton on "Super Predators" (C-SPAN)."

[208] Coates, Ta-Nehisi. "The Black Family in the Age of Mass Incarceration." The Atlantic, Oct. 2015. Web. 19 Jan. 2018.

[209] Katz, Jonathan M. "The Clintons Didn't Screw Up Haiti Alone. You Helped." Slate, 22 Sept. 2016. Web. 19 Jan. 2018.

voter suppression, a constant battleground for Black women[210] and a war that is largely ignored by white people. Because, after all, addressing that would mean white people could no longer perpetuate the narrative of their inherent benevolence and goodness.

Black women, we're told, are here to save others, not ourselves. As we are asked to be strong Black women[211], capable of saving the world from itself[212], we are also told we can't save ourselves from our male rapists[213] and male abusers[214]; we aren't legally protected[215], and we aren't socially protected[216]. We aren't even protected by our fathers, brothers, sons[217], or lovers[218]…instead we

---

[210] Newkirk, Vann R. "What's Missing from Reports on Alabama's Black Turnout." The Atlantic, 07 Dec. 2017. Web. 19 Jan. 2018.

[211] Williams, Vanessa. "Maxine Waters and the Burden of the 'Strong Black Woman.'" The Lily, 26 Aug. 2017. 19 Jan. 2018.

[212] Jones, Feminista. "Mammy 2.0: Black Women Won't Save You, So Stop Asking." Feminista Jones, 01 Aug. 2017. Web. 19 Jan. 2018.

[213] Birman, Daniel H. "Me Facing Life: Cyntoia's Story." PBS, 01 March 2011. Web. 19 Jan. 2018.

[214] Stahl, Aviva. "Behind Bars for 6 Months, Teen Accused of Killing Abusive Father Awaits Justice." Broadly, 19 Jan. 2017. Web. 19 Jan. 2018.

[215] "Marissa Alexander, Jailed for 3 Years, Speaks Out on Intimate Partner Violence & Building Movements." Democracy Now, 04 May 2017. Web. 19 Jan. 2018.

[216] Kel, TaLynn. "Leslie Jones Embodies the Least Protected Blackness of All." The Establishment, 25 April 2016. Web. 17 Jan. 2018.

[217] Charleswell, Cherise. "Sexual Abuse and The Code of Silence in the Black Community." Role Reboot, 08 Sept. 2014. Web. 19 Jan. 2018.

[218] Hutchinson, Sikivu. "The Wars Inside: Black Women and Deadly Intimate Partner Violence." Huffington Post, 14 April 2017. Web. 19 Jan. 2018.

---

are expected to save them[219], too, all while being happy we got a man to protect. We are taught to deny ourselves the love of anyone not Black[220], while being subjected to the misogynoir rampant in our society[221].

This is what it means to navigate the world as a Black woman. This is what it means to be disposable while refusing to be disposed of.

But I am not disposable. You can try. You do try. But I have spent my life refusing to be someone's trash, and instead I am this amazing and accomplished Black woman. I live a life of joy and struggle, but I do what I can, embrace my humanity, and keep moving forward. I do it because that's what I must do.

And I'm not alone. Studies consistently find[222] that Black women have higher self-esteem and self-worth[223] than non-Black women. We fight for our space to exist because we know we're worthy of the effort. I don't want it to be this way. I want Black women to have the freedom to be human in all its complexities and contradictions. I want us to have spaces where we can fail without worrying about it destroying our entire lives and families. I want us to be able to be vulnerable without having it exploited and

---

[219] Belton, Danielle C. "Black Women and the Savior Complex." Clutch, May 2014. 19 Jan. 2018.

[220] D'Oyley, Demetria Lucas. "If You're a Black Man Mad About Serena Williams' Engagement, I Have Questions." The Root, 30 Dec. 2016. Web. 19 Jan. 2018.

[221] Staff. "Black Men, We Need to Acknowledge that We Are the Problem. Let's Talk Toxic Masculinity." Black Youth Project, 25 April 2017. Web. 19 Jan. 2018.

[222] Dreisbach, Shaun. "Black Women Are More Confident Than Any Other Group of Females: Survey." Glamour, 01 Aug. 2017. Web. 19 Jan. 2018.

[223] Wilson, Julee. "Black Women Have Amazing Confidence, Survey Shows." Huffington Post, 08 Jan. 2012. Web. 19 Jan. 2018.

weaponized against us[224]. I want to see award-winning movies about Black life and have them be boring or mundane or transcendent without them being about slavery, poverty, drugs, or struggle. I want the freedom to be excellent or mediocre and have neither be representative of my Blackness. I want the freedom in this society to be me.

I know I am valuable. I know I am indispensable. I know my life matters. Too bad this country will not see that until it's strangling itself to death.

This story first appeared at TheEstablishment.co, a multimedia site entirely run and funded by women, on December 13, 2017.

---

[224] Karazin, Christelyn. "How Glamour Confidence Survey Hurts Black Women Part II." Beyond Black & White, 03 Aug. 2017. Web. 19 Jan. 2018.

Make yourself indispensable. Overcompensate. When they steal your work, learn to let it go. When they lie, protect yourself, just not at their expense. When they harm you, learn how to manage it without accusing them of anything. Do not make waves. Do not call them racist. Do not call them sexist. Smile, pretend everything is great, and then come home and let everything out. And always remember, they don't want you there, so do everything you can to avoid giving them a reason to dispose of you. They will never let you belong.

– TaLynn Kel, White Male Patriarchy Says I'm Disposable — Until White People Need Us to Save Them from Themselves

Internalized Anti-Blackness

When you're Black and living in an imperialist country that was colonized, you grow up learning to hate yourself.

You learn it in the most basic of ways like hating dark brown skin or your tightly curled hair, to bigger things like preferring your white teachers to your Black ones or choosing to only date people who aren't Black. Then there are the big-ticket items, the ways you are taught to ignore the suffering of other Black people, or better yet, blame them for being born into a system that is designed to exploit or kill us. The ones who actively capitalize on it - Black people who will denigrate other Black people and exploit them for access to white spaces and financial gain.

I know some of this is done for survival. We live in a society that intentionally limits access to resources for Black and Indigenous People of Color (BIPoCs). White men molded to provide maximum opportunities for other white men and their families while restricting access to everyone else. When your economic and physical survival is rooted in appeasing people who only see you as a resource to be exploited, then survival itself is rooted in toxic behaviors and practices.

It's fucked up when you gotta take poison to survive, and yet, that is what it's like living in a white supremacist, patriarchal, ableist, xenophobic, heteronormative, cisgendering society. You learn that every interaction is laced with some bullshit and you can learn to ignore or tolerate the taste. You can risk being completely ostracized and marginalized by fighting back. You can try to create something new.

Or you can decide that bullshit tastes good and take heaping spoonfuls as often as possible.

Ben Carson, Clarence Thomas, Omarosa, Stacy Dash, Condoleezza Rice, Herman Cain, Alan Keyes, Angela McGlowan, Paris Dennard, Katrina Pierson…these are Black people who have decided to exploit their Blackness and protect white supremacy in exchange for power. Doing this can open doors for you. You have to be willing to turn your back on friends, family, just about everyone who helped raise you.

I won't lie, I've canceled these fuckers. And I'm not one who is quick to cancel Black people. We grow up having our instincts twisted and turned against us. We are taught that pain is normal, and harm is progress. We are taught to hate ourselves before we know ourselves. Our history is hidden, and we are taught to love and support our oppressors. I honestly wonder how we manage to stay on top of anything in this. So, understanding that our environment is a warped den of poison, I'm hesitant to turn my back on other Black people. I want to be sure that they know the choices they are making and that they have the space to fuck up. We all need the space to fuck up. But the above list? Nah. Fuck them. They know what they are doing; the just don't care about its impact on anyone else.

I remember thinking my parents were overreacting when they told me not to trust white people. I remember how I'd say things are different and these people were my friends. My parents addressed racism in different ways. My mom was a fighter. If you tried something on her, she'd get right in your face regardless of consequences. My father was strategic. He was responsible for our survival, so he played the game of balancing pandering to white supremacists while maintaining economic stability. Did it lead to conflicting messaging? Sure did. But, again, that's the reality of being a Black person in a white supremacist country – you engage in toxic behaviors to survive.

While both of my parents knew the deal, my mom would only confront the overt racist things, like being called a n***er or white people spitting at her. When it came to the subtle attacks, she would make it an individual problem and not address the systemic nature of it. That was how she emotionally managed. My father navigated by being two-faced. At home, he was open about the issues he faced as a Black man but at work, he pretended everything was fine. He did his work behind the scenes, pushing for programs that would benefit his students, and working on sponsorships to pay for school programs. He would tell me not to react, that showing my anger or fear would give them power over me. He'd advise me to be silent in public but make moves in private. He survived by working within the system and funneling that anger into action.

For many years, I dismissed their words and assumed I knew better. I downplayed the racism I experienced. I internalized it and blamed myself. I numbed myself to the pain of the people around me and when I challenged power dynamics, I learned quickly that somehow, I wasn't subject to the same rules as the white people around me.

I was in my early thirties when I realized how much I passively hated myself.

And even when I realized it, I didn't know how deep the hole was. I didn't realize how much I hated my Blackness. I didn't think I hated it at all. I felt like I accepted myself for who I am and that I appreciated every aspect of myself.

It was a lie.

It's a lie that I have to remind myself of daily. It's a lie I hear repeated by other Black people around me all the time. I see it in the news. I see it in advertising. I see it in the pop culture I consume. I hear it in the music on the radio. And I see it in who is visible and who isn't.

It takes work to shatter the lie. I don't think I've done it yet, but I'm working on it.

And nothing hurts more than hearing the "respectable" Black people around me denigrate and blame less accomplished Black people for their problems. The lack or empathy, the casual disregard...especially by those who say they are pro-Black.

I've been in groups with other Black people who have argued against centering our Blackness. They thought it was too militant or would be a negative descriptor. I've had them push back against admitting racist practices were happening. I've heard them say Black people can be racist, and then undermine the impact of racism, anti-Blackness, and colorism on the world.

I've listened and challenged and sometimes compromised because we are people trying to heal ourselves while drowning in poison and sometimes we can't do it fast enough to save ourselves.

It's been interesting watching Black people realize the white people they protected aren't interested in protecting them. It's been sad to see them learn that all those white people they trusted and defended didn't actually see them as human.

I took social hits for my stance on racism. I'm still taking hits because the more I see, the more I understand and the less bullshit I'm willing to tolerate. Where one time I would have said "we're all one race, the human race" now I know that a large swath of the population takes pride ensuring that's not the case legally, ethically, socially, or financially. Too many of us lie to maintain that illusion.

Othering the Self: Learning to Recognize My Anti-Blackness

When I was in high school, we were required to meet with our guidance counselor to discuss what colleges we wanted to apply to. I remember my counselor, after looking at my list, asking me if I'd considered any historically Black colleges and universities (HBCUs). I'd chosen schools with widely accepted, excellent reputations, so his question threw me. In fact, his question offended me. I remember wondering if he thought I wasn't good enough to get into the schools on my list and if he asked white students the same question. And that thought is an example of the pervasiveness of white supremacy.

Let's take a moment to unpack that because there are a lot of assumptions in my reaction to the counselor.

Assumption 1: That HBCUs were not academically equal to the colleges on my list. In all fairness, many of the schools on my list were ivy league, or one tier below. But who ranked these schools? What standard was used? I was using a list developed by people who may not understand the value of an HBCU, specifically the self-esteem and social value one could gain there.

Assumption 2: That the system ranking the schools was trustworthy. These days, the mechanisms behind why some things are considered superior to others is a lot more transparent than in the past, so we understand that these rankings have more to do with who manipulates the criteria rather than the actual worth of the school for students.

Assumption 3: That asking me to consider an HBCU meant he thought I wasn't good enough to attend a non-HBCU. Not only didn't I meet his approval, but I wouldn't meet the approval of these historically white colleges and universities.

My response to him was something along the lines of, "Do we live in a historically Black country? Am I going to work in a historically Black company? Or am I going to be surrounded by white people all the time, so I may as well get used to functioning in that world?" Needless to say, the conversation became a lot less productive.

When I look back, a part of me is sad at the anger and defensiveness I felt at the question. I kind of wish I'd looked into HBCUs more, but at the time, I didn't think they would prepare me to live in white culture. And I couldn't fathom a world where I wouldn't live, if not in then side by side, with white culture. But maybe attending an HBCU would have instilled me with the confidence I needed to understand and refute the bullshit of white supremacy earlier in my life. Or maybe I'd be in the same place I am now. Who knows?

What I do know is that that was an example of my belief that Black owned, Black controlled environments were inferior to white establishment. It's a belief I struggle with now, and, unfortunately, I'm not alone in that belief.

We are living in an amazing and fucked up time. That's not saying
that the past 500 years have been great for Black people in
America. It hasn't. But compared to when I was growing up, we talk
openly about racism in a lot more spaces than I've ever seen. I grew
up knowing I could only talk about racism with other Black people,
mainly because I was living, playing and learning alongside openly
racist white people and talking about racism was dangerous. When
white kids told racist jokes in school, or called me the N-word, I
didn't have the support of teachers when I reported them. When I
was excluded from activities by the white kids, I felt ashamed.
When I was picked on and called racist names, it wasn't because
they were racist – somehow I'd done something to provoke them.
Sometimes my skin provoked them; imagine how provoked they'd
be if I'd actually confronted their racism? Yet, I was forced to play
with these ugly humans who were repeating what they learned
from their parents, because integration and diversity and all that.

I silently and resentfully endured teachers picking on me,
challenging me, questioning my ability. I learned through a myriad
of ways that I was different and would receive different treatment
and different punishments than the white kids. And as I learned
more, I started to understand that the reason for that difference in
treatment was because of something superficial and out of my
control. And I learned that for me to succeed, I'd need white
approval.

And white approval is ridiculous and terrible. It's arbitrary and conditional. And overall, it's degrading. Many of my authority figures outside my home were white people. People who controlled how I was perceived and therefore, controlled what I learned and was exposed to. Year after year I'd meet a teacher, learn what their assumptions were about me, and learn how to meet their expectations so that I could advance. I'd experience their biases and prejudices in the classroom without context and absorb them into a learned pattern of behavior. The majority of my classes were white, as well as the faculty, so I learned to navigate those spaces, with their invisible land mines, as best I could.

Now, to be fair, I was a smart and inquisitive kid who talked to adults as if they were my peers. I also got bored easily. Unfortunately, this was often seen as insolence, or a behavioral problem and punished. I spent many recesses inside being punished for some classroom infraction, and studies have shown that Black students are often punished more often and more severely[225] for certain behaviors than white students. We are held to a standard of behavior that is higher than our non-Black peers and childish behavior is perceived as an inherent racial defect, not just me being a bored kid.

---

[225] Moser, Laura. "Schools in the South Suspend and Expel Black Students Way More Than White Ones." Slate 25 Aug. 2015. Web. 20 Feb. 2016.

As I got older, the way to please white people changed. I learned to avoid talking about racism, slavery and anything pro-Black because I'd be socially punished for it. Pushing back on someone's racist comment made me the problem. I was being too sensitive. I didn't know how to take a joke. People would say fucked up shit about Black people then turn to me and say, "But you're different," and I was supposed to be proud of that. My defense was often silence. But it was also isolation. I didn't consider these people to be my friends, because when I did, I got hurt.

It was clear that the less I associated with other Black students, the more I was approved by my white peers. I never really boarded that train, but that doesn't mean that I didn't visit the station. I started to internalize the thoughts and actions sanctioned by the white people around me. By the time I hit college — my predominately white, ivy league school — I was surrounded by a lot of Black people who were "not like those other Black people." Interestingly, we simultaneously gravitated toward one another while rejecting each other. So many conversations about how we felt more comfortable together but didn't want to pretend to be friends with each other because we're all Black. Or how we didn't want to be associated with the local residents, who were predominately Black and worked for the school.

And it was in this environment that my belief in my superiority to those "other" Black people was reinforced. This was where I learned how to "other[226,227]" those who looked like me. The line between me and them was so pronounced that I could clearly articulate a difference. I was educated and trying to make something of myself. I was exemplary.

At the same time, I rejected the elitism of my college peers. I often left campus and hung out in town. I went to local bars, moved off campus, got a job in the mall. I was still "different," but I wasn't like those elitist assholes who thought they were better than other Black people. I was better than them, too.

But that othering never stuck for me. On some level, I was always aware that I was one confrontation away from having my "good Black person" status revoked. I've sat through meetings sorting through resumes and watching the team mock people's names for being too "different." I've participated. I've sat in silence when illness was inexplicably tied to race and didn't challenge it out of worry for repercussions. I've made disparaging comments about predominantly Black parts of town without considering the things contributing to that perspective. And I knew it was wrong.

---

[226] Hooks, bell. "Eating the Other: Desire and Resistance." 1992. Web. 21 Feb. 2016.

[227] Zevallos, Zuleyka. "What is Otherness?" The Other Sociologist, 14 Oct. 2011 Web. 21 Feb. 2016.

I'm not sure what finally raised my awareness and consciousness enough to make me speak more openly about these things. I think it's the shift in the public conversation. I feel slightly safer expressing these thoughts and exercising the empathy I feel for people experiencing a reality that's different from my own. Also, I was raised by parents who believed in helping others and taught me about meeting people where they are in life rather than imposing my values onto them. They reminded me of my privilege (we called it *luck* and *fortune*) and that many people didn't have access to the opportunities I had. So, even though I spouted ignorance about Black people needing to do better and get their shit right, another part of me learned why they needed to in the first place. That part of me started paying attention to inequality. I started learning about the systems in place that created this environment — and I started trying to figure out how I could help.

So, what did I do?

The first thing I needed to realize is that I live in a toxic environment that tells me that, as a Black person, I am not important. It is crucial that to refute this lie. I cannot believe what popular culture tells me about Black people - that we do not contribute to society in any meaningful or positive way. It's not true. Regardless of what role we play, popular culture finds a way to malign and belittle it. Black athletes are "thugs."

Affirmative action is perceived as a way of advancing unqualified Black candidates and pushing out qualified white candidates from universities and jobs. HBCUs are perceived as less, despite needing to meet the same standards as other accredited universities and colleges. They are ranked on a separate scale than the national college ranking list, implying that somehow, they are incomparable to the majority of U.S. colleges and universities. Whether that's a good thing or a bad thing is at your discretion, but when applying for jobs in a mostly white workforce, I have no illusions about how it will be perceived.

Other lies they tell: Black neighborhoods are "sketchy" — dirty, dangerous, bastions of crime. Black hair is ugly. Black hair care is dirty. Black features are ugly. Black actors aren't as capable as white actors, so they can't be cast. Movies with all Black casts aren't just movies, they are "Black movies" so that white people know it's not for them. And if Black people accomplish interesting or fun things, they are quickly appropriated by popular culture and credit is given to the white people who copied it.

Which brings me to the second thing I needed to do: *stop seeking white approval.* I am constantly exposed to a media campaign telling me that I am less. That isn't going to change. I am told that I am not enough. This will not change. I am told that I am less than nothing, through police violence, mass media and daily interactions. If you have managed to carve out a self-sufficient life in the midst of this, you are amazing because the psychological battlefield that is being Black in America is brutal. And deadly. Just ask the many Black women[228] and Black men[229] killed by police. Look at the cities experiencing a constant terror campaign[230] against their daily lives. We do not need the approval of these people through their awards or support of our work. The support these people offer is contingent upon upholding white supremacist ideology. Just ask Beyoncé[231].

[228] Abbey-Lambertz, Kate. "These 15 Black Women Were Killed During Police Encounters. Their Lives Matter, Too." Huffington Post, 13 Feb. 2015. Web. 1 Feb 2016.

[229] Swaine, Jon; Laughland, Oliver; Lartey; James; McCarthy, Ciara. "Young Black Men Killed by U.S. Police at Highest Rate in Year of 1,134 Deaths." Alternet 02 Jan. 2016. Web. 21 Feb. 2016.

[230] Berman, Mark; Lowery, Wesley. "The 12 key highlights from the DOJ's scathing Ferguson report." The Washington Post 04 March 2015. Web. 21 Feb. 2016.

[231] Boggioni, Tom. "New York City police union threatens to join Miami cops in Beyoncé boycott: 'Stop portraying us as bad guys'." Rawstory, 19 Feb. 2016. Web. 21 Feb. 2016.

Being told I'm not like those "other Black people" or "regular Black people" is racist. It is a way to justify why they aren't discriminating against me like they would other Black people. It is a form of denial used to separate Black people they like from the ones they can act against. It upholds the idea that overall, Black people deserved to be treated as less, but I am the exception to that rule. If you find yourself generalizing about Black people, really think about that shit. Think about what you are saying and think about why you would choose to promote that message. Why is that negative talk about people who look like you the message you want to share?

Modern day racism is subtle. It sounds like progress when really it's just the same old racism in a less obvious package. Learn the language. Recognize when you use it. I'm working to find the strings that manipulate me, so I can cut them and set myself free.

I don't deserve to think like a slave. No one does.

This story first appeared at BlackGirlNerds.com on March 2, 2016

It was clear that the less I associated with other Black students, the more I was approved by my white peers. I never really boarded that train, but that doesn't mean that I didn't visit the station. I started to internalize the thoughts and actions sanctioned by the white people around me.

– TaLynn Kel, Othering the Self: Learning to Recognize My Anti-Blackness

Question the Narrative

I spent the last week on an unintentional break from the news, writing, media, etc. and spent the week streaming movies. I looked for various titles, but many times just looked through the visual catalog Netflix provided. Nothing demonstrates how inclusive the movie industry is like seeing white face after white face on your screen as you try to decide what to watch. But I didn't let that bother me, I was sick, and I wanted to feel comforted, so I chose movies that made me feel nostalgic.

Now that I am more critical of what I consume, watching movies I previously enjoyed is challenging. I don't see tropes as harmless anymore. Every single image, every choice, every character is a message. It is a way to influence our thoughts. So, when I watch movies, I pay more attention to the messages being promoted. I am not the best at it. There are tons of nuance that I still miss, but it still makes a huge difference in how I see things that I once viewed as mere entertainment, and that scares and saddens me.

I watched *Small Soldiers*, a movie whose message I thought, in addition to being anti-war, was "just because something looks monstrous, doesn't mean it is." And while that message was still a big take away, there were even bigger messages about white saviorism and tolerating toxic masculinity that I'd missed. And I missed then because of how we are programmed to watch movies – the protagonist is sympathetic. They deserve our empathy. We should always seek to understand their motives unless we are explicitly told that they are evil. In *Small Soldiers*, the protagonist is a white teenager who'd been expelled from two high schools for illegal activities (downplayed as pranks) who cannot take "no" for an answer from a girl that he likes. The entire movie, he repeatedly asks his neighbor out despite her many refusals because who cares what she wants. He wants her to go out with him and he's not going to give up.

This kid is a resentful teen, angry that his parents don't trust him, despite his violating that trust at every turn. He lies to his parents. He convinces a delivery man to "lose" a shipment of toys that he plans to sell while his father is away on business – toys that violate his father's deeply held belief against promoting violence. This kid, this criminal, who cannot abide simple rules and laws is the hero, and at one point I found myself actually sympathizing with this degenerate.

Movies are fucking insidious.

This movie presented the soldier toys as extreme examples of hyper-masculinity and then bombarded us with a less extreme version of toxic masculinity, masked as the hero, to soften our perspective. We see his persistence with the girl as a heroic quality – look at how he doesn't give up. Why don't his parents believe him about the toys? Sure, he's lied in the past, but they should trust him! Why can't they trust him? Look at him try to save his family from the problem that he created with his lies and machinations? He's a hero!

Fuckery.

And then there's the peaceful toys that the degenerate works to save...the peaceful Gorgonites who he has to pressure into saving themselves. Toys who "sacrifice" themselves to save the humans. It's pretty easy to see this storyline in so many narratives about people of color – that we appear dangerous, need to be contained and destroyed, cannot save ourselves and that in order to be redeemable, we must offer to sacrifice our very beings. Blah, blah, blah. It's fucking gross.

So yeah, *Small Soldiers* sucked.

A couple days later I followed that shit up with *Good Will Hunting* and OH MY GOD that movie made me so angry!

That movie, which put the poster boys for white liberal Hollywood bullshit on the national radar, is the epitome of white male privilege. It is the magnum opus of forgiveness of toxic masculinity. It is the fuckshittiest of fuckshit when it comes to the hypocrisy of how people are treated in this country. We spend an entire movie learning to empathize with a man who is willfully violent, angry, dangerous, and destructive. We are taught to afford him opportunity after opportunity, to bend over backwards to help accommodate this white man who consistently rejected every overture. Yes, he'd been abused. Yes, he had a hard life. This man transformed himself from a victim to a predator. He picked fights. He treated people like shit. He lied, repeatedly. And yet, we were supposed to empathize, sympathize, understand, and forgive.

Bullshit.

They talked to women like shit, treated them like shit, and fought over them like prizes to be won. And the entire movie, this grown ass man who made shitty, dangerous, violent decisions was referred to as a boy and forgiven his transgressions. And the take away? He's just misunderstood. So, when your boyfriend screams at you and beats on the wall when you confront him about his lies, when that man spits on the job interviews you set up for him and mocks you incessantly, just remember that he may be a misunderstood boy who always deserves the benefit of the doubt.

This type of messaging is why the Charleston shooter got a bulletproof vest and McDonald's when he was taken alive after murdering 9 innocent people.

This type of messaging is why white men shoot at cops and are talked down.

This type of messaging is why people blame women for their abuse.

This type of messaging is why people blame Black people for racism.

We are continually bombarded with the message that white men deserve our trust, our forgiveness, our leniency, and our support and anyone who denies them these things is the enemy. White men feel entitled to these things, and when they are denied, the outcry reverberates throughout the land. This is white supremacist, patriarchal conditioning. And we are its victims.

Every time we turn on a television, watch a movie, and read a book, we are taught how to forgive white men and then men like GW Bush Jr, a man who was mediocre at best, become president for 8 years. Men like Bill Clinton fuck their interns and stay in power. Men like Trump lie, cheat, and steal but become viable presidential candidates. They are flawed. They made mistakes. They deserve our respect.

Except they don't and that we give it to them is disgusting.

So, next time you find yourself watching a movie with a white, male protagonist, assess their actions. Take a long, hard look at the main character and ask yourself if what they are doing is legal and moral. Ask yourself if you empathize with them. Ask yourself if they earned the benefit of the doubt. Ask yourself whether you'd like this person in real life.

Ask yourself, does this person deserve your regard and respect, or are you entitling them to something they haven't earned...and ask yourself why.

Always question the narrative.

I'm out.

We are continually bombarded with the message that white men deserve our trust, our forgiveness, our leniency, and our support and anyone who denies them these things is the enemy.

– TaLynn Kel, Question the Narrative

Question the Narrative Revisited — Perspective and Nuance

Yesterday, I saw that Netflix was making a new series based from *Altered Carbon*, a novel by white British author Richard Morgan. That novel was my introduction to cyber punk. A friend, who I no longer trust to recommend books to me, was the one who put the book on my radar. This was back in 2006–2007 and I remember because I bought Morgan's next novel, *Th1rte3n*, in hardcover — something I rarely did back then.

Altered Carbon fascinated me. The idea of being uploaded into different bodies and living my life with shifting identities was, for lack of a better word, cool. And the protagonist, Takeshi Kovacs, was a super-soldier so I was down with that. I bought *Th1rte3n* seeking the same kind of futuristic badassery that I like in my action novels. I don't remember much of the book, as I used to mindlessly read, looking to immerse myself into any reality other than my own. I didn't look at the authors. I didn't think about the social, political, gender, or sexual oppressions that are a constant backdrop to published narratives. I just wanted an escape and *Th1rte3n* provided that.

That France cover is so telling…

Fast forward to yesterday. I watched the trailer for *Altered Carbon* and at first, I was excited. I remember liking the book, even if I don't remember it well. Then, as I'm watching the trailer about a future where you can exist in any body, I realize the main character is a white man. Even in a future of everybody, where you can live as anybody, you still end up seeing the story of a white, male body. This was something that wouldn't have clicked with me 10 years ago. It wouldn't have crossed my mind. But since then my perspective has grown. I am less numb to racism and less forgiving of its benefactors. I am a lot more careful with who and what I choose to read, and if I see something problematic in what I'm reading/watching/listening to, I make note of it and examine it. And when I fuck up, I learn from it.

That's why, when I saw the trailer for *Altered Carbon*, I decided to take a closer look at this author whose work I'd read a decade ago. That's when I learned that *Th1rte3n* was a giant racist trope that I was too ignorant to recognize. In all honesty, what really clued me in was when I searched for the book, by the author's name, I kept finding a book called *Black Man* with the cover I recognized as *Th1rte3n*. The book is about the big, scary Black man, the physical embodiment of white fear. The protagonist, Carl Marsalis is "one of a new breed. Literally. Genetically engineered by the U.S. government to embody the naked aggression and primal survival skills that centuries of civilization have erased from humankind, Thirteens were intended to be the ultimate military fighting force."

Sigh

The book was renamed *Th1rte3n* for the U.S., which is how this racist nonsense slipped under my, admittedly, underdeveloped white nonsense radar. It's an intentional choice to make the protagonist Black. It's an intentional choice to make him a "genetic throwback" to humanity's violent tendencies. Is it a commentary on identity politics? Do we spend this book learning to accept this man's humanity? Is that a narrative a white man can address in any meaningful way?

Well, if it's possible, Morgan didn't do it.

And to be honest, it's been so long since I read any of Morgan's books that I don't even care. What I do care about is that I didn't question it back then. It didn't even register as remotely problematic back then. And while I am ashamed of that, it's also part of this journey. Seeing how we grow and how we start making decisions about how we interact with the world is additional evidence that we are no longer the same person we were 5, 10, 20 years ago. In this part of my journey, I want to be aware of how media is influencing me, including my perceptions of myself. Reading this book starring a Black protagonist described as a violent, aggressive, genetic throwback isn't something I'm interested in at this time in my life. The cyberpunk version of humanizing the Other through the eyes of whiteness is not the narrative I want to read and where *Th1rte3n* is the Black version, *Altered Carbon* seems to be the Asian version of the same type of narrative.

There are people out there who will enjoy this story, and that's cool. But question it. Question the author. Question casting. Question the director. Why this book? Why this story? Why does identity matter and why so many stories seem to be about white men? Why are stories about Black people fixed on our aggression, violence, and rage and why does our humanity always seem to be in question?

You need to ask yourself why this is important, and you need to ask yourself how to can change it.

Even now, I'm still learning how to challenge these "norms" and understand the layers of anti-Blackness that may seem like a positive, but really feed us the same anti-Black bullshit. Or sexist bullshit. Or racist bullshit. And I do this by listening, learning, and challenging my beliefs.

I learn this by questioning the narrative.

It's an intentional choice to make the protagonist Black. It's an intentional choice to make him a "genetic throwback" to humanity's violent tendencies. Is it a commentary on identity politics? Do we spend this book learning to accept this man's humanity? Is that a narrative a white man can address in any meaningful way?
Well, if it's possible, Morgan didn't do it.

— TaLynn Kel Question the Narrative Revisited — Perspective and Nuance

Keeping It Real About Interracial Relationships as A Person of Color

I will admit, I'm super annoyed that it took the election of Donald Trump as our next president to make white people admit to racism. And while I'm sad and worried about the coming days, I'm not surprised by this outcome. This was not a shock for me, or any Black people I know. It was just the confirmation of everything we'd been saying, our parents said, our great grandparents said, etc. Racism has always been a part of America.

White people just can't hide it as well anymore.

And they are still trying. The rhetoric around Trump's rise and his supporters is being downplayed. Revisionist history is taking place before our eyes. The main stream media is pretending that he's not racist and everyone from President Obama to Oprah is begging us to forgive his racist as fuck supporters and work with that dusty Cheeto.

I think I'm going to pass on that hypocritical bullshit.

Despite that, there are a lot of us people of color (POCs) who have white people in our lives. Some of us have friends who are white. In my case, my spouse is white and we had to do a shit ton of work to get us to a decent place. But that work wasn't soft shoeing around the issues. It was both of us coming to some hard truths and admitting some shit that was painful as hell. And once we understood who we were, we could work on being better for each other. I learned a lot from that experience and thought I'd share some things I applied to all my interracial relationships.

Reality #1 – If your white friend/lover was raised in America, that person is racist.

There are no exceptions to this. The very best version is the white person who knows and understands they were raised this way. They understand that they still live in a white supremacist environment and benefits from systemic racism. They also understand that they will need to challenge this in themselves for the rest of their lives.

The issue I've had is that white people refuse to admit they are racist. They will flat out deny it without the hint of reflection. To them, racist is a slur, not a set of actions, attitudes, beliefs, and assumptions that can be challenged and changed. Instead they get defensive and upset. Then, in many cases, they lash out at you. Many times, they will call you a racist, and at that point you know that this person does not understand what racism is or how it works. They haven't done the work and that makes them untrustworthy. Hell, it makes them dangerous.

Reality #2 – Call out culture will be a part of your relationship.

This is the part that kind of sucks because it requires that you constantly confront the white people in your life about their racism. You will be the one to challenge their assertions. You will be the one to point out that they are fucking up. It's uncomfortable and a buzzkill for them but then again, their racist comment was a buzzkill for you. Then again, why should you be the only one on the shitty experience train?

When I do this, it's not fun for me. But it's necessary. I don't want to be in a room with a bunch of people saying derogatory things about POCs. I don't want to entertain it in my life and I definitely don't want them to feel comfortable doing it around me. I know for a fact that it has made me persona non-grata in many white spaces but it's also made my social events more relaxed and fun. The thing to remember is that racism is abuse. It can be psychological or physical, but it's abuse and your relationship is toxic. You will need to decide how to address that toxicity but you don't have to live with it. It's not healthy for you.

Reality #3 – Anti-Blackness transcends race and you need to learn about yours.

To have a real conversation with white people about race, you are going to have to examine your anti-Blackness. Otherwise, you won't have honest conversations. While Black people cannot be racist, they can believe and do racist things, also known as practicing anti-Blackness. This is a very nuanced view because it means looking at a system verses individual actions. As an individual, I can discriminate against other Black people, but this is within a system that was designed to exploit and exclude Black people. As such, it can benefit Black people to harm other Black people.

If you've spent a lot of time in white spaces, you see the subtle approval you receive when you don't confront someone's racism. You see how popular media is that portrays Black people as drug addicts, prostitutes, violent criminals, and such. You've probably also seen how trying to advance or protect Black people can result in negative criticism from your employer. Over time you learn to choose when you will challenge people's assumptions and depending on how hostile your work environment, you may learn to never challenge it. You learn to join in on the jokes about Black people's names and how Black people speak. You learn that you'll receive subtle approval for making disparaging remarks about certain neighborhoods or certain behaviors associated with Black people. You learn to hate the things associated with being Black.

This is a tough one because it is a behavior rooted in self-preservation but it's dangerous and damaging. It's self-hate, which Black people learn in childhood that must be unlearned constantly. I still find myself questioning some of the things I say and having to self-correct. But I learn and I improve and I fight when it creeps back up on me.

And the thing with anti-Blackness is that anyone can practice it. When Peter Liang murdered Akai Gurley[232] in New York, Chinese people protested his arrest because white people got away with murdering Black people, so he should too. And while he was convicted, he got no jail time. I've seen Asian blackface[233], seen racist commercials, and they use racist depictions of Black people in anime[234]. Anti-Blackness is real, and it is practiced by all.

Reality #4 – You can't lie to yourself about reality.

The hardest thing I had to face in my relationship was being honest about the fact that I'd married a racist. Sure, he wasn't an angry, violent racist, but he was a product of his environment. America is a terribly racist, violent, and hypocritical country. It is a country that constantly and consistently lies to itself about how great it is. Then it tells that lie to the world despite the overwhelming evidence to the contrary. The lie of American exceptionalism has eroded this country into a massive human rights violation with leaders who lack the ability to address its problems because they can't stop lying

---

[232] "No Prison Time for Ex-NYPD Officer Peter Liang in Fatal Shooting of Akai Gurley." Los Angeles Times, 19, April 2916. Web. 15 Nov. 2016.

[233] Winn, Patrick. "Asia Embraces Blackface-Style Ads. Get Ready to Cringe." PRI, 01 July 2014. Web. 15 Nov. 2016.

[234] Kel, TaLynn. "One Punch Man." Breaking Normal, 22 Dec. 2015. Web. 15 Nov. 2016.

long enough. We elected a racist, sexist, ableist, xenophobic, pro-corporation, anti-environment, anti-LGBTQIA, unqualified man for president because people in this country cannot admit to their fucking biases. White people were surprised that their friends and neighbors supported Trump because they spent too much time trying to convince Black people that we were misinterpreting racist situations instead of listening and recognizing racism in their white circles.

It is this lying, this self-deception, and this ridiculous need to control how people see you instead of doing the work to be better human beings that leads to fucked up, life changing, toxic situations. If you can't admit your biases and limitations to yourself, they will damage your relationships. If you can't admit that you are a product of your environment and figure out how that harms you, it will harm your relationship. There's a reason why Black people must confront their own anti-Blackness – it is to see the ways you harm yourself so that you fix it before you harm others. And white people need to take a long hard look at themselves and accept that they were raised immersed in racism and white supremacy. Only then can they begin to dismantle it.

You can't be honest with others if you can't be honest with yourself. You also can't fix shit if you won't admit it's broken. Be honest with yourself and then fix your shit.

Reality #5 – They won't always understand.

The thing is, these experiences are personal and are rooted in how we interact with the world and the way the world interacts with us. While there are some similarities, no white person can truly understand how racism affects me. And that's ok.

What I needed was support and caring. I need my white friends to believe me and accept my truth, regardless of how it differs from theirs. For any relationship to work, there must be trust and if they are denying my reality, we aren't friends. They are allowed not to understand but they cannot dismiss or deny. That is bullshit.

Reality #6 – The work to confront racism doesn't stop.

It's constant. It's necessary and makes self-care[235] hella important. Please remember to take care of yourself and to put yourself first. You don't have to do maintain your interracial relationships. They are optional. In fact, if it's harming you, it's okay to break up. Hell, I encourage it. This is a deal-breaker issue. The work that you need to do will always exist and it is exhausting. The people with whom I've been successful did a lot of work to prove to me that they were worth the effort and I've embraced that this might change. They may still cross a line that will destroy our relationship because this is too important to treat casually. I'd be lying if I didn't share that there were days I'd cry and ask why I chose this path for myself. It hurt and it took a long time to get to a place of healing. We know that we still have work to do and we accept that it will never stop.

This concludes the six hard realities I faced in my interracial relationships. They are not the only truths, but they are the ones I needed to understand to manage my relationships.

If you are a person of color and plan to have close relationships with white people you need to understand that it's work. It's constant, messy work. It's work that makes you feel vulnerable. It's

---

235 Pérez, Miriam Zoila. "4 Self-Care Resources for Days When the World is Terrible." Colorlines, 07 July 2016. Web. 09 Dec. 2016.

work that will empower you. It's work that will hurt and heal you. And, if that person isn't worthy, it's work that's optional. I chose to do this work in some of my relationships and while I have been successful in some, I've failed in others and I can't count the number of people with whom I didn't bother to try. In many cases, they weren't worth the effort and frankly, everyone isn't capable or willing to have real dialogue about racism.

Maybe it's time for white people to get out of their feelings and fucking accept what they are. It won't kill them. In fact, it'll heal a bunch of shit that's wrong with this country and eventually make it a better place for everyone.

Or we'll burn it to the ground. I don't know what to expect anymore.

The hardest thing I had to face in my relationship was being honest about the fact that I'd married a racist. Sure, he wasn't an angry, violent racist, but he was a product of his environment. America is a terribly racist, violent, and hypocritical country.

– TaLynn Kel, Keeping It Real About Interracial Relationships as a Person of Color

Becoming an Agent of Whiteness

Do you know what white supremacy is? It's the doubt you have about your safety in predominantly Black neighborhoods. It's that skepticism you feel when your doctor isn't white. It's the hesitation you have when you question a Black person's abilities. It's the surprise you have that a Black person is good at something…anything. It's the devaluing you do when someone like me accomplishes something a white person cannot. It's the excuses you make to explain why and how I outperformed white people.

If you are a person of color (POC) in this white supremacist society, you are taught to hate yourself before you know what hate is. You are trained to prioritize white people at all costs. Self-destructive behaviors, like silencing yourself, are normalized, while protective behaviors, like self-respect, are weaponized against you.

You spend your life being conditioned into thinking you are less than white people—less intelligent, less capable, less trustworthy. You learn that no matter what you do, you are a problem. You find ways to survive, muting and hiding yourself as much as possible. Accepting verbal abuse and ridicule for things out of your control. You suppress, suppress, suppress, and prove, prove, prove, until that is all you know. Or you lash out and find your completely understandable and protective behavior deemed illegal and regulated at the potential cost of your life.

You learn that approval is gained from self-deprecating behaviors. That diminishing yourself and those who look like you can provide growing returns. You learn that your proximity to whiteness, while painful, allows you access to things you've been taught to desire. Money. Status. Power. You learn that little pieces of your dignity, pride, and self-respect hold value on the white open market.

The thing that you don't learn is that this is a form of self-abuse.

It is complicated navigating white spaces as a person of color. Your appearance plays a huge role in how much or little you will be accepted. The less you resemble a POC, the easier time you will have navigating whiteness. Provided you ritually sacrifice aspects of your identity for white acceptance, you will be allowed on the fringe of these groups. You learn to hear, see, and say no to Otherness, to embrace whiteness in all its false glory. You are told that if you are Black, you should renounce your Blackness. Remove all its trappings from your life. Embrace the light that is white Jesus, white pride, white supremacy, and know your true worth—as a footstool upon which whiteness rests. Learn your place and you shall be held high, a lord among peasants—the price being all that makes you...you.

So, you eat the apple, gain the access, and allow the insidious, sleeping protector of whiteness into your body, because survival requires it, success dictates it, and you, on some level, want it. It is, superficially, an easier path to walk. That protector, be it large or small, is poison to you, incompatible with who and what you are, ingesting you from the inside out. White supremacy is poison to all who touch it and is currently engineering the global destruction of humanity through methods like global warming, continued consumption of fossil fuels, and unending genocide.

"Consume, consume, consume," it chants, normalizing the cannibalization of others. Normalizing the cannibalization of self. Nestled inside you, aware, awake, guiding your every decision. Shadowing your every move. It is the echo chamber in your head, confusing your need to survive with the need to absorb and ingest the otherness of yourself and the otherness of others. Repackage yourself, your friends, your lovers. Soften your edges to appeal to more palates. Strip yourself of your history, individuality, nuance just enough to intrigue without overwhelming. Hide, dissect, and serve yourself to whiteness in small, manageable pieces. Exotify your experiences. Be that delicious tidbit that whiteness loves to devour. Let it absorb, reshape, and regurgitate an empty version of yourself to continue the work of white consumption in its stead.

You become, in part, the poison of whiteness, wolf in sheep's clothing, infecting everyone you touch until they also become ever-consuming agents of destruction.

This is what whiteness is. This is what whiteness does. And when you defend those who promote it, when you rationalize their intentions, empathize with their motives, sympathize with their actions, defend their rhetoric, and support being open and understanding, you are its agent, corrupting from the inside out.

For white supremacy doesn't embrace the humanity of all. It embraces the humanity of whiteness. All others are sustenance for its insatiable hunger for domination and control.

This story first appeared at TheEstablishment.co, a multimedia site entirely run and funded by women, on December 5, 2016.

You learn that your proximity to whiteness, while painful, allows you access to things you've been taught to desire. Money. Status. Power. You learn that little pieces of your dignity, pride, and self-respect hold value on the white open market.

– TaLynn Kel, Becoming an Agent of Whiteness

To the Black Women Who Align Themselves with White Supremacy

To the Black women who think that close proximity to or intimacy with whiteness means you are successful...

To the Black women who think that supporting anti-Blackness will protect them...

To the Black women who speak out against and separate themselves from Black people, consider themselves one of the "good ones," and think they are protected by the whiteness around them...

You are ignorant and misguided.

That hurt, I know. And you might have already stopped reading, but I hope you'll give me a chance, like I gave your excuse of a rationale for supporting a white supremacist candidate a chance[236]. Stay with me here.

I get why you'd do this. I understand the safety that whiteness represents. The white people public relations campaign proffers a beautifully malevolent message that worms its way into our subconscious and unconscious before we realize it's happening.

I understand the belief that white equals right. I grew up in this stew of racist patriarchy and I learned to drink my bathwater to survive[237], just like you. I understand wanting to live in what they

---

[236] HBCU Editors. "Two Howard University Students Support Trump: He Will Make Our Neighborhoods, Our Cities and Our Country Safe Again." PBS, Jan. 2017. Web. 19 Jan. 2018.

[237] Kel, TaLynn. "Surviving Whiteness." Breaking Normal, 05 Feb 2017. Web. 19 Jan. 2018.

tell us is the light. I understand the appeal of manicured lawns, clean streets, and large houses filled with white neighbors, good schools, fancy cars, and infinite consumerism. I understand how these things seem to represent safety and security.

I get how Blackness seems bleak and insecure[238]. I've heard the constant messaging from media, institutions, teachers, bosses, comedians, news anchors, authors, and musicians that promote the lies white supremacy tells us. That our dark skin means shady thoughts. That our darkness, our Blackness, is ineptitude, ignorance, and dishonesty. That Black neighborhoods are less safe and secure than white neighborhoods. That Black employees are less capable than white employees. That Black students aren't as intelligent as white students. That we, Black women, are gold-digging, disease-ridden, baby-making predators constantly seeking our next victim. I 100% understand how and why you think rejecting your Blackness rejects these ideas.

The problem is that you're Black and every fucking negative thing you believe about Black people is what you believe about yourself.

I know it doesn't feel that way. You're smart, you make excellent grades, and gosh darn it, white people love you. You speak like them. You dress like them. You went to all the same schools, live in the same neighborhoods, like the same shit that is distinctly not Black.

You are taught through media, school, and society that white people are amazing. They are smart, funny, interesting, even when doing the most mundane of tasks, heroes even when being

---

[238] Kel, TaLynn. "Othering the Self: Learning to Recognize My Anti-Blackness." Black Girl Nerds, 02 March 2016. Web. 19 Jan. 2018.

assholes. Their day to day lives are the dream everyone aspires to have. If only these bastions of greatness could be near you. Love you. Accept you. If you are one of them, then you are a success.

They tell you that you aren't like the rest of them. That you are smarter. More aware. That you are thinking independently. The other Black people are sheep, following the herd to their demise, but you… you're special. You *get it*. And all you need to do to succeed here is admit they, other Black people, aren't good enough.

You pause, because that's not quite what you think. But then you look at the shiny white people with their generational wealth gathered off the backs of the exploited labor of Black people. You see the external trappings that they say they earned through hard work and sacrifice, when often it was gifted as a benefit Black people were excluded from receiving. You look at the blood and bodies and sacrifices of countless Black people wasted by greedy liars who shine like false gods peddling snake oil cures.

"Well, I am different," you tell yourself. "I am breaking away from my family. I get it."

But do you?

You are the product of history without context and curated lies. You know what they want you to know, see what they want you to see, and believe what they want you to believe. You are the conservative rebel, the one person in your family brave enough to say your family is wrong. And why are they wrong? Because they aren't wealthy? Because life isn't easy? Because money is finite? Because they aren't the visage of pale success you've yearned to be?

So, you decide to leave the dark and live in the light. And in return? All you need to do is reject those who love you. Turn away from them. Blame them for the choices you've had to make. Pathologize the human cruelty you experienced into a characteristic of Blackness and leave it all behind.

Belittle them. Undermine them. Disparage them. Sabotage them.

Ignore them and the failures they represent. Ignore how it was engineered. Ignore how it was intentionally inflicted. Ignore the toxic tongues and poisonous actions of those with whom you've aligned yourself. If other Black people had been smarter, they'd be where you are — alone in a crowded nest of snakes where you…survive.

The pain in your chest? It's nothing. The ache in your throat? Minor. The cramping, teeth grinding, headaches, insomnia, depression…those are just growing pains. It has nothing to do with the brown visage you see every time you look in the mirror and that you tell yourself is irrelevant as you navigate your chosen minefield of whiteness. You've convinced yourself that the mediocre people surrounding you, born into the "success" that you skewer your soul to attain, is harmless. That your isolation is the price of ambition. And that one day you will prove that you belong.

You keep proving your loyalty over and over and over with acts of increasing cruelty. You disassociate from your family — the people who watched you grow into this person who is now ashamed of them.

And then, one day, you realize there is no "one day," and no matter how perfectly you emulate and perform, you're still tainted. It could be the day your in-laws refer to your friends as a gang, despite your coming from a higher educated background than their entire family.

It could be the many times you are passed over for promotion in favor of less qualified white people you trained, or when — upon inquiring about this — you're told it was because of your nonexistent attitude. Or when your white in-laws tell you your children will be beautiful because their skin will be lighter. Or maybe it'll be the day you listen to all the white people around you justify the murder of a Black child who was playing with his sibling in the park.

When you realize this, you will truly see how you've isolated and harmed yourself and your relationships. And you'll have to face a question you've been avoiding since starting down this path.

Who are you?

You aren't the "good" Black person you thought you were, and the white people you thought loved you don't. And now you're in this between space you've chosen, denying reality, trading truth for white lies only to learn that your humanity was never in question. It was denied by the very people to whom you sold your integrity to gain proximity.

I don't know when you'll learn that lesson, but you will. And it will hurt. Because one day, when you're swimming fully in the sea of falsehoods that white supremacy sells, you'll realize that the problem was never being good enough — it was our audacity to continue to exist at all.

I understand the belief that white equals right. I grew up in this stew of racist patriarchy and I learned to drink my bathwater to survive , just like you. I understand wanting to live in what they tell us is the light. I understand the appeal of manicured lawns, clean streets, and large houses filled with white neighbors, good schools, fancy cars, and infinite consumerism. I understand how these things seem to represent safety and security.

– TaLynn Kel, To the Black Women Who Align Themselves with White Supremacy

Oppression Is Rarely One Big Defining Moment

Over the years, I've spoken out a lot about the intersection of oppressions I've faced. These are always interesting, and potentially volatile conversations because if the other person isn't a member of enough oppressed groups, they struggle to understand how these oppressed identities feed into each other.

Inevitably, that person asks me for an example of racism/sexism/sizeism that I experienced. They always seem to want some pivotal moment that I can share that will help them see what it's like to live in this space.

The thing is, there isn't just one moment. It's a compilation of moments that create a pattern. It's the matching your pattern to others and seeing the overlap. It's expanding your view to include the experiences of others and seeing the bigger picture that's influencing your experiences and opportunities. But it's never just one definable moment because American society is especially gifted in lying to itself about its motives.

It's that moment you learn that you are the only person in class who lost points for skipping a step in solving the equation despite having the correct answer and you just happen to be the only Black person in the class. It's the moment when you discover that you are the only student punished for fidgeting. It's when you learn that the professor doesn't ask every student to meet them after class to ask how they developed their topic. It's when you learn that other students' concerns are validated while yours are always questioned.

It's when you cosplay at a convention and somehow never see yourself in any of the images. It's when you look through a photographer's photo reel and see all the people photographed before and after you, but none of you. It's when you see a photographer take special care with every cosplayer on site, but they rush you through the queue so quickly that you wonder if they took a picture. It's reading posts looking for cosplayers who are "fit" when they really mean not fat. And when they say canon which means very few, if any, people of color.

It's realizing that people have an image in their head of how certain activities and environments are supposed to look and realizing that those environments don't include you because the casting director didn't think having actors of color mattered. It's understanding that as long as people are using media that doesn't include the breadth of human experience and appearance, it will always be a lie. And people will replicate that lie over and over while displaying images of this lie and declaring it as truth.

It's when you, hesitatingly, mention your experiences to other people who look like you and you realize it's not unique. That it isn't isolated. That these experiences happen to people who share physical characteristics with you all the time. I am not the only Black woman who's been told she isn't a team player because of her facial expressions. I am not the only Black woman who has been ignored in meetings and had her ideas dismissed immediately only to watch a white colleague suggest the same idea and be praised for it. I'm not the only Black woman who has had to pass her ideas through other co-workers just to have them considered. Virtually every Black woman working in a predominately white workplace has the same stories.

At first, you don't think it's them. You look internally. You rehash interactions. Rethink conversations. Revisit all your believed flaws as you try to figure out where shit went sideways and learn how you failed. And you recalibrate. Adapt. Change. Try a different approach. Up your game. Increase your skills. Soften your approach.

You twist yourself into a maze of altered behaviors as you try to navigate the pathway to success, minor success. Sometimes, just one person's approval.

And still you fail. You wonder how. Your skills are greater than all those around you. You know the answers because you studied. You learned the ins and outs of the process; anticipated every possible failure and avoided them. You made no mistakes, unlike those around you. And when you ask why you weren't good enough *this time*, they tell you it's because you're too perfect. Too arrogant. Too much of a know it all. Too capable. Too resistant to other people's ideas.

You fail for being too competent. And that is when you have your confirmation that it's not you. It can't be. Competence is the goal, not evidence of failure. The impetus for this treatment is bigger than you.

So, you observe. You watch. You listen. You look for similarities, commonalities, things to make this nonsense make any kind of sense. And finally, a pattern emerges. It's superficial, so superficial that you cannot believe this is the reason, but you learn it's about your looks. It's your skin color. Your size. The way you wear your hair. It's your uterus. Your breasts. Your sexuality or lack thereof. It's things about you that you can't change. Things that shouldn't matter but do. It's these things that matter least in your skills and performance that mean the most for those evaluating it. Be it at work or at play, these are the deal breakers. And now that you know, you wonder what you can do to level the playing field.

And you try. For years, you continue changing your approach, anticipating what's going to be the trigger for your next reprimand or sidelining. You try to anticipate what thing will be responsible for your marginalization. And then, after months, if not years of trying to comport yourself in a way that "normal" people will find acceptable, you realize there is *nothing* you can do to change it. Confronting it gets you fired and ignoring it gets you fired. All of it gets you fired. Or demoted. Or stagnant in your position, if you're lucky.

If you're lucky it doesn't land you in a financial hole. Because resisting is expensive when you are in a marginalized group. It can cost you your job, your home, your family's security. The ability to resist is a privilege, and one many people standing at the intersection of oppressed identities cannot afford.

Because sometimes your survival comes down to just one moment.

But oppression is everywhere. It's in the gatekeepers who don't think you fit the image of the organization. It's in the participants who don't believe that you represent their group. It's in the protectors who don't believe you have the right to be in that space. It's in all the assumptions that people make about your skills, abilities, intelligence based on "the norm."

It's how the norm is carefully created and curated to appeal to people who believe they are inherently superior despite piles of evidence to the contrary.

I've been in the rooms where people decide what image best represents some identity and I've listened as they have rejected people, laughingly, because they didn't "look right." I've seen resumes discarded because the name didn't sound white enough. I've participated in the dismissal of those names, despite my own unconventional name. I've witnessed the surprise when, despite all the screening, a POC made it past the gatekeepers and was allowed an interview. I've heard the excuses for why that person was sidelined in favor of someone else.

"People like to hear women on the phones more."

"He sounded too flamboyant. That isn't professional."

"Her appearance was too 'creative' for our office environment."

"We can't use that image. We don't want people to think we lack self-discipline."

"Her hair just isn't styled neatly enough."

"Was he wearing eyeliner?"

I've experienced this. I've participated in this. And I am ashamed of this.

Until I understood that I don't need to understand someone else's gender identity, I participated in this. Until I understood that I don't need to understand someone's sexual preferences, I participated in this. I'm sure I still unintentionally participate in this but I'm working on it. Knowing, acknowledging, recognizing, and fighting to stop doing this is the only way my actions and my thoughts will change.

Fighting ourselves is the very least of our responsibilities. The absolute least. Because when you question people on their lives, choices, experiences, you are forcing them to defend who they are. And frankly, unless it's harming other people, it's not your business. And not the bullshit harm of "it hurts my heart that you choose to live this life." Fuck that. Your approval is not needed for anyone to live the life they need. Nobody needs you to approve or tolerate shit. What we need is for you to understand that experiences are as variable as fingerprints. No two are exactly alike and whether or not it makes sense to you doesn't scrub it from existence.

Get over yourself. Recognize that there isn't one way to do shit. There isn't a perfect picture of any identity, profession, or environment. It's all different in ways you can't imagine all the damn time. And when you can finally admit this to yourself, stop getting in the fucking way of how other people live. Question your motives. When you find yourself saying shit like "it's tradition" or "it's canon" question that shit. When you balk at a character not being white, question that shit. Ask why. If everything you see, read, hear, learn is about white people, question that shit because when you look at the demographics of the planet, white people are not the majority. That does not reflect how the world looks. Recognize it as the propaganda it is.

This is why representation matters so much. Because it's not just one single moment that makes you realize you aren't included in the norm. It's a lifetime of tiny reminders that you don't belong.

The reality is we **all** belong. Always.

But oppression is everywhere. It's in the gatekeepers who don't think you fit the image of the organization. It's in the participants who don't believe that you represent their group. It's in the protectors who don't believe you have the right to be in that space. It's in all the assumptions that people make about your skills, abilities, intelligence based on "the norm."

– TaLynn Kel, Oppression Is Rarely One Big Defining Moment

Working with White People Is Both Harmful and Necessary

I live in a very white-centered world and I'm used to it. I'm used to being ignored, undermined, and disrespected despite exceptional achievements. I'm used to being hyper visible when there's an opportunity for white people to chastise or control me. This is my normal. This shit is so normal to me that I married a white man. I didn't anticipate my reaction to inviting whiteness into my intimate spaces — the strong and insistent pushback that I now engage in that continues to teach me how to be a better me.

All day, every day I'm surrounded and informed by white supremacy. I experience it at work, in my neighborhood, shopping, in my media. And while my significant other (SO) is working on being less of the monster he was raised to be, there are times when I'm fighting white supremacy in my home. Home is the one place where I see positive results. Outside, I am punished for daring to be equal. Again, normal.

What's not normal is the way the conversations around racism have changed. It is much more at the forefront, and there are Black people leading the discussions. At least, online. In academia, white people continue to center whiteness in their academic discussions and publications about racism[239]. In the age of Black Lives Matter, you are more likely to see Tim Wise talking about racism than Brittany Cooper or Feminista Jones. That said, there are actual discussions on television about racism. There are people not only acknowledging it exists but talking about ways to address it. Again, the only people who seem to be earning a living doing it is white &

---

[239] Goldhill, Olivia. "Philosophers Published a "Black Lives Matter" Series Written Entirely by White Professors." Quartz, 27 May 2017. Web. 19 Jan. 2018.

white-adjacent people but being able to see Black people push back on white supremacy is unusual.

As a child, I remember being told that white people are racist but never to tell them that. I was not supposed to talk about racism in public. It was something that could only be discussed among other Black people. But as a child, while my school was predominantly white, I didn't understand the racist waters I was navigating. My parents shielded me from it and what they couldn't protect me from, I internalized. I believed that I was the problem until I understood that it was my Blackness that was a problem for white people.

On some level, I knew racism was an issue, but as it was The Great Unspoken, it made no sense to talk about it. Anytime a Black person brought up racism, they were dismissed with extreme prejudice. Everything around me told me to never bring it up. I grew up learning to cater to white supremacy in ways that were harmful to me because that's what it meant to survive. It's not an accident that I've had high blood pressure since my mid-20s. This society is rough.

As the discussion about racism shifted in recent years, I moved from a space where I could never talk about it to a space where I can say "fuck y'all and your white supremacist bullshit." I feel freer than I ever have. I've gone from trying to avoid mentioning the possibility of racism to saying "you know all y'all racist, right? Like no question? What are you doing to fight it?"

Some of the white people I know step up to the plate. I talk about the things that matter to me and I watch them, waiting for the other shoe to drop and when it starts falling, I check them on it. If they are amenable to talking, I engage and catch the shoe. If they give me pushback, I let that shit fall and exit their lives. Needless to say, there are a lot less white people in my personal life now than there were five years ago. Like, down to one hand less. And I'm better for it.

It's beautiful and horrible. Beautiful because I no longer need to keep the white people in my life comfortable in their racism. Horrible because this is necessary to get white people to acknowledge their historic and casually violent inhumanity towards Black people and NBPOCs.

Despite these confrontations and conversations, both personal and public, I continue to encounter white people intent on hiding the truth. They find new ways to sanitize the savagery of their ancestors and the pile of bones upon which their success rests. They relentlessly engage in the passive avoidance of uncomfortable truths and fully embrace the pride of being an amerikkkan, fully ignoring the rampant genocide, patriarchy, ableism, and white supremacy that has devastated entire societies and cultures for their illusion of superiority. You gotta admit, that's some fucking superior self-delusion and denial at work. We live in a country that openly violates the human rights of others, but people still tell themselves it's the greatest country on the planet. The skill it takes to lie to themselves so completely and willfully. I won't call it a skill — it's a lie that leaves millions of people devastated in its wake.

All I can do is wonder how white people see their shittiness and actively pretend it's good.

This is something I will not tolerate from the white people in my life. If you are a self-deluded liar, fuck you. If you are passively pretending there isn't a problem? Fuck you, too. That bullshit is why we're still fighting for Black people to have rights and equity and equal treatment. It's how I grew up knowing that if too many Black people were too non-compliant[240], the city will drop a bomb on you[241] and then say it's your fault.

The emotional and psychological brutality is constant.

And white people are clearly against changing it. Just look at the election if you doubt it.

So, I find myself conflicted. I have met white people who are less resistant. Who are open to being wrong. Who seem to want to change the world. They push back on their white identity and work to de-center themselves in the narrative, but is that possible when you are white in a white supremacist society? Is that possible? I struggle and fail to do it constantly, and I'm Black. And while it somewhat benefits me to center whiteness in white spaces, it's like taking shots of sweetened rat poison. Eventually, it's gonna kill me but white supremacy can and will kill me faster if I openly fight it. Be it through poverty or violence, white people will find a way to punish any refusal to cater to their whiteness. Just ask Sandra Bland[242].

And when I meet these white people, part of me wants to protect them. Keep them learning. But then I'm centering their whiteness in my struggle. I don't want to center them. I want to center me and my Blackness. It's a dance, trying to figure out how to manage my emotional and physical well-being in the face of white supremacist

---

[240] Democracy Now! "MOVE Bombing at 30: "Barbaric" 1985 Philadelphia Police Attack Killed 11 & Burned a Neighborhood." YouTube, 13 May 2015. Web. 19 Jan. 2018.

[241] Demby, Gene. "I'm From Philly. 30 Years Later, I'm Still Trying to Make Sense of the MOVE Bombing." NPR Code Switch, 13 May 2015. Web. 19 Jan. 2018.

[242] Nathan, Debbie. "What Happened to Sandra Bland?" The Nation, 21 April 2016. Web. 19 Jan. 2018.

culture and harm. It's a struggle to decide whether I should keep white people in my life, cuz they are going to fuck up and it's going to hurt and I'm going to be the one having to manage the fallout while they bask in their white feelings of presumed superiority (see Bill Maher[243]) or perpetual white victimhood (see Katy Perry[244]).

These people swear that they are genuine and have learned but they still struggle to have basic as shit conversations about racism. They have proven themselves unworthy of the benefit of the doubt and they are fucking it up for all of you.

Yet, I persist in maintaining these relationships because I need white people to change. I keep handing out rope to see what they will do with it. And I fight decades of conditioning that tells me these people are harmless and mean well, despite hundreds of years of evidence to the contrary. Because for them to be an ally, they would have to purposely weaken themselves. They'd have to dismantle their advantages instead of using them to "help" those they oppressed gain access. They'd have to be uncomfortable and de-powered and I doubt they have the fortitude to see that to the end. Experience has shown that the best we can expect is for them to be mouthpieces and occasional amplifiers of Black messaging because anything more risks their power base and that is never the goal.

For white people, power will always trump equality. It's the amerikkkan way. Unless white people break that conditioning, divest that definition of power, and destroy the very system that

---

[243] Carmichael, Rodney. "Ice Cube Leaves Bill Maher Shaken and Stirred Over The N-Word." NPR, 12 June 2017. Web. 19 Jan. 2018.

[244] Elizabeth, De. "Katy Perry Discusses Cultural Appropriation on Deray McKesson's Podcast." Teen Vogue, 12 June 2017. Web. 19 Jan. 2018.

gives them their advantage and comfort, we'll continue this downward spiral to national self-destruction.

As the discussion about racism shifted in recent years, I moved from a space where I could never talk about it to a space where I can say "fuck y'all and your white supremacist bullshit." I feel freer than I ever have. I've gone from trying to avoid mentioning the possibility of racism to saying "you know all y'all racist, right? Like no question? What are you doing to fight it?"

– TaLynn Kel, Working with White People is Both Harmful and Necessary

White Accountability

It was never my plan to write to or about white people. I don't actually want to write about white people. It's especially frustrating because it means that I center whiteness in my work, but I've found that writing is how I cleanse my mind and sense of self. It is the avenue in which I am most able to feel, be, and express myself. The reality is that I live in a white supremacist, patriarchal society and that impacts all of my life. I married a white man, so this toxicity exists in my home. We work individually and together to push it back, but it seeps in through his family, his acquaintances, our co-workers, our hobbies, and everyday life.

White supremacy has always influenced and impacted my life. It was inescapable. In grade school, I had white teachers who operated under racist assumptions of my abilities. I've had teachers, grown ass white women, publicly embarrass me by exposing my family issues, my parent's financial issues for the class to ridicule. I've faced harsher scrutiny, assumptions of cheating, and marginalization by both teachers and classmates, as it became clear that my brown skin meant I was to be treated as "less than." White classmates had birthday parties where the entire class was invited except the Black people. White co-workers who have invited the entire team out to lunch except me. My every facial expression and body movement scrutinized and read as hostility without any additional input from me. My questions interpreted as insubordination. My work nitpicked as they looked for reasons to belittle my efforts. It's an everyday occurrence, so much so that I'd grown mostly numb to it.

Until I stopped trying to explain the pain away and decided to look at its source: white people.

Yes, all white people.

From the emotional labor I've put into my marriage to get my S.O. up to speed, to white friends who casually say dismissive things about police violence, neighborhood demographics, and stereotypical assumptions, it's everyone. White people I spend personal time with have asked me to let them know when they fuck up, which doubles my burden as they *will* fuck up but now I'm also expected to confront them about it. Maybe I will. Maybe I won't. It's exhausting living in this and then being asked to make every fucking interaction a teachable moment. Sometimes I just want to watch a movie and have fun. Sometimes I just want to eat some wings and not think about whether or not I'm playing into a stereotype. Sometimes I want to get angry and not have someone dismiss me as an angry Black woman who doesn't deserve to be listened to or respected. Sometimes I just want to live without the burden.

That is where the numbness comes in. When I must deaden my receptors because I've overwhelmed by the toxicity I'm having to manage. It's a lot. It's constant. I can't always deal with it.

So, I write.

I write because even though white people say they are ready to hear when they fuck up, they aren't. Instead, I direct them to an essay, so they can read it and process it. If they have questions, they can come back, and we'll talk about it. If not, then we don't. I've learned not to expect white people to stick around after difficult conversations. I've learned not to expect much when it comes to anti-racism except denial and strife.

This realization doesn't come lightly. It was learned through many discussions about racism with white people. It was after having yet another discussion about whether racism is real (it is), that I finally understood that they weren't interested in learning. I finally understood that the denial of my reality was their denial of having to do anything about it. Their goal was to either get me to say something "wrong" so that they could use that as an excuse to undermine everything else I said and maintain their incorrect interpretation of the world or push me into silence. It kinda worked. I don't talk to them about racism anymore. I don't talk to them at all anymore because they are liars and gaslighters. They are emotionally cruel and completely fine with that.

To live in the United States in these past five years and tell yourself that racism isn't real or, my personal favorite, that reverse racism exists but real racism does not, is fuckery of the highest form. I can understand not seeing the nuances. I can understand not knowing what it feels like, but to say it doesn't exist is such a break from reality that it makes white people untrustworthy. It makes them outright liars and I don't need that. This shit is hard enough without having dishonest people around me.

And unless they are aware and willing to address the harm they do; white people are not trustworthy.

I've accepted this work as a part of my marriage. I don't like it, but that is part of the deal with being married to a white man. Denying it only makes it harder for both of us. He works at it and I work at being patient with him while he works at it. But it is draining, and I don't have room to do this with more people. It's hard navigating this and maintaining my sense of self while also creating welcoming spaces for me and people like me.

So, I keep writing.

What I've found is that I'm starting to repeat myself on these topics. Maybe I need to read more or engage with more people to explore this in more depth, but I don't want to keep writing about the same things. Also, it gets draining. Constantly facing the violence perpetuated by white people is traumatizing. I have anxiety watching television shows that have oppressive violence, even when Black people are erased from the narrative. This type of critical thinking is detrimental to my emotional health.

All this is to say that white people have a job to do in this. White people have to want to break the systems that perpetuate the exploitation and ruthless dehumanization of Black people. We are out here living, confronting, and trying to change this shit for our survival. If white people are dedicated to changing this, they have to confront this and break it, too.

White people, you have a lot of work to do and you gotta stop demanding that we do it for you. You also gotta stop erasing us from our work and our narratives and re-centering them on you. It's a terrible practice that compounds the problem.

These essays discuss whiteness through my perspective. It highlights the harm white people do, be it intentional or not. The first seven essays are from 2016, when the illusion of the post-racial society was finally ripped away. The next five essays talk about the impact that white denial continues to have in this country.

Hopefully, they help white people realize how much work needs to be done.

When White People Consume Blackness for Personal Gain

Yesterday I woke up ready to talk about that curly-haired former boy band goofball who pulled an "all lives matter" on Twitter[245]. I was so fired up that I spent much of the day thinking about it, doing research and mentally formulating a critique of popular culture and how it nourishes itself through cannibalism of Black people.

Jesse Williams alluded to it[246]. Bell hooks intellectualized it[247]. And Black people have lived with it for hundreds of years. It's morphed some; it's no longer just the physical consumption of our Black bodies. Now it is the intellectual cannibalism of our thoughts, innovations, and inventions. It's the political consumption of our fight against injustice and inequality. It's the absorbing of our ideology as we fight for the protection of our Black bodies. It's the devouring and erasure of our creative contributions to the arts. White people have practiced cultural cannibalism in their colonization of the world. So much so that they have no identity except in their whiteness and the power they built around it, and even that is evaporating before their eyes.

Cultural cannibalism. Jesse Williams described it at the BET awards as "mining Black gold." Bell hooks called it "eating the other." At one time, cannibalism was the literal ingesting of another's heart in an attempt to absorb their strength and knowledge. In America, it's colonialism, oppression, and white, hetero, cis, male supremacy. It

---

[245] Carroll, Rebecca. "Justin Timberlake on Jesse Williams's BET speech wasn't woke, just white." The Guardian, 27 June 2016. Web. 28 June 2016.

[246] Brown, Lauren. "Read the Full Transcript of Jesse Williams' Epically Inspiring BET Awards Speech." Glamour, 27 June 2016. Web. 28 June 2016.

[247] Hooks, bell. "Eating the Other: Desire and Resistance." 1992. Web. 21 Feb. 2016.

is the utter and complete destruction of a culture that is then picked over for the tastiest morsels that is then shared among the destroyer with the rest being deemed useless and discarded.

To practice cultural cannibalism, the enactor must be so vicious, so savage, and so convinced of their superiority, that the culture they attack, consume, and destroy has to be dehumanized. Seeing yourself in those you destroy is the first thing that must be muted; otherwise the psychological damage would be overwhelming. It is why we work so hard to categorize our differences—it makes it easier to use them to create distance in our humanity. It is how we justify treating people unfairly. It makes it easier to use terrible violence to assert our superiority.

That violence is intrinsic to cultural cannibalism. How can you consume the heart of a culture if that culture isn't decimated? How can vultures feed if their food can fight back? So, you take their tools: their language, their spirituality, their education, their children, their will. You preemptively savage their bodies to demand obedience. You remove limbs, sever spines, mutilate faces, feet, hands. You limit care. You deprive sleep. Provide minimal food. You physically terrorize them until you are the boogeyman they fear. You are the savage you accuse them of being and you tell yourself it doesn't matter because they are different. They are not like you.

You attack them mentally. You make them dependent on you. Deny them language and education[248]. You separate them. Break their families. Deny them livelihood. Deny them community. And you do

---

[248] Slavery and the Making of America. Georgia Public Broadcasting. Web. 27 June 2016.

this for years upon years upon years in hopes that you break them beyond fighting.

That savagery is never far away. It often surfaces when a Black person dares to assert their freedom, think they belong, demand justice. When they say, "Look at me, I am doing everything you are doing and often I'm doing it better than you." It surfaces when Black people dare to demonstrate that we are intelligent and capable. It surfaces when we dare to be seen, when we deviate from the scripted narrative, when we dare to think we are as protected as white people.

I think back to the 2016 Oscars when Chris Rock gave his opening monologue[249]. That monologue was problematic on numerous levels, but the one thing it effectively demonstrated was the eagerness to ridicule and dismiss Black people who demanded to be recognized and how thin the layer of civility is for white people. The crowd laughed heartily at Chris' ridicule of Jada Pinkett-Smith and Will Smith's boycott of the Oscars—even as he used America's violent history of lynching to do it. He used the imagery of a murdered Black grandmother and the audience laughed. The predominantly white, rich, creative, sensitive, liberal, genteel, civilized audience laughed at a comment featuring a Black American grandmother who'd been murdered by lynching.

I wasn't prepared for that. In fact, I remember being furious with Chris Rock for providing that imagery as a joke. Now I see it for what it was—the stripping away of the veneer of white civility as they engaged in the ritual cannibalization of Blackness.

---

[249] Oscars. "Chris Rock's Opening Monologue." YouTube, 23 March. 2016. Web. 27 June 2016.

Hollywood is too enlightened to literally hang someone for entertainment these days, right? At least, not with a televised, live audience. But it is an act they engage in with clichéd regularity in other popular mediums. Movies[250], television shows[251], comics[252]... in all these mediums, they limit the visibility of Black people, murder them, and justify it as necessary[253] for the advancement of the white characters. Sophisticated savagery. Pageant cannibalism. Cannibalism they claim isn't that because Black bodies are different from white bodies so it's not the same.

White people consume everything about Black people—from our slang to our quips, to our hair, to our looks. They condemn us for how we speak[254], then laud some white artist as edgy and cool for speaking the same way. They practice our dance moves[255] and believe that no one will realize where they originated. They practice "blaccents," get butt implants, call themselves rapper artists, and win awards[256] for that bullshit. They call our features ugly, describe

<hr>

250 Campbell, Christopher. "Who Else is Upset About the Death in "X-Men: First Class"?" Indiewire, 07 June 2011. Web. 27 June 2016.

251 Shackelford, Ashleigh. "Orange is the New Black is Trauma Porn Written for White People [Spoilers]." Wear Your Voice, 20 June 2016. Web. 27 June 2016.

252Howze, Thaddeus. "On the Death of James Rhodes—War Machine." Medium, 22 June 2016. Web. 27 June 2016.

253 Nededog, Jethro. "'Fear the Walking Dead' fans aren't happy about the amount of black deaths." Business Insider, 31 August 2015. Web. 27 June 2016.

254 Paschal, Jaylin. "Smarter Than That: On the Assumptions Made About Ebonics and Intelligence." For Harriett, May 2016. Web. 27 June 2016.

255Mangum, Trey. "Hayes Grier's 'T-Rex' dance is cultural appropriation at its finest and Black Twitter is over it." Blavity, 15 Sept. 2016. Web. 27 June 2016.

256 Zoladz, Lindsay. "Please, Don't Let Iggy Azalea Win the Best Rap Album Grammy." Vulture, 06 Feb 2015. Web. 27 June 2016.

Black women as the least desirable women in the country[257], then co-op the parts of us they've exotified[258] and reject the rest.

They mine YouTube, mock our speech patterns, and make songs out of them that they sell on iTunes[259]. They consume our work and repackage it for a white audience that pays them for it. There is a proven market in cannibalizing Blackness. The repackaging is done so they can maintain their distance. *They are not like us. They are not us.* They find us interesting in a way they cannot create themselves...but still, they tell us that we do not matter.

They tell themselves as they eat us alive that this is "right." They lie and say this is how it was meant to be. They laugh at our pain and try to destroy our wonder, they eat their humanity but pretend that the difference in skin color makes it acceptable. They will lie, cheat, steal, and kill to maintain the illusion of civility and the delusion of sanity while their immortality continues to consume them from the inside.

So keep mining our tweets. Keep digging through our YouTubes. Keep convincing yourself that you are a genius because you have managed to commodify Black innovation. Keep lying to yourself. We see you. We've always seen you. That is why you work so hard to keep us invisible and silent. Truth shines too brightly for you to

---

[257] Solomon, Akiba. "The Pseudoscience of 'Black Women Are Less Attractive.'" Colorlines, 17 May 2011. Web. 27 June 2016.

[258] Harriot, Michael. "Black Bodies and the Last Frontier of Cultural Appropriation." Ebony, 20 May 2016. Web. 27 June 2016.

[259] Richardson, Riche. "'The Bed Intruder'—News Video Goes Viral: Antoine Dodson as Internet Celebrity and Commodity." Technoculture: an online journal of technology in society, vol 4, 2014. Web. 27 June 2016.

ignore it, so instead you hide in the darkness of your soul and pretend you are better than you are.

We see you and you are not worth cannibalizing because you are rotten.

*****

I woke up crying this morning. Crying because I planned to write about a culture that views me and people who look like me as food. Not literal food, but cultural, exotic, diverse, intellectual food. Creative food. Political food. Ideological food. Sexual food. Emotional food. Exploitable food. Disposable food. We are who they use to feel powerful, because if you do not have anyone to oppress, to whom are you superior? Trying to view myself through the lens of those who do not value me is painful.

That white people think it's easy for Black people to talk about racism exemplifies their ignorance about racism as well as their privilege. That they think we take some kind of special joy experiencing this and pointing it out is ridiculous. As a child, I couldn't wrap my head around racism. It wasn't real to me. I was so busy learning about the world and how to live that the racist obstacles I faced were just obstacles I faced. I didn't understand that they were deliberate. I didn't understand that they had been created specifically to make things more difficult for people who looked like me.

We like to think racism happened by accident, but it didn't. None of this happened by accident. Some of the ramifications, the health issues, are unanticipated side effects, but the conditions that created them are not accidents. It takes many people in a room and numerous years to make laws. That is very, very intentional. And many of the laws being enforced today are designed to prevent the very acts that emancipated America, and it was at the expense of a lot of people.

Thinking about racism, talking about it, is a kind of torture. When I start researching and analyzing it, I take such an emotional beating that it affects me even as I sleep. I wake up with tears streaming down my face from having to ask myself, "Why do people hate me for being brown? Why do white people work so hard to try to convince me that I'm worthless? Why do I have to push so hard to be respected as a human being? Why does anyone have to work this hard? Why are Black invisibility and Black pain the status quo?"

"Why do they wantonly kill people who look like me? Why do they defend it? Why do some people seem to hunger for it?"

I look at the white people in my life and wonder if I can trust them. I wonder if they are imagining what parts of me they can extract to improve future generations. Is it my melanin, because of the protection it provides from the sun? Is it my intellect—my children would probably be pretty smart. Is it the access I would provide to the Ivy League school from which I graduated? Is it the wealth I am slowly amassing for my retirement?

I wonder if they see me as fresh carrion that they are circling, waiting for the opportunity to feed.

I wonder, I wonder, and I wonder...until my heart aches, my throat burns, and my eyes glisten.

I wonder and then, just a little, I break inside.

This story first appeared at TheEstablishment.co, a multimedia site entirely run and funded by women on June 29, 2016.

They tell themselves as they eat us alive that this is "right." They lie and say this is how it was meant to be. They laugh at our pain and try to destroy our wonder, they eat their humanity but pretend that the difference in skin color makes it acceptable.

– TaLynn Kel, When White People Consume Blackness for Personal Gain

Demanding Black Forgiveness Is Just Another Way to Control Us

When I was six, my favorite uncle came by to visit. I loved spending time with him; He was always playful and fun. On this day for some reason I didn't want to hang out with him. When he called me to him, I refused. A few minutes later he offered me a dollar, and being six with no allowance, I went. That was when he pocketed the dollar, grabbed my wrist, and spanked me in front of my entire family while laughing at my humiliation. Afterward, he demanded I apologize for making him spank me. I refused, ran off, and never spoke to him again.

I was fortunate that my parents didn't undermine my will by insisting I forgive someone who'd overstepped my boundaries. I wasn't forced to be polite or acknowledge him ever again and I didn't. I mourned his death when he passed, but 35 years later, I still haven't forgiven him.

I've always been perplexed by the obligation to forgive. For my family, forgiveness was part of Christian belief, but I've never been able to accept church teachings without asking questions. When I think of forgiving my uncle, I'm confused; while a part of me feels like I missed out on our relationship, the rest of me thinks about a grown man who tried to control me and punished me for demonstrating my autonomy. Why would I forgive that person? What good could it possibly do?

I feel the same when I see demands, carefully designed to appear as requests, for forgiveness from grieving Black families who have lost loved ones to racial violence. We see this asked for, implicitly and sometimes explicitly, every time there's a new tragedy. We've seen

Black people punished[260] for refusing to grant it, for exposing their pain and expressing their rage; we've seen their forgiveness made into a public show for white America's consumption[261]. We've seen people forced to apologize[262] for daring to be human. We've seen this message twisted every possible way, from those saying it's the Christian thing to do[263] to others saying it's a way to help you move forward[264].

On a societal level, this public spectacle of forgiveness is complete and utter bullshit. But white people eat it up. Our forgiveness reassures them that Black people still know their place in this country; it eases their minds, reassures them that nothing has to change, that they don't have to upset their carefully crafted, artfully curated, violently maintained societal advantages. Black forgiveness sends the message that white people are still on top.

On a personal level, we are told that forgiveness is a tool for healing—that it will help us through our pain. That is a confusing message to me. Forgiveness, to me, means recognizing that the pain has dissipated. I can't recognize that when the wound is still fresh and being reopened all the time.

---

[260] Bacon, John. "Police consider charges against Michael Brown's stepdad." USA Today, 02 Dec. 2014. Web. 08 Aug. 2016.

[261] Berman, Mark "'I forgive you.' Relatives of Charleston church shooting victims address Dylann Roof." The Washington Post, 19 June 2015. Web. 08 Aug. 2016.

[262] ABC News Staff. "Michael Brown's Stepfather Apologizes for 'Burn' Outburst in Ferguson." ABC News, 03 Dec. 2014. Web. 08 Aug. 2016.

[263] Relevant Staff. "Trayvon Martin's Parents: 'As Christians We Must Forgive Zimmerman.'" Relevant, 27 Aug. 2013. Web. 08 Aug. 2016.

[264] Ortberg, Mallory; Wallace, Carvell. "You're Not Off The Hook: The White Myth Of Black Forgiveness." The Toast, 23 June 2015. Web. 08 Aug. 2016.

We are told that forgiveness will help us with our anger, that it will keep our rage from destroying us. This doesn't make sense to me either. My anger fuels me. Almost every positive change I've made in my life has been because something bothered me enough to want to do something about it. If I forgave the people and situations that outraged me, I am not sure I'd be motivated enough to change it. Change often means destroying the old, and I wouldn't destroy something I found acceptable.

We are told that forgiveness allows us to move forward. This, too, is not true. One of the few constants is that life goes on, regardless of what tragedies we face. Time is what allows us to move forward— indeed, it means that moving forward is something we can't avoid. Forgiveness is not required for progress.

We are told that forgiveness is personal. If the act of forgiveness is personal, why does it need to be shared publicly? People ask for forgiveness. They demand forgiveness. If forgiveness is personal, something I should do for myself, then you don't need it and you don't get to ask for it. That you are seeking it tells me that it's a tool for you, not me.

We are told that forgiveness and anger aren't mutually exclusive, that we can be angry and still forgive someone. I don't know what definition of "forgiveness" people are using for that one, but for me, anger is something that demands change, while forgiveness means accepting things as they are. Forgiveness is complacency. I cannot be outraged by you and forgiving of you at the same time. Either I'm angry and we're going to work on improving the situation or I've decided to accept your bullshit. It's not both. It's never both.

Forgiveness requires that I lie to myself; I choose to live my truth. It demands I rot inside; I opt to continue my growth. It expects me to swallow my anger and suppress my pain; I express my rage and refine my voice. It requires that I choke on my discomfort to appease you; I allow you to choke on your discomfort and exit, unappeased.

I do not forgive—and please, if I wrong you, I don't want you to forgive me either. I want nothing to do with a tool designed to quiet the mistreated, to manipulate them, to deny them humanity.

I do not seek your complacency. I do not want you to tell me shit is fine when it isn't. I do not want you to hide yourself, lie to yourself, deny yourself. I do not want you to cull your emotions, quell your anger, or gut your pain to meet forgiveness' demands. I do not want to keep you still, silent, and part of the status quo.

I want us to be free.

In the beginning of our relationship[265], when my S.O. said racist shit, I explained how he messed up and forgave him. I was hurt. I was angry. It hadn't been resolved, but I forgave him. Then he did it again and I went through all the forgiveness narrative a second time.

Then he did it again and that time I did not forgive him.

I let my rage fly and let my pain show through. I stopped trying to be stoic and understanding and told him that he was a shitty human being who was fucking up. I let him know that he did not make me happy and I wrestled with whether I would stay in this relationship. I did not forgive him. I do not forgive him. When he fucks up, I

[265] Kel, TaLynn. "My Husband's Unconscious Racism Nearly Destroyed Our Marriage." The Establishment, 26 May 2016. Web. 20 Aug. 2016.

express my anger and demand better. And he works to be better. I'll admit, both of us live with the fear that we will say or do something that the other cannot live with, but we accept that as a part of our relationship. This is what it means to be in an interracial relationship where racism is the norm. This is the burden we carry and work to unpack in a white supremacist world.

This is what it means to destroy the lie that is forgiveness.

Be angry. Be outraged. Feel what you feel. Do not pretend to be something you aren't. Do not pretend to be calm when you are enraged. Do not pretend to be fine when you are hurting. Do not pretend you don't care when you do. Do not suppress your emotions with those who help or harm you. Stop lying about how you fucking feel and just FEEL.

What is guiding me if not my emotions? The law? That's often wrong. Morality? That shit is fluid at the best of times. My joy and pain tell me what is happening around me. My fear and disgust protect me. My love shields me and my anger motivates me. Forgiveness sacrifices my anger, and that is too high a price to pay. There are too many people shaming others into being what they want instead of letting them be who they are. It's ugly and oppressive, all to the benefit of those controlling the narrative.

Don't let that bullshit control you anymore. Recognize, acknowledge, grieve, target, destroy, and change everything.

We all deserve to be free.

This story first appeared at TheEstablishment.co, a multimedia site entirely run and funded by women, on August 10, 2016.

I do not forgive—and please, if I wrong you, I don't want you to forgive me either. I want nothing to do with a tool designed to quiet the mistreated, to manipulate them, to deny them humanity.

– TaLynn Kel, Demanding Black Forgiveness Is Just Another Way to Control Us

White People, You Have a Lying Problem

White people, you have a motherfucking problem.

You lie too goddamn much.

You teach your kids to lie too goddamn much. You tell your families to lie too goddamn much. All you fucking do is lie and lie and lie about lying to the point that you are killing everyone, including yourselves.

You lie at the highest levels, so much so that we expect it from our elected officials. Our presidents have told lies[266] that resulted in the death of more than 50,000 American soldiers[267].

You lie about civilian massacres[268]. You lie about terrorist attacks against Black Americans[269].

You lie about sex education[270] and risk the health of your children.

 You lie about your friends' qualifications to run national agencies[271], which results in unnecessary deaths.

---

[266] Schwartz, Larry. "The 7 Biggest Liars in Presidential History." Alternet, 07 Feb. 2016. Web. 08 July 2016.

[267] National Archives. "Statistical information about casualties of the Vietnam War." National Archives, August 2013. Web. 08 July 2016.

[268] History.com Staff. "My Lai Massacre." History.com, 2009. Web. 08 July 2016.

[269] Moore, A. "8 Successful and Aspiring Black Communities Destroyed by White Neighbors." Atlanta Black Star, 04 Dec. 2013. Web. 09 July. 2016.

[270] Advocates for Youth Staff. "The Truth About Abstinence-Only Programs." Advocates for Youth, 2008. Web. 08 July 2016.

[271] Myers, Lisa; NBC Investigative Unit. "Critics Question FEMA Director's Qualifications." MSNBC, 13 Sept. 2005. Web. 08 July 2016.

You lie about your experiences while reporting[272]. You lie about American history[273]. You lie about historical heroes[274]. You lie about slavery[275].

You lie and lie and lie on a massive scale and cover up the lies, protect the liars, rehire the liars[276], and elect the liars because *shrug* everybody lies.

You lie about the littlest things, like if you ate the last cookie.

You lie to your spouse about their annoying habits.

You lie to your kids about how to make babies.

You lie to your neighbors about your debt.

You lie to your boss about sleeping in.

You lie to your co-workers about your weekend.

You lie to your doctor about your body.

You lie to everyone and say you are fine. And you lie to yourself about how wonderful and *nice* a human being you are.

---

[272] McCormack, Simon. "Brian Williams Investigation Uncovers More Alleged Lies." Huffington Post, 25 April 2015. Web. 08 July 2016.

[273] Raphael, Ray. "Are U.S. History Textbooks Still Full of Lies and Half-Truths?" History News Network, 19 Sept. 2004. Web. 08 July 2016.

[274] Blitz, Matt. "The Truth about Christopher Columbus." Today I Found Out, 26 Jan. 2016. Web. 08 July 2016.

[275] Bouie Jamelle; Onion, Rebecca. "Slavery Myths Debunked." Slate, 29 Sept. 2015. Web. 08 July 2016.

[276] Poniewozik, James "Why Brian Williams Lost His Job, and Why He Has a New One." Time, 10 June 2015. Web. 08 July 2016.

But you aren't nice. You wear a veneer of nice. You are a rotten tooth in the mouth of the world. Instead of taking care of yourself and preventing decay, you feed on the power of your whiteness like candy. When you start to smell, you use mouthwash and mints to hide it. When you start to visibly decay, you try to hide it with whitening gel. When you start to hurt, you take pain medication. When the pain becomes too great, you finally seek help—and that help is to numb yourself, pull out the nerve, then slap a crown on it so that no one can see your empty core. Instead they see a perfect veneer passing for a healthy tooth. But it is a tooth that feels no pain and only emulates the others.

In case you didn't know, that ability to feel is called empathy. And as far as I can see, white America has none.

Or maybe you do. Maybe you have empathy, but it's overshadowed by the centuries of stinky, infected rot left by your presidents, your congressmen, your police, your lawyers, your corporations, your lobbyists, your business leaders, your forefathers, and your motherland, all in the name of colonialism. Maybe you don't know what empathy even feels like anymore.

Human rights violations are so interwoven with American history that you can no longer tell what's right...if indeed you ever could.

I know, I know, not all white people. My husband is white. Except I wrote an entire fucking essay[277] about how I needed to put his ass in check for his lack of empathy. Except that I spent years tuning him into what the fuck is going on with the huge swath of the population that doesn't look like him. And I still deal with the

---

[277] Kel, TaLynn. "My Husband's Unconscious Racism Nearly Destroyed Our Marriage." The Establishment, 26 May 2016. Web. 08 July 2016.

empathy-less white people he's brought into my life. Not often, because I love myself too much to deal with that weird combination of superficiality and toxicity that permeates white society and dictates their interactions, but still. They are in my life, kind of.

And at work? The fact that these people categorize murder by cop as politics makes me want to throw a goddamn table. *"I don't talk politics at work."* People were murdered, and you liken it to the ego-stroking and ass-kissing office bullshit that I put up with for my check? Get the fuck outta here!

Seriously, get the fuck outta here.

Can you really not see the difference? Does this really not resonate with you? Does the constant replaying of the murder of Black people really not matter?

You don't have to answer that. I already know. We aren't human to you. We never have been.

But you won't admit that because it means telling the truth. And if there is one thing white people have taught me, it's that you cannot stand the truth in any of its forms.

I keep asking myself—when will they see the monster in the mirror? When will they see who they really are? What they do? How they destroy the world with their endless quest for power and the tireless subjugation of others to do it? When will they admit their fucking inability to see the humanity in difference?

Honestly, I wouldn't care if so many white people didn't have so much fucking power. But y'all do, and your consistent abuse of that power has destroyed countless lives and continues to do so. From your rapist sons[278], to your murdering daughters[279], you continue to destroy everything you touch.

But I have hope for you.

My hope is that one day, enough of you will stop lying to yourselves and heal. That one day you will stop lying to yourself and admit that you are an empty shell, existing on the continued pain of others as you beg, borrow, and steal from EVERYONE else to feel relevant.

One day you will stop killing everyone who doesn't fit your image.

One day you will stop attacking anyone who questions your decayed foundation.

One day you will actually love instead of trying to destroy people who live, love, and somehow thrive despite your oppression.

In these times of tragedy, we talk about Black healing. It's a necessary conversation about something we have a lot of practice doing. Hundreds of years' worth, actually.

What we need is white accountability. Are you strong enough to do it?

I'll wait.

This story first appeared at TheEstablishment.co, a multimedia site entirely run and funded by women, on July 8, 2016.

---

[278] Stack, Liam. "Light Sentence for Brock Turner in Stanford Rape Case Draws Outrage." The New York Times, 06 June 2016. Web. 08 July 2016.

[279] Apel, Therese. "2 Women in Truck That Ran Down Black Man Get Max Terms." USA Today, 10 April 2015. Web. 08 July 2016.

Maybe you have empathy, but it's overshadowed by the centuries of stinky, infected rot left by your presidents, your congressmen, your police, your lawyers, your corporations, your lobbyists, your business leaders, your forefathers, and your motherland, all in the name of colonialism. Maybe you don't know what empathy even feels like anymore.

– TaLynn Kel, White People, You Have a Lying Problem

America, Stop Protecting Your Monsters

Hey America: I know it's close to Halloween and you're all psyched to pull out your scary masks and get off on scaring the shit out of each other. But instead of embracing this romanticized idea of monsters as red/green/blue-faced creatures from some otherworld darkness or abyss, it's time we realized that most of our monsters can be found by looking in the mirror.

I need you to stop pretending that we don't create a slew of new monsters every damn day. It's like we have a damn kit.

You know the kit I'm talking about. The one that convinces little white boys that their opinion is fact. The one that teaches little white girls to accept bullying and controlling from white boys because submission is feminine. The kit that makes heroes of murderers, gives them holidays, and puts their faces on money. The kit that demonizes people for the color of their skin and then bends over backwards to protect white men from being punished for their crimes. Even when they are caught in the act[280]. Even when they planned, committed, and admitted[281] to it. Even when they are proud of what they've done[282].

You know that kit.

---

[280] Kingkade, Tyler. "If Not For 2 Strangers, Brock Turner May Have Never Been Arrested." Huffington Post, 06 June 2016. Web. 14 Oct. 2016.

[281] CBS News Staff. "Colorado Theater Massacre." CBS News, 2016. Web. 14 Oct. 2016.

[282] Hughes, Trevor. "Planned Parenthood Shooter 'happy' with his attack." USA Today, 11 April 2016. Web. 21 Sept. 2016.

It's the Brock Turner "prison would ruin his life but to hell with that woman he was caught raping[283]" kit.

It's the Martin Blake "yeah he raped his 12-year old daughter but all he deserves is probation[284]" kit.

It's the Dylan Roof "deserves our sympathy instead of being labeled a terrorist[285]" kit.

It's the Donald Trump "grab them by the pussy doesn't eliminate him as a presidential candidate[286]" kit.

It's the Nate Parker "he was acquitted of rape and his writing partner's case was dismissed[287]" kit.

It's the men who protect each other, the women who protect men, and the way both groups directly take a shit on anyone who tries to make the criminal justice system address criminals, instead of those who just look like they might be up to something.

It's the rabid protection of patriarchy, folks. And it's killing us.

---

[283] Schwartz, Gadi; Ortiz, Erik. "Brock Turner, Convicted Sexual Assault Offender, Released From Jail After 3 Months." NBC News, 02 Sept. 2016. Web. 14 Oct. 2016.

[284] Cahill, Tom. "Montana father gets probation after he admits to raping 12-year-old daughter." US Uncut, 13 Oct. 2016. Web. 14 Oct. 2016.

[285] Robles, Frances; Stewart, Nikita. "Dylann Roof's Past Reveals Trouble at Home and School." The New York Times, 16 July 2015. Web. 14 Oct. 2016.

[286] Smith, Candace. "Trump's Female Supporters Back Him Despite Sexual Assault Accusations." ABC News, 15 Oct. 2016. Web. 14 Oct. 2016.

[287] Shackelford, Ashleigh. "Stop Excusing Black Men's Violence – Like Nate Parker's – for the Sake of Black Liberation." Wear Your Voice Magazine, 16 Aug. 2016. Web. 14 Oct. 2016.

Let's be real. We have sexual predators in Congress[288], law enforcement[289], and the judicial system[290]. We have sexual predators in the church[291]. New stories about pastors[292] and priests[293] who have molested and raped children come out all the time. Known abusers like Roman Polanski[294] and Woody Allen[295] still haven't been punished for their crimes.

We see patriarchy being protected with the long-ass list of men who are barely punished when they are convicted of rape, like

---

[288] Raymond, Laurel. "Longest-Serving GOP Speaker In History Is A Liar And Serial Child Molester, Federal Judge Says." Think Progress, 27 April 2016. Web. 14 Oct. 2016.

[289] Queally, James. "Oakland police to fire 4 officers, suspend 7 others, in sexual misconduct scandal." Los Angeles Times, 07 Sept. 2016, Web. 14 Oct, 2016.

[290] Washington Blade Staff. "Arkansas Judge Resigns Amid Sex Scandal." Washington Blade, 11 May 2016. Web. 14 Oct. 2016.

[291] Evans, Robert. "Why I Kept My Rape by A Priest A Secret (And Can't Anymore)." Cracked, 25 July 2016. Web. 14 Oct. 2016.

[292] Fox 5 News Staff. "Pastor Charged with Rape of 10-Year Old Girl." Fox 5, 16 Sept. 2016. Web. 14 Oct. 2016.

[293] ABC News Staff. "Priest Arrested for Child Rape." ABC News, 02 May 2016. Web. 14 Oct. 2016.

[294] Lewis, Andy. "Roman Polanski Rape Victim Unveils Startling, Disturbing Photo for Book Cover (Exclusive)" The Hollywood Reporter, 24 July 2013. Web. 14 Oct. 2016.

[295] Orth, Maureen. "10 Undeniable Facts about the Woody Allen Sexual Abuse Allegation." Vanity Fair, 07 Feb. 2014. Web. 14 Oct. 2016.

Martin Blake[296], Brock Turner[297], David Becker[298], and Kraigen Grooms[299]. We see it with physical[300] and sexual abusers, the men who enable abuse[301], and the enforcers who refuse to enforce the laws[302].

We saw the affluenza teen's mother get arrested to protect her murderous son from prison. Then, in a classic example of white privilege, we saw her released on house arrest[303], after fleeing the country with her criminal kid, who is now seeking early release[304]— because white male privilege knows no limits.

---

[296] Cahill, Tom. "Montana father gets probation after he admits to raping 12-year-old daughter." US Uncut, 13 Oct. 2016. Web. 14 Oct. 2016.

[297] Grinberg, Emanuella; Shoichet, Catherine E. "Brock Turner Released from Jail after Serving 3 Months for Sexual Assault." CNN, 02 Sept. 2016. Web. 14 Oct. 2016.

[298] Johnson, Kimberley. "No Jail Time for Rapist So He Can Enjoy 'The College Experience." Liberals Unite, 22 Aug. 2016. Web. 14 Oct. 2016.

[299] Guerra, Kristine. "Teen pleads guilty to sexual abuse of a 1-year-old girl, then a judge gives him no prison time." The Washington Post, 19 Sept. 2016. Web. 14 Oct. 2016.

[300] Agorist, Matt. "Cops Beat Their Wives and Girlfriends at Double the National Rate, Still Receive Promotions." The Free Thought Project, 07 May 2014. Web. 14 Oct. 2016.

[301] Bazelon, Emily; Levin, Josh. "The Most Damning Verdict." Slate, 12 July 2012. Web. 14 Oct. 2016.

[302] Cohen, Sarah; Ruiz, Rebecca; Childress, Sarah. "Departments Are Slow to Police Their Own Abusers." The New York Times, 23 Nov. 2013. Web. 14 Oct. 2016.

[303] Crimesider Staff. "New Charge for Tonya Couch, 'Affluenza' Teen's Mom." CBS News, 26 May 2016. Web. 14 Oct, 2016.

[304] Frazier, Charise. "'Affluenza' Teen's Attorney Seeks Early Release." NewsOne, Sept. 2016. Web. 14 Oct. 2016.

Like Frankenstein's monster, patriarchy, white lies[305], and white privilege have been sutured together, helping America reach peak fuckery with this election. We have women defending Donald Trump's[306] horrific campaign built on racism, xenophobia, white supremacy, and lies. His lies are so numerous that we can't even keep track anymore[307].

And still this corrupt, immoral piece of shit is considered a better candidate than Hillary Clinton, who is guilty of being a politician, just like every other person who has run in the past 20 years. She's problematic and dangerous, especially to Black Americans[308] and brown people in other countries, but she hasn't threatened[309] more than half the population with deportation, groping, and prison.

And I get it—the bar feels pretty fucking low. The reason for that is that America has been lowering the bar since its inception. From founding fathers condemning slavery while owning slaves[310], to doctors performing non-consensual experiments on Black people[311]

---

[305] Kel, TaLynn. "White People, You Have A Lying Problem." The Establishment. 07 July 2016. Web. 14 Sept. 2016.

[306] CNN. "Trump Supporters Standing by Their Man." CNN, 11 Oct. 2016. Web. 14 Oct. 2016.

[307] Politifact Editors. "Donald Trump's File." Politifact, 2016. Web. 14 Oct. 2016.

[308] Alexander, Michelle. "Why Hillary Clinton Doesn't Deserve the Black Vote." The Nation, 10 Feb. 2016. Web. 14 Oct. 2016.

[309] Timm, Trevor. "Trumps Many Many Threats to Sue the Press Since Launching His Campaign." Columbia Journalism Review, 03 Oct. 2016. Web. 14 Oct. 2016.

[310] Iaccarino, Anthony. "The Founding Fathers and Slavery." Encyclopedia Britannica, 28 July 2016. Web. 14 Oct. 2016.

[311] Ojanuga, Durrenda. "The Medical Ethics of the 'Father of Gynaecology', Dr. Marion Sims." Journal of Medical Ethics, 1993 vol 19: 28-31. Web. 14 Oct. 2016.

and prisoners[312], America has a shitty track record on human rights[313]. From old Jim Crow to new Jim Crow[314], from women's rights[315] and reproductive rights[316] to police reform[317], America is in the red. Time and time again, we prioritize profits over people, to the point that our health system is driven solely by profit and tied to our employment, making it extremely difficult for those who are unemployed or self-employed to get health care. We see the prices of medications manipulated by shareholders, adjusted by health systems, and ultimately harming people in need[318]. Companies poison entire communities[319] and governments scramble to protect themselves[320] from fixing their damage.

---

[312] Goodman, Howard. "Studying prison experiments Research: For 20 years, a dermatologist used the inmates of a Philadelphia prison as the willing subjects of tests on shampoo, foot powder, deodorant, and later, mind-altering drugs and dioxin." The Baltimore Sun, 21 June 1998. Web. 14 Oct. 2016.

[313] Human Rights Watch. "World Report: United States - Events of 2015." HRW.org, 2015. Web. 14 Oct. 2016.

[314] Thirteen Media with Impact – WNET. "The Rise and Fall of Jim Crow." PBS Educational Broadcasting Corporation, 2002. Web. 14 Oct. 2016.

[315] ACLU.com Editors. "Women's Rights." ACLU.com, 2016. Web. 14 Oct. 2016.

[316] ACLU.com Editors. "Reproductive Freedom." ACLU.com, 2016. Web. 14 Oct. 2016.

[317] ACLU.com Editors. "Reforming Police Practices." ACLU.com, 2016. Web. 14 Oct. 2016.

[318] Thomas, Katie. "The Complex Math Behind Spiraling Prescription Drug Prices." The New York Times, 24 Aug. 2016. Web. 14 Oct. 2016.

[319] Moore, Michael. "10 Things They Won't Tell You about the Flint Water Tragedy. But I Will." MichaelMoore.com, 29 Jan. 2016. Web. 14 Oct. 2016.

[320] Judge, Monique. "State of Michigan Removes Flint's Ability to Sue Over Water Crisis." The Root, 20 Sept. 2016. Web. 14 Oct. 2016.

We are a country that looks at its neighbors, neighbors whose lawns we've poisoned, and say, "at least we're better than that." Then we pat ourselves on the back, lower the bar, and spend untold amounts of time and money hiding the damage we're doing to ourselves and everyone else.

We are a country filled with monsters who ravage and kill the vulnerable among us, but who are enabled to prowl unseen in the darkness of America.

And here's the thing: We don't have to be this way. We *can* be good and human. We can relocate residents of Flint. Buy their homes and offer them the option of moving, either temporarily or permanently as we fix the infrastructure. But will we? Nope. Instead we'll start a bureaucratic process to talk about where the funds will come from and start making excuses as to why this is too expensive an endeavor to undertake. In the meantime, people continue to live with a poisoned water supply, owing money on a home they can't sell, and facing legal repercussions for abandoning the area, not to mention ruining their credit and fucking up their financial prospects—also known as modern-day shackles.

We have homes sitting empty and food rotting in dumpsters every day because giving any of this away undermines our capitalist system.

We have avenues for police reform, but that would mean enforcing the laws on the enforcers who have always held themselves above the law.

And so, we leave people to be poisoned, starve, freeze, and die because it's just too hard.

No. It's not that it's too hard. It's that our system is designed to keep everything as it is and to protect monstrous people from their own monstrosity. Every single time we manipulate the truth, i.e. lie, we make it easier for the next person to get away with being deplorable. When you protect your fucked-up kid, brother, uncle, husband, you make it possible for the next person to use that same convoluted logic to protect themselves. We are empowering them and eventually that monster runs for president.

When your teenage son has sex with a 7-year-old, he's a pedophile. There is no defense for that.

When your grown son has sex with someone without consent, he is a rapist. There is no defense for that.

When your kid kills anyone who isn't attacking him, he's a murderer. When he kills many people, he's a mass murderer. I don't care how many family trips he took or how loving he was before he decided to shoot up a school, theater, club, park, or church. He's a mass murderer. There is no defense for that.

I'm not blaming parents for giving birth to people who do terrible things. It happens all the time. Every asshole you meet has parents. Every liar, every murderer, every rapist, every abuser. They also have extended family, friends, teachers, schools, jobs, and a slew of other people who opt out of calling people on their shit and decide to let it slide.

As a country, we spend a lot of time and energy trying to make our murderers, rapists, and abusers look like they were created in isolation instead of flourishing in the society we created. We try real hard to separate them from the rest of us, because who wants to feel like they are responsible for the horrific decisions of others? Who wants that guilt? Who wants that blood on their hands?

But we have to ask the question—how much of their monstrousness is a result of America's teachings?

Because a lot of times they learned to be better monsters by watching other monsters. They learned it by watching you.

Did you protect them from their lies? Their thefts? Their abuses? Their crimes?

Did you lie for them? Did you enable them? Did you help them inflict damage on more and more people?

Were you silent when you could have spoken? Did you cause someone else harm with your silence?

Are you complicit in the damage being done in our country? In the world?

I have been, and now I'm working to change that shit.

There comes a point when you have to accept your responsibility in unleashing American monstrosity—when you must pull it from the shadows and drag it into the light.

Every time you do, you are saving someone—including yourself.

This story first appeared at TheEstablishment.co, a multimedia site entirely run and funded by women, on October 18, 2016.

We are a country that looks at its neighbors, neighbors whose lawns we've poisoned, and say, "at least we're better than that." Then we pat ourselves on the back, lower the bar, and spend untold amounts of time and money hiding the damage we're doing to ourselves and everyone else.

– TaLynn Kel, America, Stop Protecting Your Monsters

White People: Shut the Fuck Up About Black Voters

Repeat after me:

WHITE VOTERS NOMINATED TRUMP!

WHITE VOTERS ARE ELECTING TRUMP!

WHITE VOTERS ARE ELECTING TRUMP!!!!

That's right. White voters. Your friends. Your family. Your neighbors. The polite, friendly white communities in your life who don't think they have anything to lose by electing him. The people who think that Clinton is worse than a racist, misogynistic, sexist, ableist, violent, pro-corporation, anti-climate change, pro-war, xenophobic, anti-education idiot who lies about shit he said last week - shit that's on video, who the media coddled until they created a monster who speaks to the dark heart of this country.

The dark, silent heart of this country that has always been here, quietly lurking, strengthening, and enforcing America's racist origins through legislation, redlining, policing, and entertainment.

In case you didn't realize, which apparently, a bunch of you fucking didn't, America's always been racist, sexist, and xenophobic. ALWAYS. When overt racism, sexism, and xenophobia became less popular, this country got better at talking around it and people got better at lying about it being gone. This country consistently used exceptions to the norm to lie about what the norm actually is.

"Look, we have a Black man as president! Racism is gone!"

"Women work in all kinds of jobs. I have a woman boss. Sexism is gone!"

"I have Black coworkers. My boss is a Black person. I had sex with a Black person once. I'm not racist."

"My wife/daughter/sister can work, own property, vote. If she doesn't act like a slut, she's great. Sexism is gone!"

Are you fucking kidding me? The norm is Donald Trump and white people are proving it.

I'm so angry right now. I'm fucking mad at the media for their stories about threats of violence at polling places. I'm angry at all the reports of voter suppression that people are conveniently ignoring. I'm mad at SCOTUS for gutting the biting rights act that Republicans leaped on to start changing voting laws and access to polls. I'm mad at President Obama for not fighting more for Black people in this country.

I'm mad at all the threats being made by racist shit bags who are angry that they can't unilaterally decide to only do what's best for white men. Did you know there are reports of armed white men standing at polling places, like that's not fucking frightening as hell. And law enforcement is apparently okay with it because it's in open carry states like Georgia, where I live. Fuck, we have media reporting on a militia "preparing" for post-election fallout[321] cuz I wasn't already scared enough.

I'm mad at the self-righteous third-party voters who think they have nothing to lose. I'm mad at my significant other's parents who fucking out right said, "I was raised white. This is the only thing I

---

[321] Eldridge, Ellen. "Georgia Militia Prepares for 'Fallout' After Election." Atlanta Journal Constitution, 04 Nov. 2016. Web. 08 Nov. 2016.

know to do," when talking about voting for Trump. I'm mad at the U.S. government for being dominated by out of touch, amoral, rich white people and sheltering the abundance of racists currently in law enforcement and government. I'm mad that running for public office is so expensive that only the rich can do it.

I'm mad at the fucking plethora of lies we choke down and call democracy.

And I'm scared. I'm scared for my friends, my family, myself. I'm terrified of what's next because no matter which was this goes, violence is in our future.

The past year has been nothing but psychological warfare and trauma for me and people who look like me as we watched the pile of bodies grow at the hands of police violence and then watched most of its perpetrators walk away with their jobs and crowdsourced funds for their murders. We have had to adapt to seeing brutality enacted on people who protest the wrongdoings of our police and criminal justice system over and over again.

We have had to learn what our parents and grandparents experienced first-hand as we struggle for equality and safe spaces in America. And America keeps showing us that we are lying to ourselves if we think that's possible. That shit isn't for Black Americans, Native Americans, Asian Americans, Muslim Americans, any non-white Americans, apparently. Nope. The message to us is shut up, get out, or die. And every single day I have to pretend that isn't the message I continue to receive loud and clear while I go through the motions of living. Each day it's a struggle to wake up because I am horribly depressed and anxious and scared every damn day and my body is responding as bodies do to extreme stress – by breaking down.

So, congratulations white America. You might get your fucking country back for racist, sexist, xenophobic, islamophobic, anti-human rights, anti-civil rights, pro-militarized police, pro-corporation, pro-pollution, homophobic, transphobic, ableist white people. Just remember, the straight, cisgender men get first pickings and the rest of you can fight it out for what's left. That's what's known as making America great again.

And any of you white people asking about Black voter turnout? Y'all need to take a long hard look in the mirror when you're looking for someone to blame for this fuckery called the 2016 presidential election and its after-effects. It's your fucking friends and family who nominated that shitbag. It's your friends and family voting for him. What the fuck did you do to try to keep this from happening, huh?

I'll wait.

When overt racism, sexism, and xenophobia became less popular, this country got better at talking around it and people got better at lying about it being gone. This country consistently used exceptions to the norm to lie about what the norm actually is.

– TaLynn Kel, White People: Shut the Fuck Up About Black Voters

White People, You Have a Choice to Make

Okay, people, listen up.

I know we want to think that oppression is rooted in ignorance and misunderstanding, and yes, some of it is propagated that way, but there's a lot of fucking choice in it, too.

In fact, it's all choice.

It's an administration's choice to disparage Muslims. It's a lawmaker's choice to promote anti-Islamic sentiment. It's law enforcement's choice to create actionable items to enforce. It's the individual officer's choice to enforce them. It's your choice whether or not you help them.

It's all a choice.

These think pieces and memes and constant begging for people to open their minds and hearts and understand what they are doing are worthless because they KNOW what they are doing.

Men know they are discriminating against women. They just don't care because 1. they don't see women as people and 2. it doesn't impact them. And that's what we mean when we say "equality;" it's the understanding that women are individuals who do not need their decision-making regulated, questioned, or second-guessed because they aren't men. This is not difficult to understand, but because it limits their power, men pretend not to get it. They love their feeling of superiority over women too much to release it.

This power is further supported and legislated in American culture. So, men fight our autonomy. They fight our humanity. They create obstacle courses with ever-shifting goalposts so that we spend all our energy struggling. They fucking know what they are doing — discrimination is just an accepted norm.

White people know they are discriminating against Black people. They know they benefit from white supremacy. There just aren't any negative consequences for this — and why stop voluntarily benefitting from something? Who does that?

Empathetic people...kind people...maybe. Folks interested in justice and equality, maybe. But these are not characteristics historically associated with white people, especially considering that they exist in a system that doesn't just reward them for maintaining the status quo, but actually punishes them for fighting it. Looking to them for guidance, understanding, and care is very much like asking a lion not to eat you. They have made everyone who isn't white into prey, and they are always hungry.

In other words, white people gonna white.

People of color are soylent green for white people. Women are nourishment for men. But they don't consume us to survive — they do it to compete with themselves and elevate their status among each other. They use and abuse our labor, creativity, ingenuity, and culture.

And this is all a choice. Ignoring and erasing Black people from their work is a choice. Removing us from history is a choice. Enforcing unjust laws is a choice. Treating us as sub-human is a choice.

It's ALL a choice.

You gotta *choose* to be better. You gotta *choose* to fight this shit. You gotta *choose* to no longer comply with immoral laws and leadership. You gotta *choose* whether you're going to fight this, and then choose your weapon.

White people constantly ask how they can be a better ally. Well, the first thing is to hold yourself and the people around you accountable for the choices you make. I'm telling you right now, those ICE agents are choosing to terrorize and detain people. This isn't something out of their control and if you tell yourself that, then you're a liar.

Are there consequences for rebelling? Yup. But when enough people don't rebel, we get slavery. When enough people don't rebel, we get Jim Crow. When enough people don't rebel, we get the North Dakota Access Pipeline, the Holocaust, rampant police abuse, discrimination, disenfranchisement, open white supremacists in government, president tangerine goblin, redlining, and rapists and murderers going unpunished.

You get our current reality.

Stop pretending that love is the answer. It isn't. The answer is complicated as fuck[322], but it begins with holding yourself and others accountable for your bullshit AND white people taking the fucking hit that comes with rejecting white supremacy.

And yes, it's a hit. It's gonna hurt. It's gonna keep fucking hurting because that's the society we live in. The one that hurts and oppresses Black people, people of color, LGBTQIA+, and other marginalized populations.

Our pain is constant, and it is inflicted without thought or remorse. It's constantly learning that whiteness will hold us back in every way possible.

---

[322] Oluo, Ijeoma. "Social Justice Must Be Complicated, Because Oppression Is Never Simple." The Establishment, 15 Feb 2017. Web. 22 Jan. 2018.

Oh, and you need to drop this "left" and "right" nonsense, too. If this election taught anybody in denial a damn thing, it's that racism, ableism, anti-Muslimism, anti-LGBTQIA sentiment, xenophobia, sexism, and anti-Semitism transcend political parties. They transcend religion. They transcend economic status. In fact, the one thing you should have walked away from this election understanding is that this country and many people in it are about elevating white, Christian, heterosexual, cisgendered patriarchy — and they will destroy anybody to accomplish that goal.

It's time to step up and be heroes, because too many of us need help saving ourselves from the monsters[323].

---

[323] Kel, TaLynn. "America, Stop Protecting Your Monsters." The Establishment, 18 Oct. 2016. Web. 19 Jan. 2018.

White people constantly ask how they can be a better ally. Well, the first thing is to hold yourself and the people around you accountable for the choices you make. I'm telling you right now, those ICE agents are choosing to terrorize and detain people. This isn't something out of their control and if you tell yourself that, then you're a liar.

– TaLynn Kel, White People, You Have a Choice to Make

If I Were White

Sometimes I wonder what it's like to be white.

I wonder what things I would have accomplished if I didn't have to fight so damn hard to be seen or heard. I wonder what opportunities I would have gotten…would I be a full-time writer? Would I have multiple high-profile publications under my belt? I wonder how my life would be different without the systemic obstacles placed in my path. Like my first-grade teacher who, for months, didn't believe I knew how to read and would punish me for the slightest perceived infraction despite my constant boredom in her class. This teacher went so far as to tell my mom, who helped teach me to read, that I didn't know how. Because the word of a white woman who only met me that year supposedly carried more importance than the word of the Black woman who raised me. Needless to say, I didn't stay in that class.

But I wonder, would she have believed I could read if I were white? Would I have been punished for talking out of turn, or would my behavior have been interpreted as boredom and warranted additional attention? Would I have been placed in a more rigorous academic setting without having my parents fight for teachers to recognize my abilities?

Maybe I'd have been lazy, skating by on the assumed approval of those around me. Maybe I'd never learn to be persistent, creative, inventive, and adaptable because there was never a need. Maybe I'd never develop the traits that make me proud to be me. Or maybe I would have anyway. I'd still have been a woman, just a white one.

Maybe I'd be cruel. I'm a fairly intuitive person. Maybe I'd use that ability to manipulate those around me. Maybe I wouldn't develop my empathy and would see the world as mine for the taking.

Maybe I would have voted for 45 because I felt my whiteness was being threatened.

There is one thing about being Black that makes me profoundly sad yet proud at the same time. It is knowing that my ancestors managed to weather and survive a torment that killed many others. It's knowing that we survived what most could not and what nobody should have to, and we continue to survive because that is what we do. We adapt and we survive.

We aren't coddled and catered to by society. We aren't awarded prizes for existing. In fact, we often experience punitive interactions for daring to think ourselves equal. We are reminded time and again that our place is in service to white people and that our continued existence is at their inclination. An approval that can be rescinded at any moment.

I wonder, if I was white would I have embraced that behavior? Would I be someone capable of the reflection necessary to divest myself from whiteness? Or would I meld with that identity and embrace the monster U.S. society encourages white people to be?

I watch my significant other wrestle with this. I know he wouldn't see the racism in America as clearly as he does if I hadn't challenged him. I know that it's my constant pushing that makes him think about his environment and the people in it, and to ask the hard questions about the things happening around him. Once, I asked him how he stays with me, knowing that I will always push him to examine his whiteness and the nasty shit that comes with it. He said, "I love you and that's my burden to bear. I learn to live with it.

I learn to manage the pain. But don't stop doing what you need to do because it hurts me. That's not your fault."

Sometimes I forget it's not my fault. Sometimes I forget that we are both born into a system designed to oppress me while benefiting him. I'm glad he can remind me of that.

But for him, the hits keep coming. Last week I watched my significant other's (S.O.) heart break a little bit more as he listened to his parents defend the GOP and 45. I won't call him "woke" because that's not true. What he's become is more aware of the callousness of the white people in his life, and it's fucking him up. He's finally reached the point where he openly recognizes and criticizes whiteness and he's become better at seeing the harm it does. It is both beautiful and tragic, because now he feels isolated from people he loves.

Seeing his loved ones imbued and empowered by their whiteness was his normal, and now it hurts. It hurts for him to realize the people he thought were independent thinkers were just obnoxious and disagreeable. It hurts to see them support laws and policies that inflict unnecessary harm. It hurts to hear them defend the institutions they claimed to be against. It hurts him to know that what he sees in them was once who he was, and most likely would still be had he not been forced to confront it.

He sees the people who raised him choose 45's hateful rhetoric, listens to them defend their decisions, watches them support his dangerous bullshit, and still loves them. Then he looks in the mirror and sees that same whiteness as part of him and knows that he was fucked up, still is fucked up, and has to continue to fight it. His beauty is in his willingness to own that selfishness and inhumanity that he once wielded like a sword and shield to protect his sense of self. His appeal is in his bearing of that pain and his willingness to work for a better future.

We're living in racial polarity: I grew up learning from the world to hate myself, my Blackness, and everything it represented. He grew up learning to love himself, his whiteness, and the innate superiority tied to that. Now, I'm learning to love and appreciate everything I am, as he learns that his whiteness is a monster consuming the world. His whiteness is a greedy narcissist that refuses to share, and his humanity lies in working to slaughter that thing he was raised to protect above all else.

I don't know what it's like to see my friends and family be openly complicit in the destruction of others. My parents never denigrated others. They worked in service, gave to charity, ran neighborhood organizations. Their only resentment was for the systems they struggled to survive in...and even that was sporadic because they adapted and survived as best they could.

If anything, my SO's continuing divestment from whiteness will foster resentment in those who once supported him. I feel his pain. It is similar to the pain I felt when I realized I didn't understand the core of whiteness, which is that it must protect itself and its sense of superiority regardless of cost. It was the moment I realized that I'd made myself a victim of my husband's whiteness and that I wasn't strong enough to walk away.

It is in this way that I understand the difficulty in ending relationships with people you love because of their racism/sexism/homophobia/ableism/transphobia/sizeism/etc. Love doesn't conquer all, but it will lure you into a complacency that allows those your love to fuck you over time and time again. It is an insidious feeling that convinces you to sacrifice your well-being for others. It tells you the pain is worth the reward, the well-being of the one you love, be it your friend, your parents, your SO, or your children. We are taught that personal sacrifice for the well-being of others is always worth the pain it may bring.

I lived the pain of subverting my Blackness to keep white America comfortable. Now it's time for beneficiaries of whiteness to see the pain and destruction they are inflicting upon the world, themselves included. It is time for the beneficiaries of whiteness to see that the pain they tolerate for that ideal is too destructive for humanity to continue to bear. If you must suffer, it's time to suffer for healing instead of harm. It is time to release that toxic ideal and make the world a better place for everyone, not just white people.

It's time to let the greed, rage, and false superiority go. Embrace the pain and forge yourself into a better version of yourself. Recognize there is space for everyone and that much suffering is the result of false scarcity. When you choose to suffer, choose to do it for the benefit of everyone, not a superficial ideal rooted in superiority. Caring for others is a worthy hill to die on. Embracing humanity always is.

My Blackness is, in many ways, my humanity. It is the lens through which I view the world — with compassion, empathy, honesty, and strength — qualities I developed in stark opposition to whiteness. Qualities that whiteness sacrificed in its need for the veneer of dominance. And while I wonder if the lack of these qualities are inherent to whiteness, I know that my Blackness is the excuse white people used to dehumanize me.

I don't wonder why white people need to strip their humanity as they attempt to destroy mine. That is not a question for me. As James Baldwin once said[324]:

*"What white people have to do is try to find out in their hearts why it was necessary for them to have a n*gger in the first place. Because I am not a n*gger. I'm a man. If I'm not the n*gger here, and if you invented him, you the white people invented him, then you have to find out why. And the future of the country depends on that. Whether or not it is able to ask that question."*

It's past time for white people to ask themselves that question...before their inhumanity destroys us all.

---

[324] Yo, Malory. "'I Am Not Your Negro' Gives James Baldwin's Words New Relevance." NPR, 08 Feb. 2017. Web. 26 Jan. 2018.

I lived the pain of subverting my Blackness to keep white America comfortable. Now it's time for beneficiaries of whiteness to see the pain and destruction they are inflicting upon the world, themselves included. It is time for the beneficiaries of whiteness to see that the pain they tolerate for that ideal is too destructive for humanity to continue to bear.

– TaLynn Kel, If I Were White

White People Are Racist Landmines

Last week on my personal Facebook, I posted an article about how white college women are less likely to help a Black woman at risk of rape[325]. I commented that I was tired of these articles "proving" shit to white people that we already know but don't believe about themselves. That comment resulted in a friend of my father's having to speak up to tell me that my comments about white people are offensive.

Hmmm.

To give you some background, my father was a school administrator and as such, worked with many white people. This woman was one of them. When she had health issues, he held her job while she took a leave of absence — this was before it was required by law. He often found himself being a confidant to many of the white teachers in his school, a role he respected. As a result, when he fell ill, many of the teachers he'd helped went out of their way to be there for him. Considering that he was sick for over a decade, that was a lot and this woman was one of the people who continued to visit until he passed.

---

[325] Dolan, Eric W. "Study: White College Women are Less Likely to Help a Black Woman at Risk of Rape." PsyPost, 08 March 2017. Web. 19 Jan. 2018.

Because of the care and consideration, she gave my father, I kept contact with her. I invited her to my wedding. We chatted occasionally on Facebook. She was allowed access to me that I do not grant easily. That said, I knew she was problematic. She is a white woman in her 60s with an extremely racist family. She considers herself liberal because she cares about more than white people, yet I would routinely see her support xenophobic posts and align herself with pro-America (i.e. pro-white) sentiments. Not the super obvious stuff, but enough that you knew where her allegiances lay. I allowed her access to me because I figured she'd reflect and learn some shit. But then she decided to try to silence me, and that's where I draw the line.

It's fucked up when you realize that white people are booby traps waiting to be tripped.

We went back and forth for a week where she "not all white peopled" me and denied trying to change how I speak/write while trying to change how I speak/write. She claims she just had to let me know but had no goal in mind when she did it. She reminded me of what she'd done for Black people and my family, proving that she was not part of the white people I was referring to, then claimed that nothing I said bothered her at all and that I just couldn't take people disagreeing with me. She closed out by saying that my father wasn't prejudiced like me and would be offended by me too.

Oh, the delusions of white people.

My father was the one who told me never to trust white people. He was the one who said, "You're going to have to work with them. You'll have to play by their rules. But when it comes to them having to choose between a white person and a Black person, they will always choose the white person. Don't trust them."

That is not prejudice; it's survival[326].

One of the infinite things white people refuse to admit to themselves but love to remind Black people of, is that they can fuck us up at will. How successful they are completely depends on how entwined they are in our lives and how motivated they are to wreck us. Some are direct about it — like police officers who shoot first and lie later. Or that random white person who calls you a n*gger in passing. Or threatens your life and/or employment when you step out of line.

Then there are the less obvious ones. The white co-worker who reports you as a problem for being good at your job — can't make them look bad. Or the white people who feel free to touch you whenever they feel like it. The white people who live and work side by side with you but then are surprised that you're good at what you do.

My favorite this year are the ones who think they aren't racist because they consider me to be their friend. I've had a few fun conversations with them. We don't speak anymore — they think I'm racist against white people. (For the record, "reverse racism" is some made-up shit that white people use to derail conversations and escape with their false image of colorblind humanity intact. Don't be that asshole.)

---

326 Kel, TaLynn. "Surviving Whiteness." Breaking Normal, 05 Feb 2017. Web. 19 Jan. 2018.

What is amazing to me is how white people think their willingness to talk to a Black person means they aren't racist. That is all it seems to take for them to absolve themselves of any complicity or wrongdoing. "I have Black friends" erases everything for them, including the need for reflection, self-examination, and self-analysis. It removes the need for critical thinking, much less thoughtful discourse. As far as they are concerned, their hands are clean.

But let a Black person challenge that and see what happens.

Stage one: white person tries to get you to change what you said.

Stage two: white person tries to get you to agree they are the exception.

Stage three: white person tries to discredit you.

Stage four: White person tries to destroy you.

See a pattern? It's never about white people examining themselves or their actions. It's all about changing you, the Black person who dared challenge them. It's about managing you, and if they can't "fix" how you see them, then they'll get rid of you because once you no longer exist, there are no challenges to how they want to see themselves. It's why they say talking about racism creates racism — because they refuse to look at themselves and admit what they are. It's easier to destroy the mirror than it is to accept responsibility.

I've had white people start at stage one and others at stage four. Stage four is the scariest. These are the people who will remove your financial resources, bar you from an industry, and maybe try to kill you. And you never know what stage they'll start at or what stage they'll disengage. Some are especially motivated and will sacrifice their well-being to destroy you and what you represent — white people like Dylan Roof. My husband, when activated, used to cycle through stages one through three, but now he's kind of settled at one and then starts reflecting on his actions. It took years of conversations to get us here and I think it's mainly because he's not a hyper-aggressive or violent person. That said, we hit stage four a few times and every time I had to stop and ask him what he wanted to see happen because that path meant destruction. Those were interesting times.

And that's the shitty part about interacting with white people. They legitimately have to unlearn and fucking practice recognizing, suppressing, and mitigating their reactions to Black people. They are conditioned to silence us with extreme prejudice in emotionally and physically violent ways and they have to learn to stop. It's honestly on them and most never learn because they don't have to. They have infinite systems and millions of people conditioned to support their bullshit. And they love to lie to themselves[327] about how monstrous they are[328].

[327] Kel, TaLynn. "White People, You Have a Lying Problem." The Establishment. 07 July 2016. Web. 17 Jan. 2018.

[328] Kel, TaLynn. "America, Stop Protecting Your Monsters." The Establishment, 18 Oct. 2016. Web. 19 Jan. 2018.

Some parts of navigating whiteness are survival in america. It can be challenging to find spaces where it doesn't impact your financial well-being. Mostly, it's dangerous as fuck for Black people. You are emotionally and physically attacked for existing. White people are often condescending, dismissive, and cruel to Black people. You learn to numb yourself to their barbs and avoid their traps. You silence yourself because confidence, assertiveness, and honesty are punished. If you're like me, you get fired a lot because that shit is hard, ridiculous, and complete bullshit. But I'm privileged to have a support network that helps me offset those challenges. Everybody can't be me and talking about this shit is always dangerous — you never know when you'll set off the white person who's fucked up and resourced enough to destroy you.

What is amazing to me is how white people think their willingness to talk to a Black person means they aren't racist. That is all it seems to take for them to absolve themselves of any complicity or wrongdoing. "I have Black friends" erases everything for them, including the need for reflection, self-examination, and self-analysis. It removes the need for critical thinking, much less thoughtful discourse. As far as they are concerned, their hands are clean.

– TaLynn Kel, White People Are Racist Landmines

To the Sad, Scared, Ignorant White People

Fuck you.

I have spent my entire life having to prove to you that I am human. I have spent my entire life having to demonstrate how I'm just like you, except brown. I've had to prove it to my classmates, my teachers, my school administrators, my bosses, coworkers, car salesmen, store clerks, police, doctors, nurses, white strangers walking down the street.

I've had to prove it to every fucking random ass white person I've met and didn't give a fuck about because that's what it means to live & survive in this country.

I've had to explain where my ideas came from, as if I don't fucking have the capacity to think or use my imagination.

I've had my ability to speak and write well questioned with amazement because how the fuck can a Black person have these skills.

Once, when I was in college, a classmate slapped me "as a joke" and I stood there, running through the consequences of beating her ass in my dorm room surrounded by nothing but rich white kids in a rich white school, knowing that retaliating would probably lead to my expulsion. And I backed down because my father mortgaged our fucking house so that I could be there, and I refused to fuck it up for my self-worth.

Because that's what you do to navigate whiteness in this country. You fucking back down again and again and again because to stand up means you will be outcast, quickly. Day after day, emotional hit after hit as my humanity is constantly called into question and the value of my Black life openly diminished.

Then I get to turn on any media and hear white people whining about having to share the stage. White people actively upset that everything isn't handed to them. White people who are told in every possible way that they are the best and deserve to have the best, and that if they don't, it's because some Black person or POC stole it from them. I watch unskilled men get high paid positions and fuck them up. I get told to listen to some jackass who has no experience in my field. I get to hear white boys and white men talk and say nothing, polluting the air with their toxic and useless thoughts, as we wait for them to shut up so that actual work can get done.

I get to navigate the minefield of white woman insecurity as they try to diminish me, undermine my self-worth, aggressively challenge my abilities, and steal my ideas. I get to sit in meetings where they penalize me for existing by policing my every movement until my goal stops being to do my job and instead becomes how to stay perfectly still and unnoticed, where even breathing causes the meeting to stop and them to question why my breath is so loud.

I get to watch white people be fucking disruptive and unproductive, fucking hindrances to the job — yet get raises, promotions, and experience a job security I've never known. I, who have gotten fired for being too sad in the office or being combative because I actually did my job. I don't get the benefit of the doubt or second chances. I get written up and threatened to be fired. Like I was for being sad when my father died.

So, when I see these bullshit articles, news stories, think pieces, TV shows, and movies begging me to understand where these fucking racists who are actively calling for my removal from my country by either deportation or death? When I see white people telling me I need to be understanding of the white pain of their mediocrity? When I see white people telling me I need to give my sympathy and empathy to these fuckers who were born poor but have greater access to programs and jobs to alleviate that poverty than anyone who looks like me has ever had?

Fuck them. Fuck the writers. Fuck the producers. Fuck the publishers. And fuck anyone who asks me to have any generosity of spirit to these shitty people. They know what they are doing. They've always known. Now they just don't have to hide it anymore.

In the 10 minutes I was on social media this morning I saw the following:

- **At 3 a.m., NC Senate GOP strips education funding from Democrats' districts**[329]

- **Torch-wielding protesters gather at Lee Park**[330]

- **Stephen Fry Explains Why Some People Believe Everything Donald Trump Says**[331]

---

[329] Campbell, Colin. "At 3 a.m., NC Senate GOP Strips Education Funding from Democrats' Districts." The News & Observer, 13 May 2017. Web. 19 Jan. 2018.

[330] Daily Progress Staff. "Torch-Wielding Protesters Gather at Lee Park." The Daily Progress, 13 May 2017. Web. 19 Jan. 2018.

[331] Mazza, Ed. "Stephen Fry Explains Why Some People Believe Everything Donald Trump Says." Huffington Post, 12 May 2017. Web. 19 Jan. 2018.

I'm tired of seeing shit promoting these people. I'm tired of the media and "nice" white people trying to convince me that they are deserving of my time, energy, or emotions. They aren't. I'm angry that I'm wasting my time ranting about this shit right now, except that I'm fucking being bombarded every goddamn day with messaging telling me that I should pity these fucking 45 supporters. That I should try to help them. That I should listen to their side. Well, shit. I did help them. I told them not to vote for his ass. I told them that racism doesn't actually help anyone. That oppression is dangerous and harmful. That electing that asshole was dangerous for everyone. That there is a swath of this country that believes that they deserve to live on the backs of Black people and POCs...and I said it hoping that they were not one of them.

What I learned is that they are. They are the worst kind, the ones who are but think they aren't. They are the liars, the deceivers, some too ignorant to recognize their own ignorance but capable of hearing the white power message and interpreting it as white excellence.

And some just believe in white power and white excellence, even when they won't admit it.

There is no white excellence, just white brutality. There is no white power, just white insecurity. Because throughout history, white people don't compete. Instead, they murder their competition. They enslave them. They take the useful parts of everyone's culture, viciously rip out our excellence and stuff white mediocrity in its carcass. Then they sell the message of being the best while they rot inside the corpse they made, slowly suffocating themselves and everyone around them.

Whiteness is a global parasite that has destroyed its ecosystem in its greed. And no one will destroy them because none of us want to be like them...pale skinned monsters who don't recognize their own destruction.

I'm fucking tired, y'all.

I'm tired of watching this game play out the same way it has. I'm tired of listening to the same shit. I'm tired of white supremacy. I'm tired of its intentional obliviousness to the harm it does.

I'm tired of seeing its enactors and benefactors explain away their cruelty.

I want to be the monster we need to end this. I really do. But apparently not enough because here I am, writing about it and doing nothing.

I'd love to see this come to a peaceful resolution, but white supremacists, both the powered and the empowered, make that impossible.

They are taking all their shots. Here's to hoping we continue to survive them.

Once, when I was in college, a classmate slapped me "as a joke" and I stood there, running through the consequences of beating her ass in my dorm room surrounded by nothing but rich white kids in a rich white school, knowing that retaliating would probably lead to my expulsion. And I backed down because my father mortgaged our fucking house so that I could be there, and I refused to fuck it up for my self-worth.

– TaLynn Kel, To the Sad, Scared, Ignorant White People

White People Are the Villains in This Narrative

Every day I log into social media to learn that some other anti-Black, anti-Non-Black People of Color (NBPOC) shit has gone down, usually at the expense of someone's life.

A couple of weeks it was the Greenfell Tower fire in London[332] that left hundreds of Black people and Non-Black People of Color (NBPOCs) dead because the government refused to prioritize poor people of color.

Last Saturday it was yet another cop being exonerated for murdering a Black person[333]. His defense? He was scared.

Last Sunday, it was the murder of Nabra Hassanen, age 17[334] who was killed leaving her mosque.

Last Monday, it was the murder of Charleena Lyles, age 30[335] by the very police officers she called for help in reporting a burglary.

---

[332] Hartley-Parkinson, Richard. "Grenfell Tower Fire Rescuers 'Found 42 Bodies in One Room' During Search." Metro, 20 June 2017. Web. 19 Jan. 2018.

[333] Berman, Mark. "Minnesota Officer Acquitted of Manslaughter for Shooting Philando Castile During Traffic Stop." The Washington Post, 17 June 2017. Web. 19 Jan. 2018.

[334] "Muslim Teen Killed After Being Kidnapped While Walking with Friends to Virginia Mosque: Police." KTLA 5, 19 June 2017. Web. 19 Jan. 2018.

[335] Dandridge-Lemco, Ben. "Seattle Police Killed Charleena Lyles, A Pregnant Mother of Four Who Had Called 911." Fader, 19 June 2017. Web. 19 Jan. 2018.

Friday, it was the declaring of a 2nd mistrial for the murder of Sam Dubois[336].

I don't even mention the seemingly infinite micro and macro aggressions inflicted upon Black people, Black women, and POCs in this country. If I did, I'd never move from this computer, they are that constant.

It doesn't matter whether the perpetrators are white. White people have engineered a society so inherently dangerous and unjust for Black people that we literally operate in a bubble of complete luck when interacting with almost anyone. We have zero idea if you're going to hate us, kill us, or ignore us in our day-to-day interactions[337] and that is a fucked up way to live.

We get to live on a global stage where white people enact continuous injustice and inequality on Black people and NBPOCs then dares to call itself great because of the lies they tell about their exploitation, dehumanization, and routine persecution of people who look like me. A country that has manipulated the laws, history, and perception of itself so completely, that every single white person in this country is tarred by this brush. Regardless of how much charity they do, how many selfless acts they commit, white people are the villains of world history and they cannot change that.

---

[336] Kennedy, Merrit. "Judge Declares Mistrial, Again, In Cincinnati Police Shooting Case." NPR, 23 June 2017. Web. 17 Jan. 2018.

[337] Kel, TaLynn. "White People are Racist Landmines." Breaking Normal, 21 May 2017. Web. 17 Jan. 2018.

They fought throughout Europe, Russia, and the interlocked continents until they had nothing to fight over and spread their destruction across the globe. The story is the same in Africa, Australia, and North America. They came, they killed, they killed some more, then they set down roots, called it whiteland, and slaughtered anyone who challenged them. They forced assimilation, demanded loyalty, then wrote history to absolve themselves of the guilt from their mass genocides. And today they kill to maintain that racial hierarchy. The liberals say they seek change, but only if they get to keep their ill-gotten gains while the conservatives are more honest about their belief in their superiority.

Either way, Black people and NBPOCs get fucked over with impunity. And to defend their core sense of goodness, white people lie. They lie and lie and lie and lie and lie. Our media is nothing but a huge propaganda machine designed to show how every type of white person is good, despite the horrible things they say and do. Regardless of their histories. No matter how their families got whatever little bit of power they did. And poor white people feel whatever tiny bit of superiority for being white and use that to their advantage at will. It's a shitshow, and I am tired of being the game board in white people's game of checkers. I'm fucking better than that.

But I was born into a system that was designed to silence me[338]. A system that even now profits from my labor while telling me I'm worthless. I don't know how to break the system, make anything matter, or become a hero in my own narrative because every tool I have in my arsenal is a result of the continued villainy of white people. This includes my home, car, clothes, and the computer upon which I write this. My access to the internet is a product of exploitation. And I know my continued existence is because I don't disturb the norm enough to be removed.

I don't lie to myself about it. I don't tell myself I'm not hurting people when I know I am. White people have spent hundreds of years rearranging history to leave out the damning parts, allowing them to present a humane face to the world when really, they are the savage monsters they accuse Black people of being. They are the ones creating poverty for person gain. They are the ones polluting the waters, destroying the air, initiating false wars and inhibiting progress for profits while they create artificial scarcity of resources and let people starve. They are the ones refusing to build and maintain infrastructure while they build more and more unaffordable housing, stadiums, and shopping malls while refusing to raise the minimum wage. They are the ones still using slavery under the veneer of justice, all to keep them financially elite at the expense of the people.

They know they can't call themselves heroes, so they create them, ensure they are white, and promote this illusion to the masses for consumption. And we eat up the lies like breadcrumbs leading to our demise.

---

338 Kel, TaLynn. "When It Comes to Free Speech, the 'Whites Only; is Silent." The Establishment, 2 June 2017. Web. 17 Jan. 2018.

White people are the witches in the gingerbread houses. They are the liars and the tricksters of the "free" world that ain't so free. They are the gatekeepers of information and the preventers of innovation. They are the petty tyrants of the neighborhood HOA and management in the office. They are the embodiment of failed dreams and hopes who never learned to play with others and instead kill the other children and steal their toys.

Greed. Pain. Rage. Selfishness. Murder. Self-destruction. Brutality. Death. These are the legacies of whiteness and nothing less than a complete purge of everything they value will bring the changes this society needs to embody justice.

We get to live on a global stage where white people enact continuous injustice and inequality on Black people and NBPOCs then dares to call itself great because of the lies they tell about their exploitation, dehumanization, and routine persecution of people who look like me. A country that has manipulated the laws, history, and perception of itself so completely, that every single white person in this country is tarred by this brush.

– TaLynn Kel, White People Are the Villains in this Narrative

Violence Is the White Normal

The past year we've seen more media coverage of the violence of white supremacy. This isn't new shit. We all know this isn't new. Religion has been an exploitative and vicious tool used by shitty humans since…just since. All our written history confirms it. And it's not necessarily the religion that's the issue. It is how people use it to gain and maintain power over others. From the crusades to

You can look back at the crusades, the holy wars allegedly fought to push forward christianity. We know that the true motivation was not to spread the word of some god, but to conquer other nations. Regardless of whatever religious movement you see, you have to ask yourself what someone has to gain by converting you. They say it's to save your soul, but is it really?

Regardless of the whys, we quite clearly see religion being used as a tool to discriminate, persecute, exclude, and even attack people whose religion has been declared "wrong" by dominant culture. In America, we see this with Islam, which, more than an attack on religion, is an excuse for white people to attack people of color (POCs). There are white Muslims, yet that's not who we see or hear being harassed. Much like the anti-immigration movement in amerikkka, the attacks are skin-color based. White immigrants aren't being stopped on the street and detained by immigration kidnappers; brown people are. It's not white people being snatched up for not having "appropriate" identification on them at all times; it's people who don't look white enough.

Not that white people have ever needed a reason to attack POCs. Unfortunately, this is the modus operandi for white people for as long as anyone can remember. The entire rhetoric around white history is conquer and rule. Nowhere in european history is the idea of co-existing. It is always about conquering and assimilating. They gain power through murder, subjugation, and exploitation. They maintain power through their love of torture, terrorism, and complete willingness to maim and annihilate anyone who resists them, and this includes friends and family. They protect their power (i.e. comfort) at all costs and refuse to entertain anything that challenges or contradicts it. Resistance is met with extreme violence — the police is testimony to that.

White people made themselves into the best monsters and made that shit their moral code. They normalized violence and brutality for white people then demonized and criminalized it for everyone else. Best. PR. Strategy. Ever.

Think about it. Open carry laws, the insistence on the right to bear arms, but Black people, including children[339], who have anything that might be a weapon are brutalized[340] and murdered.

---

[339] Savali, Kirsten West. "13-Year-Old Boy with Toy Gun Shot by Baltimore Police Officers." The Root, 27 April 2016. Web. 19 Jan. 2018.

[340] Cleary, Tom. "WATCH: Balch Springs Police Officers Use Taser on Handcuffed Man." Heavy, 17 May 2017. Web. 19 Jan. 2018.

There are currently self-appointed militias[341], white people with guns, actively patrolling the U.S./Mexico border[342]. Yet, the Black Panther Party is painted as violent anarchists for having any guns at all. And if you think those militias aren't murdering people, you are living a lie.

ICE agents are audaciously rounding up and detaining POCs[343] with zero oversight. Like the militias, this is something these "officials" want to do. The only difference between them is official government permission.

Torture, mutilation, and murder were considered family-friendly events by white people — so much so that postcards were made commemorating the horrors[344]. But Black people are violent and scary, Muslim people are terrorists, and Mexican people are rapists. Yeah, no.

---

[341] Bauer, Shane. "I Went Undercover with a Border Militia. Here's What I Saw." Mother Jones, Nov/Dec 2016. Web. 19 Jan. 2018.

[342] "Armed Citizens Patrol U.S.-Mexico Border in Arizona." NBC News, 17 Nov. 2016. Web. 19 Jan. 2018.

[343] Sinclair, Harriet. "ICE Officers Eat Breakfast before Raiding Michigan Restaurant, Detaining Three." Newsweek 25, May 2017. Web. 19 Jan. 2018.

[344] Meghan. "NSFW: American Terrorism… Lynching Postcards." CVLT Nation, 08 Dec. 2014. Web. 19 Jan. 2018.

White people are violent as fuck and instead of owning that shit and trying to fix it, they spend all their time trying to pathologize it to prove it is an aberration or a form of extremism, when it's not. Just this past week three people were murdered by white supremacist civilians. White supremacist police have been murdering Black people as usual, but the surge in white people both verbally[345] and physically[346] attacking POCs and Black people is outrageous and terrifying. And every fucking time, white people bend over backwards to show how those people are outliers. How they are different. How that's a one-off that just keeps happening through some fluke. Anything to avoid addressing their barbaric past and violent present.

---

[345] Video. "Man Yells at Stranger for Speaking Spanish." CNN, 23 May 2017. Web. 19 Jan. 2018.

[346] Shaw, A.R. "HBCU Student Richard Collins III Killed by White Racist Days Before Graduation." RollingOut, 22 May 2017. Web. 19 Jan. 2018.

These people aren't crazy. They are doing what white amerikkkan society has always done — enforcing white supremacy by any means necessary — even if it means killing white people, too[347]. They advocate for violence through media — there's a reason why Black characters always die. They advocate for it in the news — there's a reason why news stations use mugshots of Black people, even when they are the victim of a crime. Black people get murdered and without fail, if they have *any* criminal record, it's mentioned. In the meantime, a white man can murder people[348] and we get to hear how he was a "gentle loner[349]."

Amerikkka humanizes white savages who kill and dehumanizes Black people and POCs for dying.

---

[347] Wamsley, Laurel. "White Supremacist Charged with Killing 2 In Portland, Ore., Knife Attack." NPR, 27 May 2017. Web. 19 Jan. 2018.

[348] Borden, Jeremy; Horwitz, Sari; Markon, Jerry. "For Accused Killer Dylann Roof, a Life That Had Quietly Drifted Off Track." The Washington Post, 18 June 2015. Web. 20 Jan. 2018.

[349] Lee, Paula Young. "Robert Dear, "Gentle Loner": The New York Times Reveals a Load of Biases in Early Round of Colorado Springs Planned Parenthood Coverage." Salon, 30 Nov. 2015. Web. 20 Jan. 2018.

So, when I see white christians calling for violence[350], crying white genocide, and threatening to take this country back[351], I don't see outliers. I see the norm. These aren't fringe groups. These people are the core. Trump supporters aren't extremists — they are the majority, because even though Clinton won the popular vote, she won it with a large swath of POC voters. White people voted for 45[352]. A lot of white people voted for 45. And again, these are not outliers; they are the white norm.

And the thing is, white people know this. Every supposedly liberal white person has "conservative" friends and relatives that they say are entitled to their opinions while never acknowledging that conservative views are polite white supremacy. What we have is that phenomenally successful PR campaign that rebranded racism, sexism, ableism, xenophobia, and genocide as "conservative." Mass murder and enslavement definitely sounds better when it's just called conservative values. It also sounds great when the catchphrase is "Make America Great Again."

PR is a hell of a drug.

---

[350] Palma, Sky. "Christian Radio Host Praises Greg Gianforte: 'We Need a More Violent Christianity.'" DEADState, 28 May 2017. Web. 19 Jan. 2018.

[351] Zucchino, David. "A Militia Gets Battle Ready for a Gun Grabbing Clinton Presidency." 04 Nov. 2016. Web. 19 Jan. 2016.

[352] Sims, Alexandra; Buncombe, Andrew. "Who Voted for Donald Trump? Mostly White Men and Women, Voting Data Reveals." 09 Nov. 2016. Web. 19 Jan. 2018.

The fight for equality isn't about Black people or POCs learning to work with white people. It's about white people overcoming their genocidal tendencies and learning to accept they aren't the best. They aren't dominant. They aren't the bastion of creativity and learning they've told themselves they are. Throughout history, white people are violent, terrifying, greedy bullies willing to inflict the most horrific of atrocities on others while standing in judgment of those who inflict the same upon them. White people traveled around the world and murdered POCs into submission and did it proudly. So, this shit, this violence, isn't anything new. In fact, POCs have spent the last couple hundred years busting our asses to fucking civilize white people so they can actually coexist with us…because their usual move is to kill and enslave everyone they could and enforce their "dominance" through terrorism.

White history is terrorism. White supremacy is terrorism. White fragility is psychological terrorism, as are white tears. Denial of this is a lie. Refusal to admit and accept this is a falsehood of immeasurable proportion. If white people want to know why there are so many issues around racism, they need to look in a mirror and own their shit. They need to own their ignorance, throw that shit in the trash and start learning their real history and try to make themselves better humans.

White people insistence on pretending it didn't happen is fueling the violence we are seeing right now. It's time for them to stop rebranding their brutality and start dealing with this shit. White people have been the best monsters. How about trying to be the better humans instead.

Torture, mutilation, and murder were considered family-friendly events by white people — so much so that postcards were made commemorating the horrors. But Black people are violent and scary, Muslim people are terrorists, and Mexican people are rapists. Yeah, no.

– TaLynn Kel, Violence Is the White Normal

To the 53% and Beyond...

You keep talking about white supremacy like it's a cute little fad all the kids are into instead of the life-threatening danger that it is.

You keep acting like those white men shouting their intent to "take back" their power are just some rambunctious kids who mean no harm; even though the last time they rallied, they murdered a woman. But you pretend it was an aberration, as though their violence isn't the norm.

You pretend white men aren't dangerous. You protect them from the consequences of their actions, excuse their violent outbursts, ignore their weapon caches, disguise their assaults as boyish energy and manly urges. You tell us that their violence is our fault. That we invite it by being around. Being noticed. Being vocal. Existing.

While you protect and lie and protect and lie and protect and lie.

You rebrand oppression as normalcy and when it looks unseemly you name it something new. You help pass legislation to ensure that oppression stays the law. Then you continue to lie and lie and lie until the lies are all you hear, and truth exists only in Black rooms and back rooms, unspoken in public and ridiculed as nonsense...Leaving its speakers discredited and often found lifeless, sometimes engulfed in flames.

You protect white men from admitting the truth of their brutally violent natures because you can't admit that nature is also part of you. A part of your parentage. A part of your history. A part of your now. And because you cannot admit the poison that has helped steer your life, you call it normal and pretend its victims are the real problem...even when one of its victims is you.

Instead of fighting, you sit there, helping them justify their foulness. Instead of making the world better, you enable them to pollute it more. You protect their offspring, raising them to step into the monstrous shoes that came before, raising them full of rage and entitlement to more than they ever earned, while helping their fathers create, enforce, and enact laws brutalizing everyone else. You comfort them while they make numerous attacks on the humanity of others, specifically Black people and non-Black people of color (NBPOC). You protect their entitlement to everything while they give nothing back. You help rape the world then demand that the world help you when you finally realize you aren't exempt. And when you've healed, you, again, fight for their right to continue doing harm without consequence, and with your help they do it over and over and over.

You. The 53% who voted for it and the rest who quietly let this happen.

You demand Black women educate you. You demand that we save you. Yet your silence speaks volumes when it's our lives being decimated, and our communities being destroyed.

Your voices return when we stand tall, proud in ourselves. Then your voices ring in the backdrop, demanding we acknowledge and submit to your white womanhood.

But you've stayed in silent opposition for too long. You benefited from our pain too often. And now that the consequences of your racist divisiveness are coming home to roost, you still look to Black women to define the dynamic that's harming you...instead of looking in the mirror and admitting it to yourself.

We gave you the answers to your questions years ago. We cannot save you. You worked too hard to undermine our voices. Your silence in the face of our abuses quieted our voices of solidarity. We are untrustworthy voices of our oppression, a trust you worked to undermine. So now you need to save yourselves.

We don't take up arms. We refuse to give the masses of whiteness the excuse they salivate for to wipe us all out. We know the horror that lives in your hearts. We are the descendants of those who managed to survive your reign of terror and your thirst for death. We know the storm that's coming. We did not purge our history to hide from ourselves. We see history repeating itself, as the government aligns to stamp out everything that deviates from the white cis-het, ableist male power fantasy.

Where do you stand?

Will you stand by your monstrous man, mask off for the world to see?

Will you continue wearing the white supremacist façade of perfection while rotting from the inside?

Or will you finally admit the choices you made, own the inhumanity you project onto others, and do the work to start fixing this fucked up society? Will you fight to be a better human?

This is your fight, white women. Own it.

You protect white men from admitting the truth of their brutally violent natures because you can't admit that nature is also part of you. A part of your parentage. A part of your history. A part of your now. And because you cannot admit the poison that has helped steer your life, you call it normal and pretend its victims are the real problem…even when one of its victims is you.

– TaLynn Kel, To the 53% and Beyond

References

Intersectional Reading List

Books on Race, Gender, Sexuality, and Class

Brown, Nikki. Private Politics and Public Voices: Black Women's Activism from World War I to the New Deal.

Collier-Thomas, Bettye, and V. P. Franklin, eds. Sisters in the Struggle: African American Women in the Civil Rights-Black Power Movement.

Collins, Patricia Hill. Black Feminist Thought: Knowledge, Consciousness, and the Politics of Empowerment.

Cooper, Anna Julia. A Voice from the South.

Crenshaw, Kimberle. "Mapping the Margins: Intersectionality, Identity Politics, and Violence Against Women of Color." Stanford Law Review 43, no. 6 (July 1991): 1241-1299.

Davis, Angela. Women, Race, & Class.

Giddings, Paula. Ida: A Sword Among Lions: Ida B. Wells.

Giddings, Paula. When and Where I Enter the Impact of Black Women on Race and Sex in America.

Guy-Shefthall, Beverly. Words of Fire: An Anthology of African-American Feminist Thought.

Harris-Perry, Melissa. Sister Citizen: Shame, Stereotypes and Black Women in America.

hooks, bell. Ain't I a Woman: Black Women and Feminism.

hooks, bell. Feminist Theory: From Margin to Center.

Hunter, Tera. To 'Joy My Freedom: Southern Black Women's Lives and Labors After the Civil War.

James, Stanlie M., Frances Smith Foster, and Beverly Guy-Sheftall, eds. Still Brave: The Evolution of Black Women's Studies.

Jordan, June. Some of Us Did Not Die.

Lorde, Audre. Sister Outsider: Essays and Speeches.

Lorde, Audre. Zami: A New Spelling of My Name.

Marby, Marcus. Twice as Good: Condoleezza Rice and Her Path to Power.

Morgan, Joan. When Chickenheads Come Home to Roost: A Hip-Hop Feminist Breaks It Down.

Ransby, Barbara. Ella Baker and the Black Freedom Movement: A Radical Democratic Vision.

Richie, Beth. Compelled to Crime: The Gender Entrapment of Battered Black Women.

Shange, Ntozke. For colored girls who have considered suicide/When the rainbow is enuf.

Shakur, Assata. Assata: An Autobiography.

Smith, Susan L. Sick and Tired of Being Sick and Tired: Black Women's Health Activism in America, 1890-1950.

Theoharis, Jeanne. The Rebellious Life of Mrs. Rosa Parks.

My Marriage

My Husband's Unconscious Racism Nearly Destroyed Our Marriage

Clark-Flory, Tracy. "John Mayer's Johnson Hates Black Women." Salon, 10 Feb. 2010. Web. 21 Feb. 2016.

The Danger of Unchallenged Racism in Interracial Relationships

Kel, TaLynn. "Othering the Self – Learning to Recognize My Anti-Blackness." Black Girl Nerds, 02 March 2016. Web. 20 July 2016.
Kel, TaLynn. "My Husband's Unconscious Racism Nearly Destroyed Our Marriage." The Establishment, 05 May. 2016. Web. 20 August 2016.
Chelsie. "When Suddenly No Lives Matter." 2 Boys 1 Blog and Me, 09 July 2016. Web. 20 August 2016.
Broadnax, Jamie. "Cosplay or No Cosplay: The Homicide of Darrien Hunt." Black Girl Nerds, 17 Sept. 2014. Web. 20 August 2016.
Graham, David A. "Sandra Bland and the Long History of Racism in Waller County, Texas." The Atlantic, 21 June 2015. Web. 20 Aug. 2016.
Neyfakh, Leon. "50-Year-Old Black Woman Who Died in Jail Was Denied Water and Medication, Court Filings Allege." Slate, 25 Feb. 2016. Web. 20 Aug. 2016.
Manuel-Logan, Ruth. "Police: Man Says He Killed Teen Seeking Help After Crash 'Accidentally.'" NewsOne, 2014. Web. 20 Aug. 2016.
Agorist, Matt. "Parents on a Date Were Asleep in Car When Cops Arrived and Killed Them Both." The Free Thought Project, 25. Feb 2016. Web. 20 Aug. 2016.

Why I Cut My Racist In-Laws Out of My Life

Kel, TaLynn. "My Husband's Unconscious Racism Nearly Destroyed Our Marriage." The Establishment, 26 May 2016. Web. 31 July 2016.

Kel, TaLynn. "White People, You Have a Lying Problem." The Establishment. 07 July 2016. Web. 31 July. 2016.

Wright, Kai. "Why Alton Sterling and Philando Castile Are Dead." The Nation, 07 July 2016. Web. 31 July 2016.

When the Space You Promised Hurts Like Hell

The Breakfast Club Power 105.1 FM. "Trevor Noah Talks Tomi Lahren, Donald Trump, Racism in America & More." YouTube, 07 Dec. 2016. Web. 09 Dec. 2016.

Kel, TaLynn. "Becoming an Agent of Whiteness." The Establishment, 05 Dec. 2016. Web. 09 Dec. 2016.

Noah, Trevor. "Trevor Noah: Let's Not Be Divided. Divided People Are Easier to Rule." The New York Times, 05 Dec. 2016. Web. 09 Dec. 2016.

Viera, Bené. "Here's the Problem with Black Men Like Trevor Noah and Charlamagne Tha God." The Frisky, 07 Dec. 2016. Web. 09 Dec. 2016.

History.com Staff. "Harriet Tubman." History.com. Web. 09 Dec. 2016.

Loewen, James W.; Kaplan, Fran; Smith, Robert. "Sundown Towns: Racial Segregation Past and Present." America's Black Holocaust Museum. Web. 09 Dec. 2016.

Sanders, Brandee. "History's Lost Black Towns." The Root, 27 Jan. 2016. Web. 09 Dec. 2016.

The Establishment. "Every Day a Funeral." The Establishment, 20 Sept. 2016. Web. 09 Dec. 2016.

Moore, A. "8 Successful and Aspiring Black Communities Destroyed by White Neighbors." Atlanta Black Star, 04 Dec. 2013. Web. 09 Dec. 2016.

Oluo, Ijeoma. "You Don't Have to Like Me — You Just Have to Believe I'm A Human Being." The Establishment, 29 Nov. 2016. Web. 09 Dec. 2016.

"It's Fine..." How "Get Out" Has Me Questioning My Instincts (Again) About My Interracial Marriage

Son of Baldwin. "Get the Fuck Outta Here: A Dialogue on Jordan Peele's GET OUT." Medium, 27 Feb. 2017. Web. 17 Jan. 2018.

Brooks, Kinitra. "What Becky Gotta Do to Get Murked? White Womanhood in Jordan Peele's Get Out." Very Smart Brothers, 03 March 2017. Web. 17 Jan. 2018.

Kel, TaLynn. "My Husband's Unconscious Racism Nearly Destroyed Our Marriage." The Establishment, 05 May. 2016. Web. 17 Jan. 2018.

NPR. "The 'Racial Cleansing' That Drove 1,100 Black Residents Out of Forsyth County, Ga." Fresh Air, 15 Sept. 2016. Web. 17 Jan. 2018.

Kel, TaLynn. "Why I Cut My Racist In-Laws Out of My Life." The Establishment, 2 Aug. 2016. Web. 17 Jan. 2018.

When Your White Significant Other Says Something Racist

White, Adam. "Swedish Music Festival to Go 'Women-Only' Following String of Sexual Assaults." The Telegraph, 6 July 2017. Web. 17 Jan. 2018.

Cauterucci, Christina. "After 27 Sexual Assault Reports, Swedish Music Festival Replaced with Man-Free Event in 2018." Slate, 5, July 2017. Web. 17 Jan. 2018.

Pollard, Alexandra. "Blaming the Swedish Festival Rapes on Migrants Isn't Just Wrong – It's Dangerous." The Guardian, 6, July 2016. Web. 17 Jan. 2018.

Kel, TaLynn. "American, Stop Protecting Your Monsters." The Establishment, 10 Oct. 2016. Web. 17 Jan. 2018.

Kel, TaLynn. "I Promised My White Husband the Space to Fuck Up on Racism – And It Hurts Like Hell." The Establishment, 16 Jan. 2017. Web. 17 Jan. 2018.

Pache, Juliana and Starling, Lakin. "A Candid Conversation About Rap Culture's Pervasive Disrespect Against Black Women." Fader, 09 May 2017. Web. 17 Jan. 2018.

Herriott, Arianna. "6 African Countries That Are Hostile Toward Black People." Atlanta Black Star, 03 June. 2017. Web. 17 Jan. 2018.

Helm, Angela. "Recent College Grad Beaten to Death in Greece." The Root, 09 July 2017. Web. 17 Jan. 2018.

Edwards, Breanna. "2 Brooklyn, NY, Men Charged with Shouting Racial Slurs at Interracial Couple, Beating Up and Threatening to 'Lynch' Black Boyfriend." The Root, 12 July 2017. Web. 17 Jan. 2018.

Tesfaye, Sophia. "Washington Man Stabs Kissing Interracial Couple, Cites Donald Trump When Arrested." Salon, 19 Aug. 2016. Web. 17 Jan. 2018.

Associate Press. "Third Mistrial Declared in Case of White Ex-Cop Accused of Killing Daughter's Black Boyfriend." Los Angeles Times, 08 July 2017. Web. 17 Jan. 2018.

Kel, TaLynn. "White People Are the Villains in This Narrative." Breaking Normal, 26 June 2017. Web. 17 Jan. 2017.

Fandom

Hathaway, Jay. "What Is Gamergate, and Why? An Explainer for Non-Geeks." Gawker, 10 Oct. 2014. Web. 19 Jan. 2018.

Waldman, Katy. "How Sci-Fi's Hugo Awards Got Their Own Full-Blown Gamergate." Slate, 08 April 2015. Web. 19 Jan. 2018.

Chu, Arthur. "Sci-fi's Right-Wing Backlash: Never Doubt that a Small Group of Deranged Trolls Can Ruin Anything (Even the Hugo Awards)." Salon, 06 April 2015. Web. 19 Jan. 2018.

Campbell, Colin. "Anita Sarkeesian's Astounding 'Garbage Human' Moment." Polygon, 27 June 2017. Web. 19 Jan. 2018.

Blackface Isn't a Compliment

Blaque, Kat. "Are Zwarte Pieten Racist?" YouTube, 19 Oct. 2014. Web. 27 Sept. 2016.

Blaque, Kat. "Cultures are Not Costumes" YouTube, 08 Oct. 2014. Web. 27 Sept. 2016.

Blaque, Kat. "Veds 28: What Is Blackface?" YouTube, 29 Sept. 2014. Web. 27 Sept. 2016.

Kel, Talynn. "The Face that Paused a Thousand Meetings." Breaking Normal, 28 April 2016. Web. 27 Sept. 2016.

Biography.com Editors. "Trayvon Martin Biography." The Biography.com Website, 09 Feb. 2016. Web. 27 Sept. 2016.

Josefczyk, Aaron. "Community Gathers to Mourn 13-Year-Ole Tyre King Who Was Killed by Cops." The Huffington Post, 26 Sept. 2016. Web. 27 Sept. 2016.

Williams, Joseph P. "Tamir Rice Shooting: Not Just a Tragedy." U.S. News and World Reports, 29 Dec. 2015. Web. 27 Sept. 2016.

Kel, TaLynn. "White People, You Have a Lying Problem." The Establishment. 07 July 2016. Web. 27 Sept. 2016.

Kel, TaLynn. "When White People Consume Blackness for Personal Gain." The Establishment. 29 June 2016. Web. 27 Sept. 2016.

On Cosplay: My Humanity Is Not Optional

Kel, TaLynn. "As a Fat, Black Woman, Cosplay Has Tried to Make Me Invisible" renamed "The Cosplay Community Has Tried to Make Me Invisible Because I'm a Fat, Black Woman." The Establishment, 20 Sept. 2016. Web. 17. Jan. 2018.

On Logan and the Death of Black People

TV Tropes.Org. "Black Index." TCTropes.Org. Web. 17 Jan. 2018.

Valerie Complex. "Will It Get Better for Black People in the Horror Genre?" Black Girl Nerds, 15 July 2015. Web. 17 Jan. 2018.

Ross, Indigo. "Trauma Porn: Hyper-Consumption of Black Death and Pain." Odyssey, 12 July 2016. Web. 17 Jan. 2018.

Downs, Kenya. "When Black Death Goes Viral, It Can Trigger PTSD-like Trauma." PBS News Hour, 22 July 2016. Web. 17 Jan. 2018.

Costandi, Mo. "A Physiological Marker for False Memories." The Guardian, 27 Jan. 2012. Web. 17 Jan. 2018.

At the Intersection of Blackness & Nerdom

Ziyad, Hari. "BLM Philly Did Not 'Ban White People from Its Meetings' but Created Necessary 'Black Only Spaces.'" AfroPunk, 04, April 2017. Web. 17 Jan. 2017.

Glover, Cameron. "No, Black-Only Safe Spaces Are Not Racist." Wear Your Voice, 31, May 2017. Web. 17. Jan. 2017.

Kel, TaLynn. "When Inclusion Becomes Erasure." Breaking Normal, 30 May 2017. Web. 17 Jan. 2017.

Protecting Becky at All Costs — Peak White Feminism in Wonder Woman

Storey, Kate. "Inside the Lives of White Supremacist Women." Marie Claire, 10 Jan. 2017. Web. 17 Jan. 2018.

Brooks, Kinitra. "What Becky Gotta Do to Get Murked? White Womanhood in Jordan Peele's Get Out." Very Smart Brothers, 03 March 2017. Web. 17 Jan. 2018.

Jionde, Elexus. "Racist White Women: An American Legacy." Intelexual Media, 8 March 2017. Web. 17 Jan. 2018.

Workneh, Lilly. "Emmett Till's Accuser Admits She Lied About Claims That Led to His Murder." Huffington Post, 27 Jan. 2017. 17 Jan. 2018.

Roberts, Laura Morgan; Ely, Robin J. "Why Did So Many White Women Vote for Donald Trump?" Fortune, 18 Nov. 2016. Web. 17 Jan. 2018.

Kuntzman, Gersh. "Donald Trump is Still Abusing Women — with His Wife Melania the Latest Victim." New York Daily News, 18 Oct. 2016. Web. 17 Jan. 2018.

Patton, Stacey. "White Women, Please Don't Expect Me to Wipe Away Your Tears." Dame, 15 Dec. 2014. Web. 17 Jan. 2018.

Kel, TaLynn. "Demanding Black Forgiveness Is Just Another Way to Control Us." The Establishment. 10 Aug. 2016. Web. 17 Jan. 2018.

Kel, TaLynn. "American, Stop Protecting Your Monsters." The Establishment, 10 Oct. 2016. Web. 17 Jan. 2018.

Kel, TaLynn. "White People, You Have a Lying Problem." The Establishment. 07 July 2016. Web. 17 Jan. 2018.

Kel, TaLynn. "Violence is the White Normal." Breaking Normal, 26 June 2017. Web. 17 Jan. 2017.

The Terror of the Now

Kel, TaLynn. "White People are Racist Landmines." Breaking Normal, 21 May 2017. Web. 17 Jan. 2018.

Johnston, Rich. "The Supergirl Cosplayer Who Went to Charlottesville – Guess Whose Side She Was On." Bleeding Cool, 18 Aug. 2017. Web. 17 Jan. 2018.

Kel, TaLynn. "When Inclusion Becomes Erasure." Breaking Normal, 30 May 2017. Web. 17 Jan. 2018.

Barnes, Mo. "Black Heroes Matter: Black Geeks Rise at DragonCon 2017." Rollingout, 05 Sept. 2017. Web. 17 Jan. 2018.

Eldridge, Ellen. "Two Women at DragonCon Hit by Chairs Thrown from Hotel Balcony." Atlanta Journal Constitution, 04 Sept. 2017. Web. 17 Jan. 2018.

Dickerson, Caitlin. "For DACA Recipients, Losing Protection and Work Permits Is Just the Start." The New York Times, 07 Sept. 2017. Web. 17 Jan. 2018.

America's Whiteness Problem is Part of Your Fandom

White, D.S. "Is Doctor Who's Black Companion Really Traveling Back In Time, This Time?" Black Girl Nerds, 11 May 2017. Web. 17 Jan. 2018.

Duncan, Amy. "New Doctor Who Sidekick Pearl Mackie 'Given the Boot after Just One Series.'" Metro, 03 April 2017. Web. 17 Jan. 2018.

Ohlheiser, Abby. "PewDiePie Said the N-Word on YouTube. The Internet's Most Famous Gamer is Out of Excuses." The Washington Post, 12 Sept. 2018.

Hernandez, Patricia. "YouTubers Worry About Blowback from New PewDiePie Controversy." Kotaku, 11 Sept. 2017. 17 Jan. 2018.

Winkler, Rolfe; Nicas, Jack; and Fritz, Ben. "Disney Severs Ties with YouTube Star PewDiePie After Anti-Semitic Posts." The Wall Street Journal, 12 Feb. 2017. Web. 17 Jan. 2018.

Hernandez, Patricia. "Indie Dev Calls for Copyright Strikes Against Pewdiepie After He Says N-Word on Stream." Kotaku, 10 Sept. 2017. 17 Jan. 2018.

Khosaravi, Rye. "Racist Reaction to Black D.Va Cosplayer Shows the Struggles of Being a Nerd of Color." Mic, 8, June 2017. Web. 17 Jan. 2018.

Doll, DeLa. "Blackface Is Ugly, And I'm Being Harassed: A Tale of Cosplay and Cosplayers Gone Wrong." Huffington Post, 07, Sept. 2016. Web. 17 Jan. 2018.

"The World of Black Cosplay: Discrimination, Rejection, Invisibility of the Black Cosplaying Community." The Columbia Chronicle, 1, Mar. 2015. Web. 17 Jan. 2018.

Faroughm, Amanda. "GeekGirlCon 2017 Controversy: Tensions Boil Over and Leads Key Organization Staff Members to Quit." Mic, 14 Aug. 2017. Web. 17 Jan. 2018.

Kel, TaLynn. "When Inclusion Becomes Erasure." Breaking Normal, 30 May 2017. Web. 17 Jan. 2017.

"'Good Shall Triumph over Evil': The Comic Book Code of 1954." History Matters: The U.S. Survey Course on the Web. Web. 17. Jan. 2018.

Kel, TaLynn. "Black Characters and Non-Black Writers: An Imperfect Union." Black Girl Nerds, 21 June 2017. Web. 17 Jan. 2018.

Trumbore, Dave. "Scarlett Johansson on Black Widow: 'The Character Is Right for a Standalone.'" Collider, 13, Feb. 2017. Web. 17 Jan. 2018.

Davis, Lauren. "Paul Dini: Superhero Cartoon Execs Don't Want Largely Female Audiences." Io9, 15 Dec. 2013. Web. 17 Jan. 2018.

Rose, Steve. "Ghost in the Shell's Whitewashing: Does Hollywood Have an Asian Problem?" The Guardian, 21 Mar. 2017. 17 Jan. 2018.

Hoffman, C.P. "Guardians of the Galaxy Vol 2 Turned Mantis into the Butt of a Joke." CBR.com, 11 May 2017. Web. 17 Jan. 2018.

Kel, TaLynn. "On "Logan" and the Tropes of Black Folks." Black Girl Nerds, 18, April 2017. Web. 17 Jan. 2018.

Johnston, Rich. "The Supergirl Cosplayer Who Went to Charlottesville – Guess Whose Side She Was On." Bleeding Cool, 18 Aug. 2017. Web. 17 Jan. 2018.

Johnston, Rich. "We Talk to The Supergirl Cosplayer "Along for The Ride" at the White Nationalist Rally in Charlottesville." Bleeding Cool, 19 Aug. 2017. Web. 20 Jan. 2018.

McKenzie, Mia. "How to Tell the Difference Between Real Solidarity and 'Ally Theater.'" Black Girl Dangerous, 04 Nov. 2015. Web. 17 Jan. 2018.

Witt, Laura. "No, You Can't Be Friends with a White Supremacist and Not Be One Yourself." Wear Your Voice, 06 June 2017. 17 Jan. 2018.

Berlatsky, Noah. "The Incoherent Backlashes to Black Actors Playing 'White' Superheroes." The Atlantic, 20 Feb. 2014. Web. 17 Jan. 2018.

Wallace, Edward. "As Expected, There Are Idiots Who Find the Black Panther Trailer Racist." Fortress, 15 June 2017. Web. 17 Jan. 2018.

"Disney Creates a New Character Just to Cast a White Actor in Latest Aladdin Film." The New Arab, 08 Sept. 2017. Web. 17 Jan. 2018.

Judge, Monique. "White People Commit Welfare Fraud, State Creates Amnesty Program so They Won't Go to Jail." The Root, 11 Sept. 2017. Web. 17 Jan. 2018.

Mechanic, Jesse. "When A Drug Epidemic Hit White America, Addiction Became A Disease." Huffington Post, 10 July 2017. Web. 17 Jan. 2018.

Kunzelman, Michael. "White Man Arrested in Slayings of 2 Black Men in Louisiana." Chicago Tribune, 19 Sept. 2017. Web. 17 Jan. 2018.

Is 'Thor: Ragnarok' A Subversive Takedown of White Supremacy?

"Thomas Jefferson: A Film by Ken Burns." PBS, Public Broadcasting Service, 1997. Web. 20 Jan. 2018.

Robinson, Nathan L. "A Quick Reminder of Why Colonialism was Bad." Current Affairs, 14 Sept. 2017. Web. 17 Jan. 2018.

"Atrocities Against Native Americans." United End to Genocide, 2016. Web. 17 Jan. 2018.

Rogers, David; Bowman, Moira. "A History: The Construction of Race and Racism." Racial Equity Tools. Web. 17 Jan. 2018.

Thompson, Tracy. "The South Still Lies about the Civil War." Salon, 16 March 2013. Web. 17 Jan. 2018.

Nazaryan, Alexander. "California Slaughter: The State-Sanctioned Genocide of Native Americans." Newsweek, 17 Aug. 2016. Web. 17 Jan. 2018.

Kel, TaLynn. "White People, You Have a Lying Problem." The Establishment. 07 July 2016. Web. 17 Jan. 2018.

Levenson, Eric. "Judge Sentences Man Who Raped Sister to Probation, Citing 'Stigma.'" CNN, 24 May 2017. Web. 17 Jan. 2018.

Robles, Frances; Stewart, Nikita. "Dylann Roof's Past Reveals Trouble at Home and School." The New York Times, 16 July 2015. Web. 17 Jan. 2018.

"Remembering the Sandy Hook Elementary School Shooting Victims." Daily News, 2017. Web. 17 Jan. 2018.

Yan, Holly; Stapleton, AnneClaire. "Authorities: Texas Church Shooter Had Three Gunshot Wounds." CNN 07 Nov. 2017. Web. 17 Jan. 2018.

Farrington, Dana. "Planned Parenthood Shooter Found Incompetent to Stand Trial." NPR, 11 May 2016. Web. 17 Jan. 2018.

Bouie, Jamelle. "The Deadly History of 'They're Raping Our Women.'" Slate, 18, June 2015. Web. 17 Jan. 2018.

Gilmore, Stephanie. "On Using White Womanhood to Justify Racism and White Terrorism." Mic, 25 June 2015. Web. 17 Jan. 2018.

Your Fandom Is Racist and So Are You

Johnston, Rich. "The Supergirl Cosplayer Who Went to Charlottesville – Guess Whose Side She Was On." Bleeding Cool, 18 Aug. 2017. Web. 17 Jan. 2018.

Kel, TaLynn. "The Terror of the Now." Breaking Normal, 08 Sept. 2017. Web. 17 Jan. 2018.

"'Good Shall Triumph over Evil': The Comic Book Code of 1954." *History Matters: The U.S. Survey Course on the Web.* Web. 17. Jan. 2018.

Reed, Brad. "'White Genocide in Space': Racist Fans Seethe at Diversity in New 'Star Trek' Series." Raw Story, 24 May 2017. Web. 17 Jan. 2018.

Simon, Rachel. "'Thor: Ragnarok' Star Tessa Thompson Knows the Color of Valkyrie's Skin Is the Least Important Thing About Her." Bustle, 07 Sept. 2017. Web. 17 Jan. 2018.

Westbrook, Logan. "Black Thor Actor Talks About Racist Comic Book Fans." The Escapist, 04 May 2011. Web. 17 Jan. 2018.

"The World of Black Cosplay: Discrimination, Rejection, Invisibility of the Black Cosplaying Community." The Columbia Chronicle, 1, Mar. 2015. Web. 17 Jan. 2018.

Kel, TaLynn. "As a Fat, Black Woman, Cosplay Has Tried to Make Me Invisible" renamed "The Cosplay Community Has Tried to Make Me Invisible Because I'm a Fat, Black Woman." The Establishment, 20 Sept. 2016. Web. 17. Jan. 2018.

<u>Misogynoir</u>

Bailey, Moya. "They Aren't Talking about Me." The Crunk Feminist Collective, 14 March 2010. Web. 27 Jan. 2018.

The Face That Paused a Thousand Meetings

Hobson, Janell. "Angry or Complicated? Misrecognizing Black Women." Ms. Blog, 22 Sept. 2014. Web. 28 April 2016.

Yancy, George. "Walking While Black in the 'White Gaze.'" The New York Times, 01 Sept. 2013. Web. 28 April 2016.

Conger, Cristen. "How the 'Angry Black Woman' Stereotype Tries to Control Black Women." Everyday Feminism, 03 March 2016. Web. 28 April 2016.

Boylorn, R. "Working While Black: 10 Racial Microaggressions Experienced in the Workplace." Crunk Feminist Collective, 11 Nov. 2014. Web. 28 April 2016.

Woodard, Monique. "The White Elephant in The Room." 13 April 2016. Web. 28 April 2016.

Johnson, Maisha Z. "6 Struggles of Being Unapologetically Black in a Professional Environment." Everyday Feminism, 04 Nov. 2014. Web. 28 April 2016.

Leslie Jones is the Least Protected Blackness of Us All

Cox, Carolyn. "The Ghostbusters Trailer Backlash Shows Men Believe in the Power of Representation (But Only When It Applies to Them)." The Mary Sue, 01 May 2016. Web. 23 Aug. 2016.

Ghostbusters (2016). Rotten Tomatoes, 2016. Web. 23 Aug. 2016.

Ghostbusters (2016). Box Office Mojo, 2016. Web. 23 Aug. 2016.

Riedel, Sam. "Why Busting 'Ghostbusters' Reboot Myths May No Longer Matter." The Establishment, 19 Aug 2016. Web. 23 Aug. 2016.

For Harriet. "Leslie Jones Quits Twitter After Spending a Day Battling Racist Twitter." For Harriet, 19, July 2016. Web. 23 Aug. 2016.

Bristol, Keir. "On Moya Bailey, Misogynoir, and Why Both Are Important." The Visibility Project, 27 May 2014. Web. 23 Aug. 2016.

LaSha. "We Need to Talk About Leslie Jones and Colorism in Our Community." Ebony, 12 Aug 2016. Web. 23 Aug. 2016.

Lennard, Natasha. "'Why are Black Women Less Attractive?' asks Psychology Today." Salon, 17 May 2011. Web. 23 Aug. 2016.

Leicht, Angelica. "Suspects Arrested, Charged in #Jadapose Rape Case." Houston Press, 17 Oct. 2014. Web. 23 Aug. 2016.

Roberts, Monica. "Misgendering Attacks on A Black Woman's Femininity Aren't Funny." TransGriot, 02 June 2015. Web. 23 Aug. 2016.

Cooper, Brittney. "The World Only Has Ugliness for Black Women. That's Why Serena Williams is So Important." Salon, 15 July 2015. Web. 23 Aug. 2016.

Azalia, Loy. "My Struggle to Protect Black Men When They've Been My Abuser." Blavity, August 2016. Web. 23 Aug. 2016.

Blay, Zeba. "'Confirmation' And the Silencing of Black Women to Shield Black Men." Huffington Post, 15 April 2016. Web. 23 Aug. 2016.

Drayton, Tiffanie. "On Nate Parker's College Rape Case & Why Black Women Should Not Watch 'Birth of a Nation.'" Clutch, Aug. 2016. Web. 23 Aug. 2016.

Shackelford, Ashleigh. "Stop Excusing Black Men's Violence – Like Nate Parker's – for the Sake of Black Liberation." Wear Your Voice Magazine, 16 Aug. 2016. Web. 23 Aug. 2016.

Haimerl, Amy. "The Fastest-Growing Group of Entrepreneurs in America." Fortune, 29 June 2015. Web. 23 Aug. 2016.

Davis, Rachaell. "New Study Shows Black Women Are Among the Most Educated Group in The United States." Essence, 07 June 2016. Web. 23 Aug. 2016.

Kinks, Klassy. "White Hair Blog Claims Bantu Knots Were "Inspired" By Marc Jacobs, Black Twitter Goes Nuts." Black Girl Long Hair, 27 May 2015. Web. 23 Aug. 2016.

Wellington, Elizabeth. "When Black Girls Get Criticized and White Girls Get Celebrated." For Harriet, Oct. 2014. Web. 23 Aug. 2016.

Phillips, Kady. "Blavity Exclusive: Akilah Obviously on BuzzFeed and #StopBuzzThieves." Blavity, Aug. 2016. Web. 23 Aug. 2016.

Bowerman, Mary. "Is White Lives Matter a Movement or White Supremacist Group?" USAToday, 22 Aug. 2016. Web. 23 Aug. 2016.

Kel, TaLynn. "When White People Consume Blackness for Personal Gain." The Establishment, 29 June 2016. Web. 23 Aug. 2016.

Wilson, Julee. "The Meaning Of #BlackGirlMagic, And How You Can Get Some of It." Huffington Post, 12 Jan. 2016. Web. 23 Aug. 2016.

Men Are Shitty Friends

Kel, TaLynn. "My Husband's Unconscious Racism Nearly Destroyed Our Marriage." The Establishment, 05 May. 2016. Web. 17 Jan. 2018.

You Are Not in the Fight for Equality if You Protect Your Privilege

Kirabo, Sincere. "Why Black Men Participate in Misogynoir – And 3 Ways We Can Fight Against It." Everyday Feminism, 17 Oct. 2016. Web. 17 Jan. 2018.

"Where the Backlog Exists and What's Happening to End It." End the Backlog. Web. 17 Jan. 2018.

Phillip, Abby. "Man Who Sexually Abused 3-Year-Old Girl-Didn't 'Intend to Harm' His Victim California Judge Rules." 07 April, 2015. Web. 17 Jan. 2018.

Kel, TaLynn. "American, Stop Protecting Your Monsters." The Establishment, 10 Oct. 2016. Web. 17 Jan. 2018.

When It Comes to Free Speech, the 'Whites Only' Is Silent

Bernard, Sara. "Princeton Professor Cancels Seattle Talk Following Deluge of Racist Threats." Seattle Weekly, 31 May 2017. Web. 17 Jan. 2018.

Lieu, Johnny. "Prominent GamerGate Target Details Disturbing Harassment, All These Years Later." Mashable, 28 Feb. 2017. Web. 17 Jan 2018.

Jones, Feminista. "We Have Had to Defend Ourselves Against Online Threats." 03 Aug. 2016. Web. 17 Jan. 2018.

Klein, Rebecca. "Texas Teacher Fired After Disturbingly Racist Post in Response to Pool Party Incident." Huffington Post, 11 June 2015. Web. 20 Jan. 2018.

"US: Black Woman Forcibly Removed from Hospital Dies 2 Hours Later." Telesur, 25 Dec. 2015. Web. 17 Jan. 2018.

Oppel, Richard A.; Stolberg, Sheryl ay; Apuzzo, Matt. "Justice Department to Release Blistering Report of Racial Bias by Baltimore Police." The New York Times, 09 Aug. 2016. Web. 17 Jan. 2018.

Lee, Vic. "Department of Justice Report Cites Bias by San Francisco Police." ABC 7 News, 12, Oct. 2016. Web. 17 Jan. 2018.

Lazarus, Jeremy. "Black Patrons Turned Away from Fan Restaurant." Richmond Free Press, 04 Nov. 2016. Web. 17 Jan. 2018.

Demby, Gene. "Study Reveals Worse Outcomes for Black and Latino Defendants." NPR Code Switch, 17 July 2014. Web. 17 Jan. 2018.

Harriot, Michael. "Black Man Found Not Guilty of Crime, Still Sentenced to 7 Years in Prison." The Root, 23 May 2017. Web. 17 Jan. 2018.

Covert, Bryce. "Race Best Predicts Whether You Live Near Pollution." The Nation, 18 Feb. 2016. Web. 17 Jan. 2018.

Chira, Susan. "'You Focus on the Good': Women Who Voted for Trump, in Their Own Words." The New York Times, 14 Jan. 2017. Web. 17 Jan 2018.

Chang, David; Lozano, Alicia Victoria; Gutierrez, Gabe. "Family of Syrians Deported from Philadelphia Supported Donald Trump." NBC Philadelphia, 31 Jan. 2017. Web. 17 Jan. 2018.

Kel, TaLynn. "To the Black Women Who Align Themselves with White Supremacy." The Establishment, 27, Feb 2017. Web. 17 Jan. 2018.

McLaughlin, Eliott C. "War on Campus." CNN, 1, May 2017. Web. 17 Jan. 2018.

Interview. "The ACLU Explains Why They're Supporting the Rights of Milo Yiannopoulos." NPR, 12 Feb. 2017. Web. 17 Jan. 2018.

Stone, Geoffrey R. "Richard Spencer's Right to Speak at Auburn." The New York Times, 18 April 2017. Web. 17 Jan. 2018.

Markus, Bethania Palma. "Fresno Bar Kicks Out Two Black Women — and It Turns Out They Are Attorneys for the ACLU." Raw Story, 24 March 2016. Web. 17 Jan. 2018.

Kutner, Jenny. "Kentucky Fire Chief Refuses to Help Black Family after Traffic Accident: "We Ain't Taking No N–gers Here." Salon, 20 Nov. 2014. Web. 17 Jan. 2018.

Serwer, Adam. "Jeff Sessions's Blind Eye." The Atlantic, 05 April 2017. Web. 17 Jan. 2018.

Okeowo, Alexis. "Hate on the Rise After Trump's Election." The New Yorker, 17 Nov. 2016. Web. 17 Jan. 2018.

The Hate We Receive: On Colorism & Anti-Blackness Among Black People

Ways, Kays. "Rickey Smiley Dragged for Disgusting Joke About Dark Skin Women." Lisa A La Mode, 29, April 2017. Web. 17 Jan. 2018.

Kel, TaLynn. "Leslie Jones Embodies the Least Protected Blackness of All." The Establishment, 25 April 2016. Web. 17 Jan. 2018.

Kwateng-Clark, Danielle. "'Guerilla' Director John Ridley Says Black Women Are Erased from His Series Because He's 'In A Mixed-Race Relationship.'" Essence, 10 April 2017. Web. 17 Jan. 2018.

Pennington, Tonya. "Why Black Women in History Deserve to Have Their Stories Told." Black Girl Nerds, 19 April 2017. Web. 17 Jan. 2018.

Scott, Sydney. "Charlamagne Tha God Is Problematic Once More, Says Black Women Should Use Their Voice Like Tomi Lahren." 07 Dec. 2016. Web. 17 Jan. 2018.

"Gilbert Arenas Says Lupita Nyong'o 'Ain't Cute' in Tirade about Dark-Skinned Women." The Grio, 14 April 2017. Web. 17 Jan. 2018.

Andrews, Masai. "The UAlbany Bus Incident Is Repeating History." Huffington Post, 01 May 2017. Web. 17 Jan 2018.

White Male Patriarchy Says I'm Disposable — Until White People Need Us to Save Them from Themselves

Newkirk, Vann R. "African American Voters Made Doug Jones a U.S. Senator in Alabama." The Atlantic, 12 Dec. 2017. Web. 17 Jan. 2018.

ByBlacks.com. "The Harsh Reality of Being a Black Woman in the Workplace." Huffington Post, 24 April 2017. Web. 19 Jan. 2018.

Jeffreys, Zenobia. "Why Police Violence Against Women of Color Stays Hidden." Yes Magazine, 10 Aug. 2017. Web. 18 Jan. 2018.

Raser, Tess. "Twenty-Three Years of Resisting Police Brutality: The Life and Death of Korryn Gaines." Truthout, 19 July 2017. Web. 19 Jan. 2018.

Finn, Jessica. "Black 5ft 2in Teenage Girl Weighing 115lbs Tells of Horrific Ordeal as Police Confronted Her at Gunpoint and Punched Her in the Mouth When They Mistook Her for a 170lb Bald 5ft 10in Male Suspect." Daily Mail, 12 July 2017. Web. 20 Jan. 2018.

Levy, Pema. "Reports of Voter Suppression Tactics Pour in From Alabama Election." Mother Jones, 12 Dec. 2017. Web. 19 Jan. 2019.

Kaczynski, Andrew. "Roy Moore in 2011: Getting Rid of Amendments After 10th Would 'Eliminate Many Problems.'" CNN, 11 Dec. 2017. Web 19 Jan. 2018.

Paiella, Gabriella. "Fifth Woman Accuses Roy Moore of Sexually Assaulting Her When She Was a Teenager (Update)." The Cut, 13 Nov. 2017. Web. 19 Jan. 2018.

Burlij, Terence. "The 7 Most Revealing Findings in the Alabama Exit Polls." CNN 13 Dec. 2017. Web. 19 Jan. 2018.

Clark, Dartunorro. "Meet Doug Jones, Alabama's First Democratic Senator in 25 Years." NBCNews, 13 Dec 2017. Web. 19 Jan. 2018.

Lockhart, P.R. "The Alabama Election is the Latest Example of the Political Power of Black Women." Vox, 13 Dec. 2017. Web. 19 Jan. 2018.

Fang, Marina. "Black Women Played a Big Part in Doug Jones' Surprise Victory in Alabama." Huffington Post, 13 Dec. 2017. Web. 20 Jan. 2018.

Landers, Jackson. "When Shirley Chisholm Ran for President, Few Would Say: 'I'm With Her.'" Snithsonian.com, 25 April 2016. Web. 19 Jan. 2018.

C-SPAN. "1996: Hillary Clinton on "Super Predators" (C-SPAN)."

Coates, Ta-Nehisi. "The Black Family in the Age of Mass Incarceration." The Atlantic, Oct. 2015. Web. 19 Jan. 2018.

Katz, Jonathan M. "The Clintons Didn't Screw Up Haiti Alone. You Helped." Slate, 22 Sept. 2016. Web. 19 Jan. 2018.

Newkirk, Vann R. "What's Missing from Reports on Alabama's Black Turnout." The Atlantic, 07 Dec. 2017. Web. 19 Jan. 2018.

Williams, Vanessa. "Maxine Waters and the Burden of the 'Strong Black Woman.'" The Lily, 26 Aug. 2017. 19 Jan. 2018.

Jones, Feminista. "Mammy 2.0: Black Women Won't Save You, So Stop Asking." Feminista Jones, 01 Aug. 2017. Web. 19 Jan. 2018.

Birman, Daniel H. "Me Facing Life: Cyntoia's Story." PBS, 01 March 2011. Web. 19 Jan. 2018.

Stahl, Aviva. "Behind Bars for 6 Months, Teen Accused of Killing Abusive Father Awaits Justice." Broadly, 19 Jan. 2017. Web. 19 Jan. 2018.

"Marissa Alexander, Jailed for 3 Years, Speaks Out on Intimate Partner Violence & Building Movements." Democracy Now, 04 May 2017. Web. 19 Jan. 2018.

Kel, TaLynn. "Leslie Jones Embodies the Least Protected Blackness of All." The Establishment, 25 April 2016. Web. 17 Jan. 2018.

Charleswell, Cherise. "Sexual Abuse and The Code of Silence in the Black Community." Role Reboot, 08 Sept. 2014. Web. 19 Jan. 2018.

Hutchinson, Sikivu. "The Wars Inside: Black Women and Deadly Intimate Partner Violence." Huffington Post, 14 April 2017. Web. 19 Jan. 2018.

Belton, Danielle C. "Black Women and the Savior Complex." Clutch, May 2014. 19 Jan. 2018.

D'Oyley, Demetria Lucas. "If You're a Black Man Mad About Serena Williams' Engagement, I Have Questions." The Root, 30 Dec. 2016. Web. 19 Jan. 2018.

Staff. "Black Men, We Need to Acknowledge that We Are the Problem. Let's Talk Toxic Masculinity." Black Youth Project, 25 April 2017. Web. 19 Jan. 2018.

Dreisbach, Shaun. "Black Women Are More Confident Than Any Other Group of Females: Survey." Glamour, 01 Aug. 2017. Web. 19 Jan. 2018.

Wilson, Julee. "Black Women Have Amazing Confidence, Survey Shows." Huffington Post, 08 Jan. 2012. Web. 19 Jan. 2018.

Karazin, Christelyn. "How Glamour Confidence Survey Hurts Black Women Part II." Beyond Black & White, 03 Aug. 2017. Web. 19 Jan. 2018.

Internalized Anti-Blackness

Othering the Self: Learning to Recognize My Anti-Blackness

Kel, TaLynn. "Othering the Self – Learning to Recognize My Anti-Blackness." Black Girl Nerds, 02 March 2016. Web. 30 Dec. 2016.

Moser, Laura. "Schools in the South Suspend and Expel Black Students Way More Than White Ones." Slate 25 Aug. 2015. Web. 20 Feb. 2016.

Hooks, bell. "Eating the Other: Desire and Resistance." 1992. Web. 21 Feb. 2016.

Zevallos, Zuleyka. "What is Otherness?" The Other Sociologist, 14 Oct. 2011 Web. 21 Feb. 2016.

Abbey-Lambertz, Kate. "These 15 Black Women Were Killed During Police Encounters. Their Lives Matter, Too." Huffington Post, 13 Feb. 2015. Web. 1 Feb 2016.

Swaine, Jon; Laughland, Oliver; Lartey; James; McCarthy, Ciara. "Young Black Men Killed by U.S. Police at Highest Rate in Year of 1,134 Deaths." Alternet 02 Jan. 2016. Web. 21 Feb. 2016.

Berman, Mark; Lowery, Wesley. "The 12 key highlights from the DOJ's scathing Ferguson report." The Washington Post 04 March 2015. Web. 21 Feb. 2016.

Boggioni, Tom. "New York City police union threatens to join Miami cops in Beyoncé boycott: 'Stop portraying us as bad guys'." Rawstory, 19 Feb. 2016. Web. 21 Feb. 2016.

Keeping It Real About Interracial Relationships as a Person of Color

"No Prison Time for Ex-NYPD Officer Peter Liang in Fatal Shooting of Akai Gurley." Los Angeles Times, 19, April 2916. Web. 15 Nov. 2016.

Winn, Patrick. "Asia Embraces Blackface-Style Ads. Get Ready to Cringe." PRI, 01 July 2014. Web. 15 Nov. 2016.

Kel, TaLynn. "One Punch Man." Breaking Normal, 22 Dec. 2015. Web. 15 Nov. 2016.

Pérez, Miriam Zoila. "4 Self-Care Resources for Days When the World is Terrible." Colorlines, 07 July 2016. Web. 09 Dec. 2016.

When White People Are Too Hateful to Realize They Screwed Up

To the Black Women Who Align Themselves with White Supremacy

HBCU Editors. "Two Howard University Students Support Trump: He Will Make Our Neighborhoods, Our Cities and Our Country Safe Again." PBS, Jan. 2017. Web. 19 Jan. 2018.

Kel, TaLynn. "Surviving Whiteness." Breaking Normal, 05 Feb 2017. Web. 19 Jan. 2018.

Kel, TaLynn. "Othering the Self: Learning to Recognize My Anti Blackness." Black Girl Nerds, 02 March 2016. Web. 19 Jan. 2018.

Working with White People is Both Harmful and Necessary

Goldhill, Olivia. "Philosophers Published a "Black Lives Matter" Series Written Entirely by White Professors." Quartz, 27 May 2017. Web. 19 Jan. 2018.

Democracy Now! "MOVE Bombing at 30: "Barbaric" 1985 Philadelphia Police Attack Killed 11 & Burned a Neighborhood." YouTube, 13 May 2015. Web. 19 Jan. 2018.

Demby, Gene. "I'm From Philly. 30 Years Later, I'm Still Trying to Make Sense of the MOVE Bombing." NPR Code Switch, 13 May 2015. Web. 19 Jan. 2018.

Nathan, Debbie. "What Happened to Sandra Bland?" The Nation, 21 April 2016. Web. 19 Jan. 2018.

Carmichael, Rodney. "Ice Cube Leaves Bill Maher Shaken and Stirred Over The N-Word." NPR, 12 June 2017. Web. 19 Jan. 2018.

Elizabeth, De. "Katy Perry Discusses Cultural Appropriation on Deray McKesson's Podcast." Teen Vogue, 12 June 2017. Web. 19 Jan. 2018.

White Accountability

When White People Consume Blackness for Personal Gain

Carroll, Rebecca. "Justin Timberlake on Jesse Williams's BET Speech Wasn't Woke, Just White." The Guardian, 27 June 2016. Web. 28 June 2016.

Brown, Lauren. "Read the Full Transcript of Jesse Williams' Epically Inspiring BET Awards Speech." Glamour, 27 June 2016. Web. 28 June 2016.

Hooks, bell. "Eating the Other: Desire and Resistance." 1992. Web. 21 Feb. 2016.

Slavery and the Making of America. Georgia Public Broadcasting. Web. 27 June 2016.

Oscars. "Chris Rock's Opening Monologue." YouTube, 23 March. 2016. Web. 27 June 2016.

Campbell, Christopher. "Who Else is Upset About the Death in "X-Men: First Class"?" Indiewire, 07 June 2011. Web. 27 June 2016.

Shackelford, Ashleigh. "Orange is the New Black is Trauma Porn Written for White People [Spoilers]." Wear Your Voice, 20 June 2016. Web. 27 June 2016.

Howze, Thaddeus. "On the Death of James Rhodes — War Machine." Medium, 22 June 2016. Web. 27 June 2016.

Nededog, Jethro. "'Fear the Walking Dead' fans aren't happy about the amount of black deaths." Business Insider, 31 August 2015. Web. 27 June 2016.

Paschal, Jaylin. "Smarter Than That: On the Assumptions Made About Ebonics and Intelligence." For Harriett, May 2016. Web. 27 June 2016.

Mangum, Trey. "Hayes Grier's 'T-Rex' dance is cultural appropriation at its finest and Black Twitter is over it." Blavity, 15 Sept. 2016. Web. 27 June 2016.

Zoladz, Lindsay. "Please, Don't Let Iggy Azalea Win the Best Rap Album Grammy." Vulture, 06 Feb 2015. Web. 27 June 2016.

Solomon, Akiba. "The Pseudoscience of 'Black Women Are Less Attractive.'" Colorlines, 17 May 2011. Web. 27 June 2016.

Harriot, Michael. "Black Bodies and the Last Frontier of Cultural Appropriation." Ebony, 20 May 2016. Web. 27 June 2016.

Richardson, Riche. "'The Bed Intruder'—News Video Goes Viral: Antoine Dodson as Internet Celebrity and Commodity." Technoculture: an online journal of technology in society, vol 4, 2014. Web. 27 June 2016.

Demanding Black Forgiveness Is Just Another Way to Control Us

Bacon, John. "Police consider charges against Michael Brown's stepdad." USA Today, 02 Dec. 2014. Web. 08 Aug. 2016.

Berman, Mark. "'I forgive you.' Relatives of Charleston church shooting victims address Dylann Roof." The Washington Post, 19 June 2015. Web. 08 Aug. 2016.

ABC News Staff. "Michael Brown's Stepfather Apologizes for 'Burn' Outburst in Ferguson." ABC News, 03 Dec. 2014. Web. 08 Aug. 2016.

Relevant Staff. "Trayvon Martin's Parents: 'As Christians We Must Forgive Zimmerman.'" Relevant, 27 Aug. 2013. Web. 08 Aug. 2016.

Ortberg, Mallory; Wallace, Carvell. "You're Not Off the Hook: The White Myth of Black Forgiveness." The Toast, 23 June 2015. Web. 08 Aug. 2016.

Kel, TaLynn. "My Husband's Unconscious Racism Nearly Destroyed Our Marriage." The Establishment, 26 May 2016. Web. 20 Aug. 2016.

White People, You Have a Lying Problem

Schwartz, Larry. "The 7 Biggest Liars in Presidential History." Alternet, 07 Feb. 2016. Web. 08 July 2016.

National Archives. "Statistical information about casualties of the Vietnam War." National Archives, August 2013. Web. 08 July 2016.

History.com Staff. "My Lai Massacre." History.com, 2009. Web. 08 July 2016.

Moore, A. "8 Successful and Aspiring Black Communities Destroyed by White Neighbors." Atlanta Black Star, 04 Dec. 2013. Web. 09 July. 2016.

Advocates for Youth Staff. "The Truth About Abstinence-Only Programs." Advocates for Youth, 2008. Web. 08 July 2016.

Myers, Lisa; NBC Investigative Unit. "Critics Question FEMA Director's Qualifications." MSNBC, 13 Sept. 2005. Web. 08 July 2016.

McCormack, Simon. "Brian Williams Investigation Uncovers More Alleged Lies." Huffington Post, 25 April 2015. Web. 08 July 2016.

Raphael, Ray. "Are U.S. History Textbooks Still Full of Lies and Half-Truths?" History News Network, 19 Sept. 2004. Web. 08 July 2016.

Blitz, Matt. "The Truth about Christopher Columbus." Today I Found Out, 26 Jan. 2016. Web. 08 July 2016.

Bouie Jamelle; Onion, Rebecca. "Slavery Myths Debunked." Slate, 29 Sept. 2015. Web. 08 July 2016.

Poniewozik, James "Why Brian Williams Lost His Job, and Why He Has a New One." Time, 10 June 2015. Web. 08 July 2016.

Kel, TaLynn. "My Husband's Unconscious Racism Nearly Destroyed Our Marriage." The Establishment, 26 May 2016. Web. 08 July 2016.

Stack, Liam. "Light Sentence for Brock Turner in Stanford Rape Case Draws Outrage." The New York Times, 06 June 2016. Web. 08 July 2016.

Apel, Therese. "2 Women in Truck That Ran Down Black Man Get Max Terms." USA Today, 10 April 2015. Web. 08 July 2016.

America, Stop Protecting Your Monsters

Kingkade, Tyler. "If Not For 2 Strangers, Brock Turner May Have Never Been Arrested." Huffington Post, 06 June 2016. Web. 14 Oct. 2016.

CBS News Staff. "Colorado Theater Massacre." CBS News, 2016. Web. 14 Oct. 2016.

Hughes, Trevor. "Planned Parenthood Shooter 'happy' with his attack." USA Today, 11 April 2016. Web. 21 Sept. 2016.

Schwartz, Gadi; Ortiz, Erik. "Brock Turner, Convicted Sexual Assault Offender, Released from Jail After 3 Months." NBC News, 02 Sept. 2016. Web. 14 Oct. 2016.

Cahill, Tom. "Montana father gets probation after he admits to raping 12-year-old daughter." US Uncut, 13 Oct. 2016. Web. 14 Oct. 2016.

Robles, Frances; Stewart, Nikita. "Dylann Roof's Past Reveals Trouble at Home and School." The New York Times, 16 July 2015. Web. 14 Oct. 2016.

Smith, Candace. "Trump's Female Supporters Back Him Despite Sexual Assault Accusations." ABC News, 15 Oct. 2016. Web. 14 Oct. 2016.

Shackelford, Ashleigh. "Stop Excusing Black Men's Violence – Like Nate Parker's – for the Sake of Black Liberation." Wear Your Voice Magazine, 16 Aug. 2016. Web. 14 Oct. 2016.

Raymond, Laurel. "Longest-Serving GOP Speaker in History Is a Liar And Serial Child Molester, Federal Judge Says." Think Progress, 27 April 2016. Web. 14 Oct. 2016.

Queally, James. "Oakland police to fire 4 officers, suspend 7 others, in sexual misconduct scandal." Los Angeles Times, 07 Sept. 2016, Web. 14 Oct 2016.

Washington Blade Staff. "Arkansas Judge Resigns Amid Sex Scandal." Washington Blade, 11 May 2016. Web. 14 Oct. 2016.

Evans, Robert. "Why I Kept My Rape by A Priest a Secret (And Can't Anymore)." Cracked, 25 July 2016. Web. 14 Oct. 2016.

Fox 5 News Staff. "Pastor Charged with Rape of 10-Year Old Girl." Fox 5, 16 Sept. 2016. Web. 14 Oct. 2016.

ABC News Staff. "Priest Arrested for Child Rape." ABC News, 02 May 2016. Web. 14 Oct. 2016.

Lewis, Andy. "Roman Polanski Rape Victim Unveils Startling, Disturbing Photo for Book Cover (Exclusive)" The Hollywood Reporter, 24 July 2013. Web. 14 Oct. 2016.

Orth, Maureen. "10 Undeniable Facts about the Woody Allen Sexual Abuse Allegation." Vanity Fair, 07 Feb. 2014. Web. 14 Oct. 2016.

Cahill, Tom. "Montana Father Gets Probation after He Admits to Raping 12-Year-Old Daughter." US Uncut, 13 Oct. 2016. Web. 14 Oct. 2016.

Grinberg, Emanuella; Shoichet, Catherine E. "Brock Turner Released from Jail after Serving 3 Months for Sexual Assault." CNN, 02 Sept. 2016. Web. 14 Oct. 2016.

Johnson, Kimberley. "No Jail Time for Rapist So He Can Enjoy 'The College Experience." Liberals Unite, 22 Aug. 2016. Web. 14 Oct. 2016.

Guerra, Kristine. "Teen Pleads Guilty to Sexual Abuse of a 1-Year-Old Girl, then a Judge Gives Him No Prison Time." The Washington Post, 19 Sept. 2016. Web. 14 Oct. 2016.

Agorist, Matt. "Cops Beat Their Wives and Girlfriends at Double the National Rate, Still Receive Promotions." The Free Thought Project, 07 May 2014. Web. 14 Oct. 2016.

Bazelon, Emily; Levin, Josh. "The Most Damning Verdict." Slate, 12 July 2012. Web. 14 Oct. 2016.

Cohen, Sarah; Ruiz, Rebecca; Childress, Sarah. "Departments Are Slow to Police Their Own Abusers." The New York Times, 23 Nov. 2013. Web. 14 Oct. 2016.

Crimesider Staff. "New Charge for Tonya Couch, 'Affluenza' Teen's Mom." CBS News, 26 May 2016. Web. 14 Oct 2016.

Frazier, Charise. "'Affluenza' Teen's Attorney Seeks Early Release." NewsOne, Sept. 2016. Web. 14 Oct. 2016.

Kel, TaLynn. "White People, You Have a Lying Problem." The Establishment. 07 July 2016. Web. 14 Sept. 2016.

CNN. "Trump Supporters Standing by Their Man." CNN, 11 Oct. 2016. Web. 14 Oct. 2016.

Politifact Editors. "Donald Trump's File." Politifact, 2016. Web. 14 Oct. 2016.

Alexander, Michelle. "Why Hillary Clinton Doesn't Deserve the Black Vote." The Nation, 10 Feb. 2016. Web. 14 Oct. 2016.

Timm, Trevor. "Trumps Many Many Threats to Sue the Press Since Launching His Campaign." Columbia Journalism Review, 03 Oct. 2016. Web. 14 Oct. 2016.

Iaccarino, Anthony. "The Founding Fathers and Slavery." Encyclopedia Britannica, 28 July 2016. Web. 14 Oct. 2016.

Ojanuga, Durrenda. "The Medical Ethics of the 'Father of Gynaecology', Dr. Marion Sims." Journal of Medical Ethics, 1993 vol 19: 28-31. Web. 14 Oct. 2016.

Goodman, Howard. "Studying Prison Experiments Research: For 20 years, a Dermatologist Used the Inmates of a Philadelphia Prison as the Willing Subjects of Tests on Shampoo, Foot Powder, Deodorant, and Later, Mind-Altering Drugs and Dioxin." The Baltimore Sun, 21 June 1998. Web. 14 Oct. 2016.

Human Rights Watch. "World Report: United States - Events of 2015." HRW.org, 2015. Web. 14 Oct. 2016.

Thirteen Media with Impact – WNET. "The Rise and Fall of Jim Crow." PBS Educational Broadcasting Corporation, 2002. Web. 14 Oct. 2016.

ACLU.com Editors. "Women's Rights." ACLU.com, 2016. Web. 14 Oct. 2016.

ACLU.com Editors. "Reproductive Freedom." ACLU.com, 2016. Web. 14 Oct. 2016.

ACLU.com Editors. "Reforming Police Practices." ACLU.com, 2016. Web. 14 Oct. 2016.

Thomas, Katie. "The Complex Math Behind Spiraling Prescription Drug Prices." The New York Times, 24 Aug. 2016. Web. 14 Oct. 2016.

Moore, Michael. "10 Things They Won't Tell You about the Flint Water Tragedy. But I Will." MichaelMoore.com, 29 Jan. 2016. Web. 14 Oct. 2016.

Judge, Monique. "State of Michigan Removes Flint's Ability to Sue Over Water Crisis." The Root, 20 Sept. 2016. Web. 14 Oct. 2016.

White People: Shut the Fuck Up About Black Voters

Eldridge, Ellen. "Georgia Militia Prepares for 'Fallout' After Election." Atlanta Journal Constitution, 04 Nov. 2016. Web. 08 Nov. 2016.

White People, You Have a Choice to Make

Oluo, Ijeoma. "Social Justice Must Be Complicated, Because Oppression Is Never Simple." The Establishment, 15 Feb 2017. Web. 22 Jan. 2018.

Kel, TaLynn. "America, Stop Protecting Your Monsters." The Establishment, 18 Oct. 2016. Web. 19 Jan. 2018.

If I Were White

Yo, Malory. "'I Am Not Your Negro' Gives James Baldwin's Words New Relevance." NPR, 08 Feb. 2017. Web. 26 Jan. 2018.

White People are Racist Landmines

Dolan, Eric W. "Study: White College Women are Less Likely to Help a Black Woman at Risk of Rape." PsyPost, 08 March 2017. Web. 19 Jan. 2018.

Kel, TaLynn. "Surviving Whiteness." Breaking Normal, 05 Feb 2017. Web. 19 Jan. 2018.

Kel, TaLynn. "White People, You Have a Lying Problem." The Establishment. 07 July 2016. Web. 17 Jan. 2018.

Kel, TaLynn. "America, Stop Protecting Your Monsters." The Establishment, 18 Oct. 2016. Web. 19 Jan. 2018.

To the Sad, Scared, Ignorant White People

Campbell, Colin. "At 3 a.m., NC Senate GOP Strips Education Funding from Democrats' Districts." The News & Observer, 13 May 2017. Web. 19 Jan. 2018.

Daily Progress Staff. "Torch-Wielding Protesters Gather at Lee Park." The Daily Progress, 13 May 2017. Web. 19 Jan. 2018.

Mazza, Ed. "Stephen Fry Explains Why Some People Believe Everything Donald Trump Says." Huffington Post, 12 May 2017. Web. 19 Jan. 2018.

White People Are the Villains in This Narrative

Hartley-Parkinson, Richard. "Grenfell Tower Fire Rescuers 'Found 42 Bodies in One Room' During Search." Metro, 20 June 2017. Web. 19 Jan. 2018.

Berman, Mark. "Minnesota Officer Acquitted of Manslaughter for Shooting Philando Castile During Traffic Stop." The Washington Post, 17 June 2017. Web. 19 Jan. 2018.

"Muslim Teen Killed After Being Kidnapped While Walking with Friends to Virginia Mosque: Police." KTLA 5, 19 June 2017. Web. 19 Jan. 2018.

Dandridge-Lemco, Ben. "Seattle Police Killed Charleena Lyles, A Pregnant Mother of Four Who Had Called 911." Fader, 19 June 2017. Web. 19 Jan. 2018.

Kennedy, Merrit. "Judge Declares Mistrial, Again, In Cincinnati Police Shooting Case." NPR, 23 June 2017. Web. 17 Jan. 2018.

Kel, TaLynn. "White People are Racist Landmines." Breaking Normal, 21 May 2017. Web. 17 Jan. 2018.

Kel, TaLynn. "When It Comes to Free Speech, the 'Whites Only; is Silent." The Establishment, 2 June 2017. Web. 17 Jan. 2018.

Violence is the White Normal

Savali, Kirsten West. "13-Year-Old Boy with Toy Gun Shot by Baltimore Police Officers." The Root, 27 April 2016. Web. 19 Jan. 2018.

Cleary, Tom. "WATCH: Balch Springs Police Officers Use Taser on Handcuffed Man." Heavy, 17 May 2017. Web. 19 Jan. 2018.

Bauer, Shane. "I Went Undercover with a Border Militia. Here's What I Saw." Mother Jones, Nov/Dec 2016. Web. 19 Jan. 2018.

"Armed Citizens Patrol U.S.-Mexico Border in Arizona." NBC News, 17 Nov. 2016. Web. 19 Jan. 2018.

Sinclair, Harriet. "ICE Officers Eat Breakfast before Raiding Michigan Restaurant, Detaining Three." Newsweek 25, May 2017. Web. 19 Jan. 2018.

MacRae, Meghan. "NSFW: American Terrorism... Lynching Postcards." CVLT Nation, 08 Dec. 2014. Web. 19 Jan. 2018.

Video. "Man Yells at Stranger for Speaking Spanish." CNN, 23 May 2017. Web. 19 Jan. 2018.

Shaw, A.R. "HBCU Student Richard Collins III Killed by White Racist Days Before Graduation." RollingOut, 22 May 2017. Web. 19 Jan. 2018.

Wamsley, Laurel. "White Supremacist Charged with Killing 2 In Portland, Ore., Knife Attack." NPR, 27 May 2017. Web. 19 Jan. 2018.

Borden, Jeremy; Horwitz, Sari; Markon, Jerry. "For Accused Killer Dylann Roof, a Life That Had Quietly Drifted Off Track." The Washington Post, 18 June 2015. Web. 20 Jan. 2018.

Lee, Paula Young. "Robert Dear, "Gentle Loner": The New York Times Reveals a Load of Biases in Early Round of Colorado Springs Planned Parenthood Coverage." Salon, 30 Nov. 2015. Web. 20 Jan. 2018.

Palma, Sky. "Christian Radio Host Praises Greg Gianforte: 'We Need a More Violent Christianity.'" DEADState, 28 May 2017. Web. 19 Jan. 2018.

Zucchino, David. "A Militia Gets Battle Ready for a Gun Grabbing Clinton Presidency." 04 Nov. 2016. Web. 19 Jan. 2016.

Sims, Alexandra; Buncombe, Andrew. "Who Voted for Donald Trump? Mostly White Men and Women, Voting Data Reveals." 09 Nov. 2016. Web. 19 Jan. 2018.